New Media, Knowledge Practices and Multiliteracies

AF775236

Will W.K. Ma • Allan H.K. Yuen
Jae Park • Wilfred W.F. Lau • Liping Deng
Editors

New Media, Knowledge Practices and Multiliteracies

HKAECT 2014 International Conference

Springer

Editors
Will W.K. Ma
Hong Kong Shue Yan University
Hong Kong, China

Allan H.K. Yuen
The University of Hong Kong
Hong Kong, China

Jae Park
Hong Kong Institute of Education
Hong Kong, China

Wilfred W.F. Lau
The University of Hong Kong
Hong Kong, China

Liping Deng
Hong Kong Baptist University
Hong Kong, China

ISBN 978-981-10-1358-4 ISBN 978-981-287-209-8 (eBook)
DOI 10.1007/978-981-287-209-8
Springer Singapore Heidelberg New York Dordrecht London

© Springer Science+Business Media Singapore 2015
Softcover reprint of the hardcover 1st edition 2015
This work is subject to copyright. All rights are reserved by the Publisher, whether the whole or part of the material is concerned, specifically the rights of translation, reprinting, reuse of illustrations, recitation, broadcasting, reproduction on microfilms or in any other physical way, and transmission or information storage and retrieval, electronic adaptation, computer software, or by similar or dissimilar methodology now known or hereafter developed. Exempted from this legal reservation are brief excerpts in connection with reviews or scholarly analysis or material supplied specifically for the purpose of being entered and executed on a computer system, for exclusive use by the purchaser of the work. Duplication of this publication or parts thereof is permitted only under the provisions of the Copyright Law of the Publisher's location, in its current version, and permission for use must always be obtained from Springer. Permissions for use may be obtained through RightsLink at the Copyright Clearance Center. Violations are liable to prosecution under the respective Copyright Law.
The use of general descriptive names, registered names, trademarks, service marks, etc. in this publication does not imply, even in the absence of a specific statement, that such names are exempt from the relevant protective laws and regulations and therefore free for general use.
While the advice and information in this book are believed to be true and accurate at the date of publication, neither the authors nor the editors nor the publisher can accept any legal responsibility for any errors or omissions that may be made. The publisher makes no warranty, express or implied, with respect to the material contained herein.

Printed on acid-free paper

Springer is part of Springer Science+Business Media (www.springer.com)

Preface

The HKAECT International Conference 2014 on *New Media, Knowledge Practices and Multiliteracies* (HKAECT 2014) is organized by The Hong Kong Association for Educational Communications and Technology (HKAECT) and sponsored by a number of higher institutions and organizations including China Association for Educational Technology (CAET), Journal of Communication and Education, Centre for Information Technology in Education (CITE, HKU), Online Communication Research Centre and Department of Journalism and Communication (Hong Kong Shue Yan University), Centre for Learning, Teaching and Technology (Hong Kong Institute of Education), and Knowledgement Ltd. It is held at The University of Hong Kong, Hong Kong, China, during 8–10 December, 2014.

New media appear both with multimedia presentation elements and interactive knowledge units, which call for emergent knowledge practices. All these multifaceted ways of communication require the ability to understand multiliteracies in terms of culture, disciplines, media, and technology. We are calling papers to discuss new media, emergent knowledge practices, and multiliteracies in three main aspects: (1) Communication, (2) Education, and (3) Technology. HKAECT 2014 provides such a platform for knowledge exchange on education, communication, and technology among educators, researchers, and practitioners who share a common goal to better teaching and learning on the one hand and effective and meaningful media communication on the other with the support of technology advancement.

It is our pleasure to have one of the keynote speakers, Professor J. Michael Spector, from the Department of Learning Technologies, College of Information, at the University of North Texas to kick off the Conference. Dr. Spector served on the International Board of Standards for Training, Performance and Instruction (IBSTPI) as Executive Vice President; he is on the Executive Committee of the IEEE Learning Technology Task Force. He is the editor of the Development Section of ETR&D and serves on numerous other editorial boards. He coedited the third edition of the *Handbook of Research on Educational Communications and Technology* and has more than 100 journal articles, book chapters, and books to his credit. He is former President-elect of the Association for Educational and

Communications Technology (AECT). He is surely the right person and an old friend to represent AECT to celebrate the 25th anniversary of HKAECT at the Conference.

We greatly appreciate the excellent work and contributions of all the reviewers and authors to this monograph. This monograph serves as a rich and resourceful exchange between academics and practitioners.

Hong Kong, China
December 2014

Will W.K. Ma
Allan H.K. Yuen
Jae Park
Wilfred W.F. Lau
Liping Deng

Organization

International Advisory Committee

Dick Cornell, University of Central Florida, United States
Kedong Li, South China Normal University, China
Leo Yam, HKAECT
Allan H.K. Yuen, HKAECT

Organizing Committee

Conference Chair	Will W.K. Ma, Hong Kong Shue Yan University, Hong Kong
Program Chairs	Wilfred W.F. Lau, The University of Hong Kong, Hong Kong
	Jae Park, Hong Kong Institute of Education, Hong Kong
Publication Chairs	Alex C.K. Chan, Hong Kong Shue Yan University, Hong Kong
	Liping Deng, Hong Kong Baptist University, Hong Kong
Sponsors Chair	Kar-wai Tong, Knowledgement Ltd., Hong Kong
Publicity Chair	Heidi Fung, Hong Kong Shue Yan University, Hong Kong
Social Event Chair	Wendy W.L. Chan, Hong Kong Baptist University, Hong Kong
Financial Chair	Rose Chang, Community College of City University of Hong Kong, Hong Kong
Local Arrangement Chair	Vincent H.K. Hung, Hong Kong Institute of Education, Hong Kong
Honorary Legal Advisor	Raymond Kong
Web Master	Albert Chan, The University of Hong Kong, Hong Kong

International Programme Committee

Albert Chan	*The University of Hong Kong, Hong Kong, China*
Alex C.K. Chan	*Hong Kong Shue Yan University, Hong Kong, China*
Wendy W.L. Chan	*Hong Kong Baptist University, Hong Kong, China*
Rose Chang	*Community College of City University of Hong Kong, Hong Kong, China*
Chi-Bin Cheng	*Tamkang University, Taiwan*
Debbie Mei-Tai Chu	*La Trobe University, Australia*
Rebecca Hsiang-Ning Chu	*I-Shou University, Taiwan*
Rose Wan-Mui Chu	*Metropolitan State University, Minnesota, United States*
Lesa M. Covington Clarkson	*University of Minnesota, United States*
Liping Deng	*Hong Kong Baptist University, Hong Kong, China*
Heidi Fung	*Hong Kong Shue Yan University, Hong Kong, China*
Kenneth N.K. Fong	*The Hong Kong Polytechnic University, Hong Kong, China*
Kevin K.W. Ho	*University of Guam, United States*
Huang-Yao Hong	*National Cheng-chi University, Taiwan*
Vincent H.K. Hung	*Hong Kong Institute of Education, Hong Kong, China*
Timothy C.H. Kwong	*Community College of City University of Hong Kong, Hong Kong, China*
Yew Meng Lai	*Universiti Malaysia Sabah, Malaysia*
Anthony S.K. Lam	*Hong Kong Shue Yan University, Hong Kong, China*
Wilfred W.F. Lau	*The University of Hong Kong, Hong Kong, China*
Silver Lee	*The Chinese University of Hong Kong, Hong Kong, China*
Kaman Lee	*Hong Kong Shue Yan University, Hong Kong, China*
Wenguang Li	*Shenzhen University, China*
Lin Lin	*University of North Texas, United States*
Mike Lindstrom	*SciMathMN (Minnesota), United States*
Pey-Yan Liou	*National Central University, Taiwan*
Olivine Lo	*Hong Kong Shue Yan University, Hong Kong, China*
Carrie Lui	*James Cook University, Australia*
Will W.K. Ma	*Hong Kong Shue Yan University, Hong Kong, China*
Scott Mcleod	*University of Kentucky, United States*
Francis K.T. Mok	*Hong Kong Institute of Education, Hong Kong, China*
Shaun Nykvist	*Queensland University of Technology, Australia*
Anatoly Oleksiyenko	*The University of Hong Kong, Hong Kong, China*
Ann Ooms	*Kingston University London & St. George's, University of London, United Kingdom*
Jae Park	*Hong Kong Institute of Education, Hong Kong, China*
Jim Ridgway	*Durham University, United Kingdom*
Howard Zhaoxun Song	*Hang Seng Management College, Hong Kong, China*
Kar-wai Tong	*Knowledgement Ltd., Hong Kong, China*
Rebecca Vivian	*University of Adelaide, Australia*
Amy Wu	*University of Maryland, United States*
Eunice P.Y. Yim	*The Open University of Hong Kong, Hong Kong, China*
Jingjing Zhang	*Beijing Normal University, China*

Organizers

Hong Kong Association for Educational, Communications & Technology (HKAECT)

China Association for Educational Technology (CAET)

Sponsors

Journal of Communication and Education

Centre for Information Technology in Education, The University of Hong Kong

Online Communication Research Centre, Hong Kong Shue Yan University

Department of Journalism and Communication, Hong Kong Shue Yan University

Knowledgement Ltd.

Centre for Learning, Teaching and Technology, Hong Kong Institute of Education

Contents

Part I
Introduction

Chapter 1
The Changing Face of Educational Technology: New Media, Knowledge Practices, and Multiliteracies

Allan H.K. Yuen

Abstract This chapter aims to provide an introduction to the present edited volume. Saettler (2004) argues that educational technology is essentially the product of a great historical stream consisting of trial and error, long practice and imitation, and sporadic manifestations of unusual individual creativity and persuasion. A trace of the definitions of educational technology showed that researchers have strived to propose different frameworks to be flexible enough to embrace new development of technology and educational practices. This edited volume is an attempt to depict the changing face of educational technology focusing on the development of new media, knowledge practices, and multiliteracies.

Keywords Communication • Education • Media • Practice • Literacy

1.1 Introduction

The Hong Kong Association for Educational Communications and Technology (HKAECT; see http://www.hkaect.org/) was established in 1989. The HKAECT organized the first conference in 1990 with the theme "*The Role of Educational Communications and Educational Technology in Year 2000*" and invited speakers from the USA, China, and Taiwan to address and discuss the outlook on educational communications and technology (see Appendix for the themes of HKAECT conferences since 1990). The 1990 conference theme signified the HKAECT started to go in quest of its identity in the field of educational communications and technology. About 300 researchers, educators, and practitioners from local and international tertiary institutions attended the conference. The silver anniversary annual meeting will be held at the University of Hong Kong in December 2014 with the theme "*New Media, Knowledge Practices and Multiliteracies*". Educational technology is a

---

A.H.K. Yuen (✉)
The University of Hong Kong, Hong Kong, China
e-mail: hkyuen@hku.hk

© Springer Science+Business Media Singapore 2015

W.W.K. Ma et al. (eds.), *New Media, Knowledge Practices and Multiliteracies*,
DOI 10.1007/978-981-287-209-8_1

well-researched academic area. However, the theory and practice of educational technology change over time. The 2014 annual meeting aims to provide a forum for academic exchange and discuss the evolving changes of educational technology.

With the invention of different technologies, from the early 1910s to 1920s, films, slides, pictures, and the likes were used as visual aids for presentation as well as instruction to provide 'seeing experience' for audience and students (Reiser 2012). The situation started to change due to the advancement of technology. Later, the use of audiovisual media in instruction became a trend, the so-called audiovisual movement with the popularity of television in the 1950s (Roblyer et al. 1997). At that time, the form of instruction was enhanced from visual to audiovisual, and the media has begun to be an important element in educational technology. Herbert Marshall McLuhan (1964) believed that media have effects in that they continually shape and reshape the ways in which individuals, societies, and cultures perceive and understand the world. This edited volume presents research studies to discuss the shaping and changing issues focusing on new media, knowledge practices, and multiliteracies.

1.2 New Media

Educational technology was first formally defined by Donald Ely in 1963 as "audiovisual communications is that branch of educational theory and practice primarily concerned with the design and use of messages which control the learning process. It undertakes (a) the study of the unique and relative strengths and weaknesses of both pictorial and nonrepresentational messages which may be employed in the learning process for any purpose; and (b) the structuring and systematizing of messages by men and instruments in educational environment" (Januszewski 2001, p. 18).

In accordance with the Commission of Instructional Technology, educational technology "goes beyond any particular medium or device. In this sense, instructional technology is more than the sum of its parts. It is a systemic way of designing, carrying out, and evaluating the whole process of learning and teaching in terms of specific objectives, based on research on human learning and communication, and employing a combination of human and non-human resources to bring about more effective instruction" (Commission of Instruction Technology 1970, p. 21).

The 1963 definition spells out clearly the nature of educational technology that 'audiovisual communications' is educational technology. Educational technology is no mere technology. First, technology is about communication, and education is conceptualized as such accordingly. If education is about communication, then various issues pertinent to teaching and learning need to be addressed. Second, the audiovisual technology in the 1960s and 1970s refers to media such as photography, films, and television, all being labeled as 'old media' in contrast to 'new media' developed and flourished in the wake of digitalization from the 1980s onward. The 1970 definition then goes beyond particular medium or device and proposes a systemic approach to manage the process of teaching and learning.

New media in general refers to on-demand access to content anytime, anywhere, on any digital device, as well as interactive user feedback, and creative participation, and it also refers the real-time generation of new and unregulated content. Jan van Dijk (2012) provides a definition of the new media as a combination of two structural and two technical characteristics. They are media at the turn of the twentieth and twenty-first centuries which are both integrated and interactive in the structural terms and use digital code and hypertext as technical means. This volume includes seven chapters under the New Media section, which cover the discussion of old as well as new media, such as newspaper, television, mass media, online media, tablet, and social media.

1.3 Knowledge Practices

In 1977, the Association for Educational Communications and Technology (AECT) proposed a definition on educational technology as "a complex, integrated process, involving people, procedures, ideas, devices and organization, for analyzing problems and devising, implementing, evaluating and managing solutions to those problems, involved in all aspects of human learning. ... takes the form of all the Learning Resources that are designed, selected, used, or all three, to bring about learning; these resources are identified as Messages, People, Materials, Devices, Techniques, and Settings" (AECT 1977, p. 1).

On the one hand, AECT's definition of educational technology in 1977 was similar with the one proposed by the Commission of Instructional Technology in 1970, as both of them stressed that educational technology as a complex and integrated process of teaching and learning. On the other hand, however, the two definitions were not the same. Differed from previous definition, at least, AECT added the element of 'analyzing problem' into the concept of educational technology.

New technologies, such as the Internet and personal computer, emerged and triggered the redefinition of educational technology in the 1990s. When compared with the past, the performances of new technologies improved greatly. What is more, the cost in using the technologies also reduced sharply. As a result, more users, including teachers and students, can afford to purchase their own personal computers at home and access to the Internet. This, in return, facilitated and promoted the application of technology in education.

Another reasons for the need of redefining the concept of educational technology was the rise of the cognitive and constructivist learning theories. Rather than being guided by the behavioral learning theory, the cognitive and constructivist learning theories affected the planning and design of educational technology in teaching and learning. Thus, a new definition of educational technology was suggested (Reiser 2012).

In view of the above, in 1994, AECT redefined educational technology as: "the theory and practice of design, development, utilization, management, and evaluation of processes and resources for learning" (Seels and Richey 1994, p. 1). In this definition, five interrelated elements were added into the concept of educational technology, namely, design, development, utilization, management, and evaluation. Concepts of these five fields have fallen in and out of favor at various times over the years by educational technology researchers and practitioners (Ely 2008).

More than a decade later, in 2008, AECT updated the definition of educational technology and define it as "the study and ethical practice of facilitating learning and improving performance by creating, using, and managing appropriate technological processes and resources" (AECT Definition and Terminology Committee 2008, p. 1).

A new element which never be seen before was added into the new definition of the educational technology, which was 'ethical practice'. The element of ethical practice was missing, whether the educational technology was regarded as media or process. However, the appearance of 1994 and 2008 definitions emphasizes the practice of educational technology in teaching and learning. Educational technology involves and changes human practices that deserve special attention.

Recently, Hakkarainen (2009) refers 'knowledge practices' to "personal and social practices related to working with knowledge. [...] Knowledge practices, while sometimes just supporting routine learning (transmission), at their creative edge diverge from other routine social practices in that they take place in specific purposefully dynamic and fluid settings designed for the furtherance of innovation and knowledge" (p. 215). He argues that technology enhances learning through transformed social practices. In order to truly contribute to educational transformation, pedagogical approaches have to be embedded in locally cultivated knowledge practices that channel the participants' intellectual efforts in a way that elicits collective advancement of knowledge. This volume includes ten chapters under the Knowledge Practices section, which cover the discussion of a range of human or knowledge practices in connection to technology, such as dating attitude and love style, school management, mathematics learning experience, learning oral English, online knowledge sharing, engagement with digital technologies outside school, building knowledge repository, addiction and social relations, cultural differences, and blended learning.

1.4 Multiliteracies

A definition of twenty-first century literacy offered by the New Media Consortium is "the set of abilities and skills where aural, visual, and digital literacy overlap. These include the ability to understand the power of images and sounds, to recognize and use that power, to manipulate and transform digital media, to distribute them pervasively, and to easily adapt them to new forms" (Jenkins et al. 2009, p. 28). It is further argued that new media literacies should include the traditional literacy that evolved with print culture as well as the newer forms of literacy within mass media and digital media (Jenkins et al. 2009).

Members of the digital generation actively engage with different new media forms and with their recombinations, for example, they take and send pictures with their mobile phones, they produce websites and personal blogs, they use camcorders for filmmaking, and they edit music and refashion avatars downloaded from the net and play online games. Due to its multimodal nature, all these activities implicitly require and develop new forms of literacy or multiliteracies (Drotner 2008; Herring 2008).

Nowadays, the digital technology is deeply embedded in everyday experience (McCarthy and Wright 2004), and it has been enabling the use of multimodal interfaces that combine speech, touch, gesture, pens, and haptic interfaces (Rowe 2013). This volume includes six chapters under the section of Multiliteracies, which cover the discussion of a range of literacy issues such as learning style inventory, interdisciplinary approach, ePortfolios for learning, video production and generic skills, mobile-assisted collaborative learning, and reading and mathematics.

Conclusions

Nye (2006) argues that "a technology is not merely a system of machines with certain functions; rather, it is an expression of a social world" (p. 47). And human–computer interactions in the future would be more like human-to-human communication (Rowe 2013). With the advances in information and communication technology, the Internet and new media are enabling the emergence of new mechanism of human associations as well as social connections which are shaped by—yet also shape—the development of human practices and literacies in a participatory culture (Slevin 2000; Jenkins et al. 2009).

As "educational technology is essentially the product of a great historical stream consisting of trial and error, long practice and imitation, and sporadic manifestations of unusual individual creativity and persuasion" (Saettler 2004, p. 4). Through a historical account of the definitions of educational technology, it is showed that researchers have strived to propose different frameworks to be flexible enough to embrace new development of technology and educational practices. This edited volume is an attempt to depict the changing face of educational technology focusing on the development of new media, knowledge practices, and multiliteracies.

Appendix: Themes of the HKAECT Conferences Since 1990

1990 The Role of Educational Communications and Educational Technology in Year 2000
1992 Instructional Technology: Design, Utilization and Evaluation
1994 Telecommunications in Education
1996 Innovations and Quality in Teaching and Learning

1997 Tertiary Teaching in the Use of Technology: Vision and Practice
1998 New Challenges and Innovations in Teaching and Training into the Twenty-First Century
2001 Education Reform: Integrating Information Technology, Communication, and Curriculum
2004 Media Innovations in Education: Input and Outcome in New Society
2007 Educational Communications and Technology as Learning Experiences
2010 Multiliteracies for the Twenty-First Century: Education, Communication, and Technology
2014 New Media, Knowledge Practices, and Multiliteracies

References

AECT Definition and Terminology Committee. (2008). Definition. In A. Januszewski & M. Molenda (Eds.), *Educational technology: A definition with commentary*. New York: Lawrence Erlbaum.

Association for Educational Communications and Technology. (1977). *Educational technology: Definition and glossary of terms*. Washington, DC: Association for Educational Communications and Technology.

Commission on Instructional Technology. (1970). *To improve learning: An evaluation of instructional technology*. Washington, DC: U.S. Government Printing Office.

Drotner, K. (2008). Leisure is hard work: Digital practices and future competencies. In D. Buckingham (Ed.), *Youth, identity, and digital media* (The John D. and Catherine T. MacArthur Foundation series on digital media and learning, pp. 167–184). Cambridge, MA: The MIT Press.

Ely, D. (2008). Frameworks of educational technology. *British Journal of Educational Technology, 39*(2), 244–250.

Hakkarainen, K. (2009). A knowledge-practice perspective on technology-mediated learning. *Computer-Supported Collaborative Learning, 4*, 213–231.

Herring, S. C. (2008). Questioning the generational divide: Technological exoticism and adult constructions of online youth identity. In D. Buckingham (Ed.), *Youth, identity, and digital media* (The John D. and Catherine T. MacArthur Foundation series on digital media and learning, pp. 71–92). Cambridge, MA: The MIT Press.

Januszewski, A. (2001). *Educational technology: The development of a concept*. Englewood: Libraries Unlimited, Inc.

Jenkins, H., with Purushotma, R., Weigel, M., Clinton, K., & Robison, A. J. (2009). *Confronting the challenges of participatory culture: Media education for the 21st century*. Cambridge, MA: MIT Press.

McCarthy, J. J., & Wright, P. (2004). *Technology as experience*. Cambridge, MA: MIT Press.

McLuhan, H. M. (1964). *Understanding media: The extensions of man*. New York: McGraw-Hill.

Nye, D. E. (2006). *Technology matters: Questions to live with*. Cambridge, MA: MIT Press.

Reiser, R. A. (2012). What field did you say you were in? Defining and naming our field. In R. A. Reiser & J. V. Dempsey (Eds.), *Trends and issues in instructional design and technology* (3rd ed., pp. 1–7). Boston: Pearson.

Roblyer, M. D., Edwards, J., & Havriluk, M. A. (1997). *Integrating educational technology into teaching*. Upper Saddle River: Prentice-Hall.

Rowe, L. A. (2013, October). Looking forward 10 years to multimedia successes. *ACM Transactions on Multimedia Computing, Communications and Applications, 9*(1s, Article 37), 1–7.

Saettler, P. (2004). *The evolution of American educational technology*. Greenwich: Information Age Publishing.
Seels, B. B., & Richey, R. C. (1994). *Instructional technology: The definition and domains of the field*. Washington, DC: Association for Educational Communications and Technology.
Slevin, J. (2000). *Internet and society*. Cambridge: Polity Press.
van Dijk, J. (2012). *The network society* (3rd ed.). London: Sage.

Part II
New Media

Chapter 2
Cultivation Effects of Television Broadcasting and Online Media

Hey Yeung Lau

Abstract In the era of social media, Online Media is so popular that everyone can use their electronic devices to access in anytime and anywhere. At the same time, although Television is named as traditional media, it is still influential owing to its popularity and attractiveness. In the past few decades, Cultivation Theory was developed by George Gerbner which examined the long-term effects of Television. Since Online Media has similar function as Television, it is important to find out the possibility of Online Media having cultivating effect. Besides, it is crucial to examine the application of cultivating effects of Television. This study is under quantitative analysis with using a survey questionnaire administered to a sample of 258 undergraduate students. The results indicate that TV Viewing is an important determinant of Changes of Concept of Social Realities, with beta = .296 ($p < 0.001$) and $R^2 = 0.114$. Also, Use of Online Media is an important determinant of Behavioral Intention, with beta = 0.379 ($p < 0.001$) and $R^2 = 0.141$.

Keywords Television • Online media • Social realities • Intention • Behavior

2.1 Introduction

Cultivation Theory is significant in mass communication. It states if a heavy viewer is exposed to more violence content eventually effected by the Mean World Syndrome, an idea that the world is worse than it actually is (Gerbner and Gross 1976). It showed that after a prolonged exposure to television will affect the concept of social realities of the viewer. "In general, the relation between viewing and various types of judgments is modest but reliable (Shrum et al. 2011)."

Until now, the emergence of Internet has changed people concepts of media usage. As Internet can also perform the function of TV, it is possible for Internet having cultivation and worth to be discussed.

H.Y. Lau (✉)
Online Communication Research Centre, Department of Journalism and Communication, Hong Kong Shue Yan University, Hong Kong, China
e-mail: cyrus924@gmail.com

© Springer Science+Business Media Singapore 2015

W.W.K. Ma et al. (eds.), *New Media, Knowledge Practices and Multiliteracies*,
DOI 10.1007/978-981-287-209-8_2

After reviewing of databases EBSCO in the last 8 years, studies concerning the cultivation effects of TV broadcasting are plenty, but examining of having cultivation effects in online media is very few, and it is even rare of discussing both cultivation effects of TV broadcasting and online media. Besides, researchers has called in question about there should be one or more factor which associated with the factor of heavy viewing. In order to come up with the results of shaping heavy viewers' concept on social realities, therefore, it comes up with two research questions:

1. What is/are the factor(s) affecting viewers in the concept of social realities?
2. Can frequent use of online media affect the users' concept of social realities?

This study extends previous research and provides an alternative perspective, with particular reference to "TV Viewing" and "Use of Online Media".

2.2 Literature Review

In this study, Behavioral Intention as a contingency factor is added to the research framework to find out the relationship between each factors regarding cultivation theory.

2.2.1 Changes of Concept of Social Realities

Firstly, Appel (2008) said that the self-reported frequency of watching fiction on television is positively related to the belief in a just real world, and at the same time, the general amount of television viewing was positively related to mean and scary world.

It is investigated that Flemish crime drama viewing predicted a higher perceived risk in sexual violence, the relationship is especially stronger in women who has a higher socioeconomic status and with no direct experience with crime. On the other hand, News Viewing predicted a lower perceived risk, since that the relative lack of exemplars in news and victim blaming giving viewers an impression of the risk of sexual victimization did not apply to themselves (Lee and Niederdeppe 2011).

It is found that after watching a violent television program, viewers with more vivid memories of blood and gore gave a higher prevalence estimate of real-world crime and violence (Riddle et al. 2011).

2.2.2 TV Viewing

It is examined that viewers watching a TV legal drama program were more likely to endorse to false beliefs than those viewers exposed to the program immediately (Jensen et al. 2011).

It is founded that a general television consumption has a significant relationship with first- and second-order rape myth beliefs among male and female. The study also indicated that soap opera viewing has a positive relationship with both rape myth acceptance and the overestimation of false rape accusations (Kahlor and Eastin 2011).

2.2.3 Use of Online Media

It is found that the perceptions of the quality of the content and empathy affect three benefit expectations of control, inclusion, and affection, and these three benefit expectations affected the forwarding intention of the users (Huang et al. 2012).

Lewis and Shewmaker (2011) found that the minor celebrities as the Internet users follow the same pattern seen in adult celebrities, in that the female presented sexualized dress and submissive posture as compared to demure dress and assertive posturing on the male website.

Some analysts has investigated that the heavy viewers of a particular program tend to visit the respective program's official website more than the light viewers, who building a better website loyalty. This loyalty leads to an increase in the use of Interactive Online Product Placement, which has a positive influence on the viewer's attitude toward the sponsor, and their purchase intentions (Lin and Cho 2010).

2.2.4 Contingency Factor: Behavioral Intention

Beullens and the colleagues (2011) found that adolescent's viewing music video is one of the significant marker risky driving behavior, and at the same time, this relationship is mediated through their attitudes and intention. At the same research, they have combined Cultivation Theory and the Theory of Planned Behavior or the Problem Behavior Theory to explain the above relationship of viewing music video and risky driving behavior. It is stated that the relationship is mediated through the viewer's attitudes and intentions. However, it is found that there is no association between music video viewing and Problem Behavior Theory. A conclusion has drawn that the combination of Cultivation Theory and Theory of Planned Behavior can provide a better framework for explaining the above relationship (Beullens et al. 2011).

With respect to the literature review, the hypotheses are as follow (see Fig. 2.1):

H_1: The level of Television Viewing has a direct and positive relationship with the Behavioral Intention.

H_2: The level of Use of Online Media has a direct and positive relationship with the Behavioral Intention.

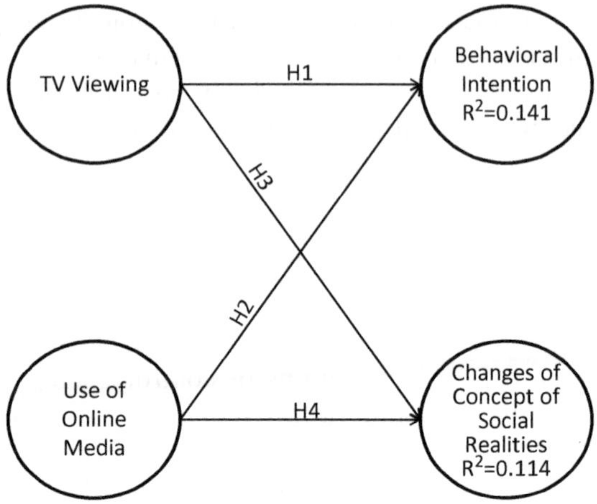

Fig. 2.1 Hypothesized model for media effects

H_3: The level of Television Viewing has a direct and positive relationship with the Changes of Concept of Social Realities.

H_4: The level of Use of Online Media has a direct and positive relationship with the Changes of Concept of Social Realities.

2.3 Methodology

2.3.1 Background

One of the major local television broadcasting company, Television Broadcasts Limited (TVB), and two of the most popular online video sharing platform, Youtube and MyTV, would be used as referencing in the following study.

2.3.2 Subjects

The subjects in this study are the Local university students, major in Journalism and Mass Communication, who have a habit in viewing Television and using the online media. We focus on how these two media affect their concepts in social realities.

2.3.3 Data Collection

In order to reach our target, we conducted and distributed a paper questionnaire for students in campuses in Hong Kong Shue Yan University. 258 completed questionnaires were collected. The data collection process took two weeks to complete (see Tables 2.1 and 2.2).

Table 2.1 Descriptive statistics of age group and gender ($n = 258$)

	Number	Percent
Age group		
11–20	114	44.2
21–30	144	55.8
Gender		
Male	72	27.9
Female	186	72.1

Table 2.2 Descriptive statistics of watching TV and using online media

	Mean
Average hour(s) of watching TV per weekday	1.73
Average hour(s) of watching TV per day in weekend	2.79
Average day(s) of watching TV per week	4.42
Average hour(s) of using online media per day	4.10
Average day(s) of using online media per week	6.58

2.3.4 Measures

The subjects will be asked to report demographics data in the first half of the questionnaire, including ages, gender, the experience in watching TV and using online media, and then to answer the statements in responding to TV Viewing, Use of Online Media, Behavioral Intention and Changes of Concept of Social Realities in with Likert's scale ranged from 1 (*strongly disagree*) to 7 (*strongly agree*).

2.4 Findings

2.4.1 Descriptive Summary and Reliability Testing of the Observed Variables

The respondents had generally neutral between TV viewing and Use of Online Media to Behavioral Intention, Changes of Social Realities, Changes of Moral Value, and the behavioral changes, with the mean value range from 3.08 to 5.70.

2.4.2 Instrument Validation

The Cronbach's α values for each of the constructs exceeded the suggested threshold value of 0.7, with a range from 0.699 to 0.876. Although one of the construct, Changes of Concept of Social Realities—Moral Value, just get a Cronbach's $\alpha = 0.699$, it is already very close to 0.7, which is acceptable to be used

Table 2.3 Descriptive Statistic of Each Constructs

	Minimum	Maximum	Mean	Std. deviation
TV viewing	1.00	7.00	4.3594	1.2272
Use of online media	1.00	7.00	4.8740	1.1547
Behavioral intention	2.00	7.00	5.4472	0.8995
Changes of concept of social realities	1.00	5.40	3.2581	0.9262

in further analysis. These findings indicate that the constructs were reliable and internally consistent.

Factor analysis is used after testing the reliability of the constructs. After several times of using principal component varimax rotation and removing some questions, and as a result, four components are clearly identified without lumping and no cross-loading among components. Besides, most of the values >0.7 or very close to 0.7, and they are consistent as well, exhibiting there is a convergent validity with high factor loadings.

2.4.3 *Model Testing Results*

The following table has shown the data of mean and standard deviation of the summed mean score of each constructs (see Table 2.3).

The corresponding constructs were examined using linear regression in several times.

First, the relations between TV Viewing and Use of Online Media with the dependent variable, Behavioral Intention has been examined, which indicated that the model has a R^2 of 0.141, and $p<0.001$. All of these and the other indices exceeded the suggested values, indicating that the model fit the data well.

However, there is only one factor "Use of Online Media" which is supported, with the Beta = 0.379, and $p<0.001$. It indicates a relatively strong, direct, and significant relationship to Behavioral Intention. Since the other factor "TV Viewing" has no significance, it is not supported (see Tables 2.4 and 2.5).

Second, the relations between TV viewing and Use of Online Media with the dependent variable, Changes of Concept of Social Realities has been examined. The results indicated that the model has a R^2 of 0.114, and $p<0.001$. All of these and the other indices exceeded the suggested values, indicating that the model fit the data well.

After examining the coefficient, only "TV Viewing" is supported, with the Beta = 0.296, and $p<0.001$. It reflects a relatively strong, direct, and significant relationship to political participation. All of the others have no significant so they are not supported (see Tables 2.6 and 2.7).

After model testing, a complete form of model is formed which exhibiting the relationships between constructs (see Fig. 2.2 and Table 2.8).

Table 2.4 Summary of model and ANOVA of TV viewing and use of online media with behavioral intention

Model				ANOVA	
R	R^2	Adjusted R^2	Std. error of the estimate	*F*	Sig.
0.376	0.141	0.134	0.8385	20.178	0.000

Table 2.5 Coefficients of TV viewing and use of online media with behavioral intention

	Unstandardized coefficients		Standardized coefficients		
Model	*B*	Std. error	Beta	*t*	Sig.
Constant	4.075	0.279		14.624	0.000
TV viewing	−0.015	0.044	−0.021	−0.347	0.729
Use of online media	0.296	0.047	0.379	6.314	0.000

Table 2.6 Summary of model and ANOVA of TV viewing and use of online media on changes of social realities

Model				ANOVA	
R	R^2	Adjusted R^2	Std. error of the estimate	*F*	Sig.
0.338	0.114	0.103	0.86233	10.091	0.000

Table 2.7 Coefficients of TV viewing and use of online media on changes of social realities

		Unstandardized coefficients		Standardized coefficients		
Model		*B*	Std. error	Beta	*t*	Sig.
	Constant	1.815	0.408		4.450	0.000
	TV viewing	0.221	0.047	0.296	4.749	0.000
	Use of online media	0.095	0.053	0.120	1.801	0.073

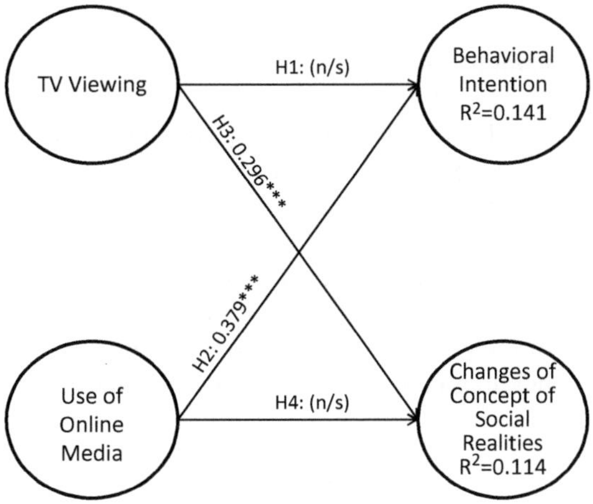

Fig. 2.2 Model testing for the factors relating to behavioral intention and changes of concept of social realities

Table 2.8 Summary of model testing

Hypothesis	Causal paths	Coefficients	*t*-values	Results
H1	TV viewing → Behavioral intention	−0.21 ($n-s$)	−0.347	*Not supported*
H2	Use of online media → Behavioral intention	0.379 ($p<.001$)	6.314	*Supported*
H3	TV viewing → Changes of concept of social realities	0.296 ($p<.001$)	4.749	*Supported*
H4	Use of online media → Changes of concept of social realities	0.120 ($n-s$)	1.801	*Not supported*

2.5 Discussion

The findings of this study indicate a strong relationship between TV Viewing and Changes of the Concept of Social Realities. Thus, an individual who prolonged exposed in television, or in other words, being a heavy user of TV, his/her concept of social realities will be changed.

On the other hand, the findings also show that there is a strong relationship between Use of Online Media and Behavioral Intention, which means if an individual is a intensive user of Online Media, he/she would intended to act in some activities and after a period of time, altered and to become a kind of behavior.

In this study, the findings can only partially answer the research questions. With respect to "What is/are the factor(s) affecting viewers in the concept of social realities?", this study can only prove that the prolonged exposure of TV will lead to the changes of concept of social realities, however, cannot find any other factor. Besides, with against to the question "Is frequent use of online media can affect the users' concept of social realities?", this study found that there is no relationship between use of online media and social realities. This result may ascribe to the limitation, which is the term Online Media was narrowed to only for "Youtube and MyTV". It is possible to have a relationship between online media and social realities.

Conclusion

The effect of media is strong, especially TV broadcasting and Online Media, which they are the most popular in Hong Kong. Therefore, the senders and the receivers should use it carefully. As stated in Cultivation Theory, mean world syndrome is found on heavy TV users. Thus, TV station should take the responsibility to reduce the amount of sex and violence in shows, and the audiences should control in the time of watching TV. Besides, the consequence of intensive use of online media will lead to building up certain kind of intention. Therefore, using online media correctly and wisely can prevent building up negative and bad behavior.

References

Appel, M. (2008). Fictional narratives cultivate just-world beliefs. *Journal of Communication, 58*(1), 62–83.

Beullens, K., Roe, K., & Van den Bulck, J. (2011). The impact of adolescents' news and action movie viewing on risky driving behavior: A longitudinal study. *Human Communication Research, 37*(4), 488–508.

Gerbner, G., & Gross, L. (1976). Living with television: The violence profile. *Journal of Communication, 26*(2), 172–194.

Huang, J., Chen, R., & Wang, X. (2012). Factors influencing intention to forward short internet videos. *Social Behavior & Personality: An International Journal, 40*(1), 5–14.

Jensen, J. D., Bernat, J. K., Wilson, K. M., & Goonewardene, J. (2011). The delay hypothesis: The manifestation of media effects over time. *Human Communication Research, 37*(4), 509–528.

Kahlor, L., & Eastin, M. S. (2011). Television's role in the culture of violence toward women: A study of television viewing and the cultivation of rape myth acceptance in the United States. *Journal of Broadcasting & Electronic Media, 55*(2), 215–231.

Lee, C., & Niederdeppe, J. (2011). Genre-Specific cultivation effects: Lagged associations between overall TV viewing, local TV news viewing, and fatalistic beliefs about cancer prevention. *Communication Research, 38*(6), 731–753.

Lewis, S., & Shewmaker, J. (2011). Considering age and gender: A comparative content analysis of sexualization of teen celebrity websites. *The International Journal of Interdisciplinary Social Sciences, 5*(12), 215–224.

Lin, J., & Cho, C. (2010). Antecedents and consequences of cross-media usage: A study of a TV program's official web site. *Journal of Broadcasting & Electronic Media, 54*(2), 316–336.

Riddle, K., Potter, W., Metzger, M. J., Nabi, R. L., & Linz, D. G. (2011). Beyond cultivation: Exploring the effects of frequency, recency, and vivid autobiographical memories for violent media. *Media Psychology, 14*(2), 168–191.

Shrum, L. J., Lee, J., Burroughs, J. E., & Rindfleisch, A. (2011). An online process model of second-order cultivation effects: How television cultivates materialism and its consequences for life satisfaction. *Human Communication Research, 37*(1), 34–57.

References

Chapter 3
Online Legal Risks in Social Media: Lessons from a Few Court Cases in Hong Kong

Kar-wai Tong

Abstract There are two objectives in this research (a) it outlines some online legal risks in social media in Hong Kong and (b) it provides a basis for further discussion and research on online legal risks and/or online behaviours in the explosive growth of social media. The author conducted literature review and basic legal research on online legal risks in social media and examined court cases to illustrate such risks in Hong Kong. In particular, defamation, reasonable care by providers of social media, and criminal liability were reviewed. Limitations of the study are discussed and future directions for research are proposed at the end of the chapter.

Keywords Legal risks • Social media • Court cases • Hong Kong

3.1 Introduction

> The Internet is an open door to knowledge, entertainment, communication—*and exploitation* [with emphasis]. … Shielded by the anonymity of an assumed online name and profile, they aspire to gain the trust of their targeted victims through computer "chats" …
>
> —Fisher J sitting in the Supreme Court of Canada in *R v Legare* 2009 SCC 56 (paragraphs 1–2)

The growth of social media, or social network sites as sometimes interchangeably used, is strong. When Friedman (2006, p. 57) said, "The political constraint on individual reach collapsed with the fall of the Berlin Wall … [and] the practical constraint on individual reach collapsed with the rise of the Apple and Windows-enabled, modem connected IBM PC", social media have been exploding across the globe and becoming important social venues for people to make connections with others through the virtual world. In the USA, for instance, social media have become central to the lives of many youngsters (Lenhart et al. 2007). In Arabian countries, the Dubai School of Government reported that Arabic language was

K.-w. Tong (✉)
Part-time Lecturer, The Open University of Hong Kong,
Barrister (England & Wales), Flat B, 19/F, Block 1, Goldfield Industrial Building,
140-150 Tai Lin Pai Road, Kwai Chung, Hong Kong SAR, China
e-mail: kwtong@knowledgement.com.hk

© Springer Science+Business Media Singapore 2015

W.W.K. Ma et al. (eds.), *New Media, Knowledge Practices and Multiliteracies*,
DOI 10.1007/978-981-287-209-8_3

the fastest growing language ever on Twitter in 2012 (Mourtada and Salem 2012). In South Korea, there were 23 million unique visitors per month visiting Cyworld, a local social medium, in the first quarter of 2009 (Goh 2009). In China, a study found that 91 % of the respondents had visited a social media site in the 6 months prior to the research, and China took over Japan (30 %), the USA (67 %), and South Korea (70 %) to become the most active population using social media in the world (Chiu et al. 2012). In Hong Kong, the use of social media was also reported in 2011 to be higher than that in the USA, with 92 % of respondents in an online survey visiting Facebook, 77 % reading blogs on a weekly basis, and 52 % writing blogs (Li 2011).

3.2 Literature Review

3.2.1 Social Media

There is no formal definition of social media (Xiang and Gretzel 2010). In the definition of Kietzmann et al. (2011), for instance, a social medium is referred to as a honeycomb comprising seven functional building blocks: identity, conversations, sharing, presence, relationships, reputation, and groups. Kane et al. (2014, p. 279) updated the definition of Boyd and Ellison (2008, p. 211) and described social media to have four features, so that users of social media "(a) have a unique user profile that is constructed by the user, by members of their network, and by the platform; (b) access digital content through, and protect it from, various search mechanisms provided by the platform; (c) can articulate a list of other users with whom they share a relational connection; and (d) view and traverse their connections and those made by others on the platform".

Social media have impacted people's living and behaviours. For example, people may use social media to manage their online reputations (Madden and Smith 2010) and check health information (Vance et al. 2009). Social media have also been used for other purposes such as marketing (Mangold and Faulds 2009), public relations (Eyrich et al. 2008), and political movements (Shirky 2011).

3.2.2 Online Risks in Social Media

There is more than one definition of online risk. Especially for children, Staksrud (2013, p. 51) defined online risk as "a concept and an area of research, linking it back to the historical fear of 'new media'". Livingstone (2009, p. 157) highlighted the paedophile and the bully as two particular risks. EU Kids Online examined approximately 400 studies across 21 European countries and classified children's online risks as shown in Table 3.1 (Livingstone and Haddon 2009).

Table 3.1 Typology of online risks classified by EU kids online

	Commercial	Aggressive	Sexual	Values
Content: child as recipient	Advertising, spam, sponsorship	Violent/ gruesome/ hateful content	Pornographic/ harmful sexual content	Racist, biased information/ advice (e.g. drugs)
Contact: child as participant	Tracking/ harvesting personal information	Being bullied, harassed or stalked	Meeting strangers, being groomed	Self-harm, unwelcome persuasion
Conduct: child as actor	Gambling, illegal downloads, hacking	Bullying or harassing another	Creating and uploading porn material	Providing advice, e.g. suicide/ pro-anorexia

Note. Adapted from Livingstone and Haddon (2009, p. 10, Table 3.2)

In addition to risks to children, there are other online risks. Commercial risk is a prevalent example. Vellido et al. (1999, p. 305) referred to online risk in shopping in cyberspace as customers' perceptions of risks with regard to the trustworthiness and security of Internet vendors. Bhatnagar et al. (2000) advocated that online risk is a multidimensional construct, where product category risk and financial risk are two predominant risks of online shopping. Lim (2003) argued that in the business-to-commerce mode of e-commerce, consumers perceived technology, vendor, and product as three sources of online risks. Forsythe and Shi (2003) also pointed out that perceived online risk is useful to explain barriers to Internet shopping. The degree of how different online risks affect individuals' commercial behaviours varies. In a study, for instance, it was found that social and time risks had less influence than economic and performance-related factors on shopping in the virtual world (Crespo et al. 2009). Perceptions of online risks may have an impact not only on individuals but also on organizations as well. Perceived online risks, such as the risk of wasting time, financial loss, and functional risks in marketing communication, may deter companies from using social media (Munnukka and Järvi 2013).

3.2.3 Online Legal Risks in Social Media

If legal risk is a special branch of risks (Mahler 2007) without a universal definition, online legal risk is a sub-specialty of legal risk bearing no formal definition, either. Online legal risks may exist in different activities in the virtual environment such as e-banking (Georgescu 2006), e-commerce (Schoder and Yin 2000), and e-file sharing (Amoroso and Dembla 2009). Examples of online legal risks in social media comprise violation of terms and conditions of using a social medium, defamation, and different types of infringement such as privacy infringement, as well as trademark or copyright infringement (Savell 2010).

How people perceive legal risk in cyberspace may affect their behaviours online. For example, their perceptions may have impacts on the amount of personal data they would share in the virtual environment (Featherman and Pavlou 2003) or whether they would use pirated software (Liao et al. 2010).

3.3 Methodologies

3.3.1 Searches on Google Scholar

Online legal risk in social media in Hong Kong may not be a hot topic attracting scholars' attention. In late April 2014, the author carried out a simple search on Google Scholar with "legal online risk" in quotation marks as keywords for the search. It resulted in zero research findings. Similar searches using "online legal risk" and "legal risk online" in quotation marks, respectively, led to two findings each. Taking a closer look at these four identified documents, none of them discussed legal risks in cyberspace.

Another independent search on Google Scholar using "social media" and "legal risk" (both in quotation marks) as the two sets of keywords at one go led to a total of 141 results. When "Hong Kong" in quotation marks was included to refine the search within these 141 results, it generated 14 results: ten books, three journal articles, and one research paper. All these fourteen results were checked and they had nothing to do with legal risks in social media.

3.3.2 Searches on the Westlaw HK

Against the background of the search results on Google Scholar as described above, further searches were carried out in late April 2014 on a renowned online professional legal database, namely the Westlaw HK, for court cases in Hong Kong relevant to online legal risks. The numbers of cases identified through using "online risk", "social media", "Facebook", "Twitter", "Weibo" (微博; *wēi bó*), and "Weixin" (微信; *wēi xìn*) as keywords for the respective searches are tabulated in Table 3.2. Facebook, Twitter, Weibo, and Weixin were chosen as these social media are no strangers to Hong Kong people. A specific search using "online legal risk" as keywords was not necessary as the search using "online risk" would somehow include the results of "online legal risk".

A total of 83 court cases were found. The author then scanned the principal subjects and catchwords of these findings as shown on the legal database and read the judgments of potentially relevant ones. As a result, three cases were identified for discussion below.

Table 3.2 Search results on the Westlaw HK

Keywords used	Number of court cases in Hong Kong identified
"Online" and "risk" in the same search	57
"Social" and "media" (a computer command was set to search the two words simultaneously within the same pages of each document archived in the legal database)	0
Facebook	24
Twitter	2
Weibo	0
Weixin	0
Total:	83

3.4 A Few Online Legal Risks in Social Media in Hong Kong

3.4.1 Defamation

In *John Raymond Luciw v Wolfgang Derler* [2013] HKEC 1206, because of unsatisfactory contractual performance of Mr Derler's company, WP Engineering, in a renovation project, Mr. Luciw used a pseudonym in 2010 to post critical comments online against the performance of WP Engineering and Mr. Derler. Mr. Luciw also posted a self-produced video on YouTube, created a group on Facebook bearing a title of "Consumers against WP Engineering Ltd Hong Kong", and built a website using the URL www.bewareofwp.com. In return, Mr. Derler used the name of Mr. Luciw in 2011 to create a page on Facebook which contained some accurate personal details of Mr. Luciw and a photograph of Mr. Luciw and his wife. The Facebook page Mr. Derler created purported that Mr. Luciw was both a homosexual and a paedophile. More than that, in disguise of Mr. Luciw, Mr. Derler used the Facebook page to send messages to an online female friend asking for a sexual encounter. The female friend had more than 200 friends on Facebook herself and they could easily access the disguised Facebook page through a direct link. Playing the same tricks, Mr. Derler also wrote to Mr. Luciw's wife on Facebook, "admitting" to a desire for homosexual paedophilia. He further posted messages with paedophilic contents to three children—Mr. Luciw's two nephews and a friend of theirs. Saunders DJ sitting on the Court of First Instance agreed that alleged paedophilia is "an allegation of criminal behaviour that is of the most reprehensible nature and behaviour that is viewed with total disgust and disdain by the community" (paragraph 32). Having considered the seriousness of the acts and that the defamation was widely disseminated through Facebook, the court held that Mr. Derler had to pay about HK$1.5 million to Mr. Luciw, inclusive of damages, aggravated damages, and indemnity costs.

3.4.2 Reasonable Care by Providers of Social Media

In another case, *Oriental Press Group Ltd & Others v Fevaworks Solutions Ltd & Others* [2013] HKEC 1025, Fevaworks Solutions Ltd and others, being the respondents, are the providers, administrators, and managers hosting a popular online discussion forum in Hong Kong. The appellant, Oriental Press Group Ltd, sued the respondents for libel with regard to defamatory statements posted in that forum by some users of the forum. The questions before the Court of Final Appeal (CFA), the highest court in Hong Kong, were whether a provider of an online discussion forum may be held liable for the forum users' posting of defamatory statements, whether and to what extent the provider could be regarded in law as the publisher of the defamatory statements, and whether the provider could rely on the common law defence of innocent dissemination. The CFA held that the respondents did not authorize publication of the defamatory content. They were not the first or main publishers but like subordinate publishers, and they were entitled to rely on the common law defence of innocent dissemination. In order to escape liability, the respondents had to prove that reasonable care had been taken, and they were innocent of the posting of defamatory statements in their online discussion forum.

3.4.3 Criminal Liability

In *HKSAR v Chan Yau Hei* [2014] HKEC 383, some alleged inflammatory messages in relation to proposals for a political reform in Hong Kong were posted on an online discussion forum, saying "我哋要學猶太人炸咗中聯辦 # fire #" (*wǒ diè yào xué yóu tài rén zhá zuo zhōng lián bàn* # fire #) in Chinese or "We have to learn from the Jewish people and bomb the Liaison Office of the Central People's Government # fire #" as translated in the court judgment (paragraphs 5–6). The questions before the CFA were whether the posting of such an offending message in cyberspace would commit the common law offence of outraging public decency and whether the posting would be capable of constituting the offence. The CFA condemned the message posted but found that the public element of the offence of outraging public decency was not satisfied. The CFA allowed the appeal and quashed the appellant's conviction.

3.5 Discussion

All three court cases discussed above involved posting of statements of defamatory or even criminal nature in the virtual settings. They have provided vivid and lively lessons for users of social media in Hong Kong on how they should behave online. *John Raymond Luciw v Wolfgang Derler* [2013] HKEC 1206 has shown that legal liability arising from online defamation could be very serious. Also, people could not ignore the risk of paedophilia which has been warned by Livingstone (2009, p. 157) as one of the online predominant risks posed to children.

The CFA is the highest court in Hong Kong and its decisions bind the lower courts. The ruling of the CFA in *Oriental Press Group Ltd & Others v Fevaworks Solutions Ltd & Others* [2013] HKEC 1025 has made it clear that while users of social media posting statements or comments may be liable to claims for alleged defamation, the providers of social media should also take reasonable care to prevent publication of defamatory content on their sites, and protect others' rights not to have their reputations damaged by defamatory statements.

HKSAR v Chan Yau Hei [2014] HKEC 383 has pointed out that inappropriate online behaviours may be subject to criminal liabilities. Although the CFA approved the appeal and quashed the appellant's conviction in this case, it does not necessarily mean that the online statement in question was not serious enough to be subject to criminal liabilities. Fok PJ said, "the message posted by the appellant is deserving of condemnation" (paragraph 93). Ma CJ further added in the judgment with emphasis, "The common law offence of outraging public decency, which has a history going back at least 350 years, is not one that comfortably fits into the modern Internet age. Criminal liability in the context of the present case is one that should be determined by legislation" (paragraph 1).

3.6 Limitations

Owing to constraints of resources and space, this chapter can only briefly cover some online legal risks in social media in Hong Kong. From a legal perspective, no discussion is made on the legal principles and reasoning of the three court cases cited above. From a social perspective, no in-depth analysis is conducted, for instance, as to how people perceive legal risks when they are engaged in online activities in social media sites. Secondly, issues on jurisdiction and the conflict of laws are not dealt with in this chapter. Hong Kong is under a special context of "One Country Two Systems", where Hong Kong has inherited a common law system from the UK, and China runs a civil law system. The lack of resources and space has handicapped this study in a manner that it cannot address any potential legal risks and uncertainties if there are issues arising from online social networking activities in-between Hong Kong and China via social media sites such as Weibo or Weixin. It makes no examination either on the issues of applicable law, jurisdiction, and the conflict of laws in cross-border online activities between Hong Kong and territories other than China through social media sites such as Facebook and Twitter. Thirdly, as law changes over time and is not the same worldwide, what has been discussed in this chapter is only a snapshot of Hong Kong. To the best knowledge of the author, the law discussed in this chapter is current as of June 2014. Last but not least, there is a further technical limitation. The author has tried his best to provide the most current and accurate information such as case law and website addresses, but some may have changed after this chapter is submitted to the publisher. In brief, this study may not be able to provide a global picture about online legal risks in social media. The discussion herein may not be generalized and applied universally to other territories.

3.7 Future Directions for Research

Online legal risk in social media in Hong Kong is still a developing topic, as shown by the fact that the availability of relevant scholarly references is limited. This study examines three court cases in Hong Kong by means of literature review and basic legal research on a professional legal database. It serves two purposes. Firstly, with the support of court cases as illustrations, it outlines some legal risks in cyberspace in Hong Kong when people are engaged in online activities in social media. Secondly, this chapter may facilitate further discourse and research on online legal risks. In fact, there are few, if not none, legal and social studies, both qualitative and quantitative, conducted in the context of social media in Hong Kong. More studies are therefore proposed in these directions. In the areas of legal research, further studies on issues of jurisdiction and the conflict of laws involved in online social networking activities under the context of "One Country Two Systems" and across borders are recommended. As far as social research is concerned, empirical studies on the relationship between online legal risks and people's behaviours in social media in cyberspace are suggested, for example, how they perceive online legal risks in social media and whether their perceptions of such risks would affect their behaviours in social media.

References

Amoroso, D., & Dembla, P. (2009, March 12–14). Music sharing in China: Theoretical foundations. In *Proceedings of the Southern Association for Information Systems conference* (pp. 175–181). Charleston, South Carolina.

Bhatnagar, A., Misra, S., & Rao, H. R. (2000). On risk, convenience, and Internet shopping behavior. *Communications of the ACM, 43*(11), 98–105. doi:10.1145/353360.353371.

Boyd, D. M., & Ellison, N. B. (2008). Social network sites: Definition, history, and scholarship. *Journal of Computer-Mediated Communication, 13*(1), 210–230. doi:10.1111/j.1083-6101.2007.00393.x.

Chiu, C., Lin, D., & Silverman, A. (2012). China's social-media boom. Retrieved June 25, 2014, from http://www.mckinsey.com/insights/marketing_sales/chinas_social-media_boom

Crespo, Á. H., del Bosque, I. R., & de los Salmones Sánchez, M. M. G. (2009). The influence of perceived risk on Internet shopping behavior: A multidimensional perspective. *Journal of Risk Research, 12*(2), 259–277. doi:10.1080/13669870802497744.

Eyrich, N., Padman, M. L., & Sweetser, K. D. (2008). PR practitioners' use of social media tools and communication technology. *Public Relations Review, 34*(4), 412–414. doi:10.1016/j.pubrev.2008.09.010.

Featherman, M. S., & Pavlou, P. A. (2003). Predicting e-services adoption: A perceived risk facets perspective. *International Journal of Human-Computer Studies, 59*(4), 451–474. doi:10.1016/S1071-5819(03)00111-3.

Forsythe, S. M., & Shi, B. (2003). Consumer patronage and risk perceptions in Internet shopping. *Journal of Business Research, 56*, 867–875. doi:10.1016/S0148-2963(01)00273-9.

Friedman, T. L. (2006). *The world is flat – The globalized world in the twenty-first century* (Rev. and exp. ed.). London: Penguin Books.

Georgescu, M. (2006). Some issues about risk management for e-banking. *Social Science Research Network*. Retrieved June 25, 2014, from http://ssrn.com/abstract=903419

Goh, B. (2009, September 8). Asian social networking sites profit from virtual money. *Reuters*. Retrieved June 25, 2014, from http://www.reuters.com/article/2009/09/09/us-asia-socialnetworking-idUSTRE58800D20090909

HKSAR v Chan Yau Hei. [2014] HKEC 383. Court of Final Appeal of Hong Kong.

John Raymond Luciw v Wolfgang Derler. [2013] HKEC 1206. Court of First Instance of Hong Kong.

Kane, G. C., Alavi, M., Labianca, G.(. J.)., & Borgatti, S. P. (2014). What's different about social media network? A framework and research agenda. *MIS Quarterly, 38*(1), 275–304.

Kietzmann, J. H., Hermkens, K., McCarthy, I. P., & Silvestre, B. S. (2011). Social media? Get serious! Understanding the functional building blocks of social media. *Business Horizons, 54*(3), 241–251. doi:10.1016/j.bushor.2011.01.005.

Lenhart, A., Madden, M., Macgill, A. R., & Smith, A. (2007). *Teens and social media: The use of social media gains a greater foothold in teen life as they embrace the conversational nature of interactive online media*. Washington, DC, USA: Pew Internet & American Project. Retrieved June 25, 2014, from http://www.pewinternet.org/files/old-media//Files/Reports/2007/PIP_Teens_Social_Media_Final.pdf.pdf

Li, Z. (2011, August 24). Hong Kong social media use higher than United States. *CNN Travel*. Retrieved June 25, 2014, from http://travel.cnn.com/hong-kong/life/hong-kong-social-media-use-higher-united-states-520745

Liao, C., Lin, H.-N., & Liu, Y.-P. (2010). Predicting the use of pirated software: A contingency model integrating perceived risk with the theory of planned behavior. *Journal of Business Ethics, 91*(2), 237–252. doi:10.1007/s10551-009-0081-5.

Lim, N. (2003). Consumers' perceived risk: sources versus consequences. *Electronic Commerce Research and Applications, 2*(3), 216–228. doi:10.1016/S1567-4223(03)00025-5.

Livingstone, S. (2009). *Children and the Internet*. Cambridge, UK: Polity Press.

Livingstone, S., & Haddon, L. (2009). *EU Kids Online: final report 2009* (EU Kids Online, Deliverable D6.5). London: EU Kids Online Network. Retrieved June 25, 2014, from http://eprints.lse.ac.uk/24372/1/EU%20Kids%20Online%20final%20report%202009%28lsero%29.pdf

Madden, M., & Smith, A. (2010). *Reputation management and social media: How people monitor their identity and search for others online*. Washington, DC, USA: Pew Internet & American Life Project. Retrieved June 25, 2014, from http://www.pewinternet.org/files/old-media//Files/Reports/2010/PIP_Reputation_Management_with_topline.pdf

Mahler, T. (2007, June 13–16). Defining legal risk. In *Conference proceedings of "Commercial contracting for strategic advantage – Potentials and prospects"* (pp. 10–31). Turku University of Applied Sciences, Turku, Finland.

Mangold, W. G., & Faulds, D. J. (2009). Social media: The new hybrid element of the promotion mix. *Business Horizons, 52*(4), 357–365. doi:10.1016/j.bushor.2009.03.002.

Mourtada, R., & Salem, F. (2012). Social media in the Arab world: Influencing societal and cultural change? *Arab Social Media Report, 2*(1), 1–28.

Munnukka, J., & Järvi, P. (2013). Perceived risks and risk management of social media in an organizational context. *Electronic Markets* (published online: 1 August 2013). doi:10.1007/s12525-013-0138-2.

Oriental Press Group Ltd & Others v Fevaworks Solutions Ltd & Others. [2013] HKEC 1025. Court of Final Appeal of Hong Kong.
R v Legare 2009 SCC 56, [2009] 3 SCR 551. Supreme Court of Canada.
Savell, L. (2010). *Minimizing the legal risks of using online social networks*. Retrieved June 25, 2014,fromhttp://www.law.com/jsp/article.jsp?id=1202462946165&slreturn=20131030063802
Schoder, D., & Yin, P. L. (2000). Building firm trust online. *Communications of the ACM, 43*(12), 73–79. doi:10.1145/355112.355127.
Shirky, C. (2011). The political power of social media: Technology, the public sphere, and political change. *Foreign Affairs, 90*(1), 28–41.
Staksrud, E. (2013). *Children in the online world: Risk, regulation, rights*. Burlington: Ashgate.
Vance, K., Howe, W., & Dellavalle, R. P. (2009). Social Internet sites as a source of public health information. *Dermatologic Clinics, 27*(2), 133–136. doi:10.1016/j.det.2008.11.010.
Vellido, A., Lisboa, P. J. G., & Meehan, K. (1999). Segmentation of the on-line shopping market using neural networks. *Expert Systems with Applications, 17*(4), 303–314.
Xiang, Z., & Gretzel, U. (2010). Role of social media in online travel information search. *Tourism Management, 31*, 179–188. doi:10.1016/j.tourman.2009.02.016.

Chapter 4
The Effect of a Brief Media Intervention on Help-Seeking Attitudes Among College Students in Hong Kong

Wai Kit Wong and Chi Keung Chan

Abstract This experimental study examined the effect of a brief media preventive intervention on help-seeking attitudes among college students in Hong Kong. Sixty local university students aged 17–23 were recruited and randomly assigned to either the experimental group or the control group. Participants in the experimental group (media intervention group) watched a video clip containing a mental health preventive message while participants in the control group watched a neutral video clip without any preventive message. Attitudes toward seeking help from mental health professional were measured before and after the media intervention. The results found that help-seeking attitudes of the experimental group slightly increased from the pretest ($M=6.20$, $SD=2.25$) to the posttest ($M=6.97$, $SD=2.09$). Nevertheless, there was no significant difference on the changes in help-seeking attitudes between the experimental group and the control group.

Keywords Media intervention • Help-seeking attitudes • Mental health

4.1 Introduction

In recent years, the government of Hong Kong Special Administrative Region (HKSAR) has been implementing mass media (e.g., advertisement) intervention to promote the importance of early prevention and to raise the awareness of potential mental health patients regarding seeking professional help. In other words, this media intervention aims to increase the potential mental health patients' attitudes toward seeking help from professional mental health care services.

Previous research supported the use of mass media as a preventive and educational strategy. Vogel et al. (2005) suggested that media intervention is an alternative approach to increase the expectations of potential mental health patients in

W.K. Wong • C.K. Chan (✉)
Department of Counseling and Psychology,
Hong Kong Shue Yan University, Hong Kong, China
e-mail: jackwong615@hotmail.com; alexchan@hksyu.edu

© Springer Science+Business Media Singapore 2015

W.W.K. Ma et al. (eds.), *New Media, Knowledge Practices and Multiliteracies*,
DOI 10.1007/978-981-287-209-8_4

seeking professional help when they have psychological needs. A recent study by Demyan and Anderson (2012) aimed to find out the effects of a brief media intervention on expectations, intentions, and attitudes of seeking help among American college students. In their study, both the experimental group and the control group watched seven 10-min video segments of musical performance. In between the segments, the experimental group was exposed to nine 2-min media intervention (mental health service announcement), whereas the control group did not. They found that there was a positive effect of the use of brief media intervention on the attitudes toward seeking help from mental health professions among college students. On the contrary, Caldwell and Miaskowski (2002) argued that media intervention can only increase the awareness of potential mental health patients but may not sufficiently motivate them to seek help from mental health professional.

Locally, social welfare agencies and organizations have been adopting the brief media intervention approach by broadcasting some mental health-related advertisements to influence the public's help-seeking attitudes. Nevertheless, a recent report from the Social Indicators of the Hong Kong (2011) showed that there had been an increasing trend of teenagers' suicide rates over the past few years. More seriously, there was 52 % increase in suicide rates from 2005 to 2011 for the age group of 15–19 (Sing Tao Daily 2011; Social Indicators of Hong Kong 2011). Even with such a dramatic increase in suicide rates of the youth, the annual report from The Samaritan Befrienders Hong Kong showed that the help-seeking rates from the age group of 10–19 had been stagnated (The Samaritan Befrienders Hong Kong 2006, 2007, 2008, 2009, 2010, 2011, 2012). Some claimed that these opposite trends indicating the failure of media preventive intervention. Do these trends imply the use of media intervention to change help-seeking attitudes and to motivate help-seeking behaviors is ineffective?

In this study, we adopted Ajzen and Fishbein's (1980) Theory of Reasoned Action and Planned Behavior (TRA/PB) to establish a theoretical framework to understand the effectiveness of a brief media preventive intervention. TRA/PB can be applied to understand the changes of help-seeking attitudes and behavior. First, individuals should overcome some belief-barriers, for instance, adjusting their beliefs about seeking help from mental health professionals. After the belief has been adjusted, positive attitudes would be developed and these positive attitudes in turn influence their intention of help seeking and then the actual behaviors. Based on the TRA/PB, the media preventive intervention in mental health assumes that by adjusting the belief of potential mental health patients could influence their help-seeking attitudes, intention, and actual behaviors.

Thus, the purpose of this experimental study was to investigate the influence of a brief media intervention on the help-seeking attitudes among college students aged 17–23 in Hong Kong. This age group was chosen because they have the largest growth in attempting and committing suicide. The key objective of this study was to investigate whether a brief media preventive intervention is effective in changing the help-seeking attitudes of college students. Another objective of this study was to provide recommendations for improving the existing media preventive intervention program to motivate the help-seeking behaviors among college students in Hong Kong.

Furthermore, a previous research from Lin et al. (1978) stated that American Chinese patients were less likely to seek help from mental health professional due to various familial and cultural factors. However, very few studies have systematically examined the effectiveness of media preventive strategy on help-seeking attitudes in Chinese societies. Hence, the final objective of this study was to investigate the effect of a brief media prevention intervention on help-seeking attitudes among the youth and young adults in a Chinese society.

4.2 Theoretical Framework

The theoretical framework for this study was based on the Theory of Reasoned Action/Planned Behavior Model (TRA/PB) developed by Ajzen and Fishbein (1980). This theory states that after a continuous intervention, such as media intervention, a person's belief on some issue or behavior would be changed. With the change in belief, it may influence a person's positive attitudes toward the conditioned behavior (e.g., help-seeking behavior). A person's positive attitudes toward a behavior then influence and increase the intention to act out. Finally, an individual acts out the actual behavior (help-seeking behavior) when they need. In this experimental study, we only limited the scope on whether a brief media preventive intervention can effectively change the help-seeking attitudes among college students in Hong Kong.

Figure 4.1 shows the conceptual framework for this experimental study. The independent variable was the brief media intervention and the dependent variable was the attitudes toward help-seeking behavior among college students in Hong Kong. The independent variable was manipulated by playing a video clip including two 30-s help-seeking preventive messages (experimental condition) versus a video clip without any preventive messages (control condition). The research question was whether this one-time brief media preventive intervention (independent variable) can influence the help-seeking attitudes (dependent variable) among college students in Hong Kong. It is hypothesized that participants in the experimental group would have more positive attitudes toward help-seeking behavior than participants in the control group after the exposure to the brief media intervention.

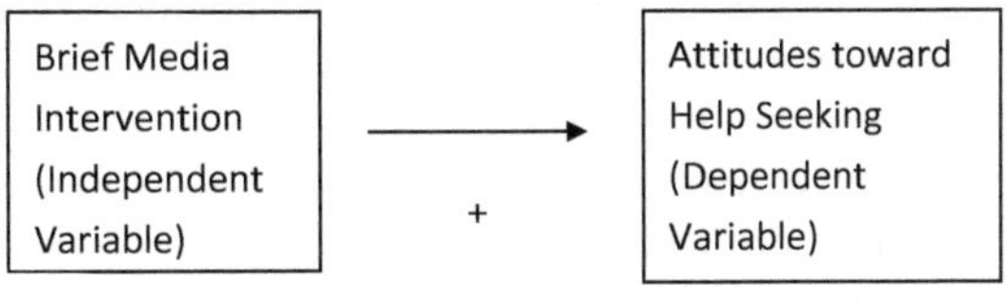

Fig. 4.1 A theoretical model for the influence of the brief media intervention on help-seeking attitudes among college students in Hong Kong

4.3 Method

4.3.1 Participants

The participants of this experiment study were Hong Kong college students aged from 17 to 23. A short version of the Mental Health Scale (Fischer and Farina 1995) was used to screen for the suitable participants in the experiment. The suitable participants were those who scored in the normal range on the Mental Health Scale (4–9 marks). This criterion was set because participants who scored from 0–3 or 10–12 were too extreme. At the end, the total number of participants in the experiment was 60 and they were evenly and randomly assigned either to the experimental group or the control group (30 participants in each group).

4.3.2 Measure

In this study, we adopted the Attitudes toward Seeking Professional Psychological Help Scale: Short Form (ATSPPH; Fischer and Farina 1995) to measure participants' attitudes toward seeking help from mental health professionals before and after the brief media intervention. The ATSPPH includes 10 items rated on a 4-point Likert scale ranging from 0 (Disagree) to 3 (Agree). The total scores ranged from 0 to 30 with higher scores indicating higher positive attitudes toward seeking help from professionals. Elhai et al. (2008) reported that the test–retest reliability ($r=0.80$) and the internal consistency ($\alpha=0.84$) are high. After pilot testing, only four items (items 1, 5, 9, and 10) with acceptable factor loadings were selected for including in both the pretest and posttest for the actual experimental study. Hence, the range of the total scores was from 0 to 12.

4.3.3 Brief Media Intervention

Two 17-min video clips were played to the experimental group and the control group, respectively. Each version of the video contained three segments of musical performance with an approximate length of 5 min for each segment. Two advertisements were played in between the three segments. For experimental group, two 30-s advertisements with help-seeking preventive message were inserted in between the segments. The help-seeking advertisement was made by The Samaritan Befrienders Hong Kong and it was an announcement to persuade an individual to seek help if he/she has a thought of attempting suicidal. For the control group, the advertisements with preventive message were replaced by two general health announcements. The length of the health-related announcements was also 30-s each. In addition, two sales promotion advertisements were included to deceive the participants about the real purpose of the experiment.

4.3.4 Procedures

At the beginning, the researcher explained the purpose and procedures of the experiment and obtained the informed consent from the participants. Then, all participants filled out the edited short version of the Mental Health Scale (Fischer and Farina 1995) which measures their level of mental health. The results of the screening test were calculated immediately and eligible participants (those scored within 4–9 marks) were then randomly assigned to either the experimental group (with media intervention) or the control group. The participants also completed a questionnaire about their attitudes toward help-seeking behavior.

Both participants in the experimental and control groups were asked to watch a 17-min video. As mentioned above, participants in experimental group watched a video clip with help-seeking preventive advertisements embedded, whereas participants in control group watched a same length video clip with general health advertisements (without help-seeking preventive message). After the brief media intervention, participants completed a questionnaire about their attitudes of help-seeking behavior (posttest). The questionnaire also included a few questions as manipulation check for the attention of participants to the media intervention.

4.4 Results

In order to test the hypothesis about the effect of mass media intervention, we conducted a series of independent sample *t*-tests to compare the pretest, posttest, and change scores on the help-seeking attitudes between the experimental group and the control group.

Table 4.1 summarizes the descriptive and inferential statistics on the help-seeking attitudes for both of the experimental and control groups. There was no significant difference on the pretest scores of help-seeking attitudes between the experimental group and the control group, $t(58)=0.066$, $p=0.947$, indicating there was no selection bias in the random assignment.

Table 4.1 Descriptive and inferential statistics on the help-seeking attitudes for experimental and control groups

	Experimental	Control	*t*-value	*p*-value
Pretest				
Mean	6.17	6.20	0.066	0.947
SD	1.60	2.25		
Posttest				
Mean	6.77	6.97	0.390	0.698
SD	1.87	2.09		
Change scores				
Mean	0.60	0.77	0.485	0.629
SD	1.40	1.25		

In addition, the within-group paired-samples *t*-test showed that there was a significant slight improvement in help-seeking attitudes for the experimental group from the pretest ($M=6.20$, SD=2.25) to the posttest ($M=6.97$, SD=2.09), $t(29)=2.34$, and $p=0.026$. Unexpectedly, there was also a significant improvement in help-seeking attitudes for the control group from the pretest ($M=6.17$, SD=1.60) to the posttest ($M=6.77$, SD=1.87), $t(29)=3.36$, and $p=0.002$.

Finally, no significant difference was found on the change scores of help-seeking attitudes between the experimental group and the control group $t(58)=0.485$, $p=0.629$. These results indicated that the mass media intervention (with a mental health preventive message) cannot significantly improve the help-seeking attitudes of the participants as compared to those who watched advertisements with general health message only. Hence, the influence of brief media preventive intervention on help-seeking attitudes among college students was limited for this study.

4.5 Discussion

The findings of this study indicated that the effect of the brief media prevention intervention on the change in help-seeking attitudes among Hong Kong college students was limited. Although the scores of the attitudes toward seeking help from mental health professionals were slightly increased after the brief intervention, there was no significant difference on the change of help-seeking attitudes between the experimental group and the control group. These results suggested that a one-time brief media intervention may not be sufficient and effective in changing help-seeking beliefs and attitudes of Chinese college students.

The results of this study were inconsistent to the findings of a similar study conducted by Demyan and Anderson (2012). Demyan and Anderson (2012) found that brief media intervention significantly increased the positive attitudes toward help-seeking behaviors among American college students. In this study, brief media intervention was not influential to help-seeking attitudes among Chinese college students. These inconsistent results were mainly due to the exposure frequency and length to the media intervention. The total exposure frequency and time were 7 times and 14-min in Demyan and Anderson's study but only 2 times and 1-min for the present study. The differences in exposure frequency and length explained the inconsistent results between the two studies.

Also, the inconsistent results may reflect the cultural differences between the Chinese and the American college students. In Chinese society, many individuals do not feel comfortable to mention their personal and emotional problems to outsiders. The Chinese usually view practitioners as outsiders (Hung-Bin and Sedlacek 2004; Kung 2003) and they think seeking help from outsiders immediately during difficulties is losing "lian" (臉). Hence, a potential reason that hinders the Chinese college students to seek help from the mental health professionals may be due to the strong stigma about psychiatric treatment in Hong Kong, the fear of social stereotype of being mentally-ill, and the avoidance of losing face.

Moreover, the Chinese have a tendency to suppress positive and negative emotions which might not be noticed easily (Sun 2013). Hung-Bin and Sedlacek (2004) suggested that the Chinese usually adopt intrafamilial coping and seek help from their family members first. If this coping strategy is failed, they tend to get confirmation from informal network (e.g., mental health resources on the Internet). Extrafamilial coping and seek help from mental health professionals are only their last step after they confirm and accept their mental illness. Future studies need to further explore the cultural differences on the relationship between mental health preventive media intervention and help-seeking attitudes.

Besides the cultural factor, there were a few possible factors that might affect the effect of the brief media preventive intervention. The first possible factor was the receiver's awareness of the media intervention. The effectiveness of the media preventive intervention could be reduced due to the inattention of the participants. Thus, in this study, the researcher adopted a manipulation check on the participants' attention to the brief media intervention. It was found that 90 % (54 out of 60) of participants did pay attention to the intervention advertisements. Therefore, there was no evidence to link inattention to the insignificant findings.

Another possible factor was the receiver's bias on the intervention message. This subjective bias may affect the effectiveness of the brief media intervention. As mentioned above, in Chinese culture, the behavior to seek help from others is a label of losing face (Mian Zi 面子) (Sun 2013). Moreover, there may be a social stigma on seeking help from mental health professional. With this cultural bias and stigmatization, the attitudes of the Chinese participants might not be easily changed and more difficult to accept the preventive message of the brief media intervention. As discussed above, this linkage needs to be further investigated.

The last possible factor was the understanding of the media preventive message. The effectiveness of the media intervention may be affected by the receiver's recognition of the preventive message. If the participants do not understand the intervention message, the effectiveness of the brief media intervention would be significantly reduced. Chan and Fang (2007) found that teenagers and youth usually watch advertisements shown on any mass media to understand the fashion trend or functions of new products. They have low incentive to extract and understand the information from the brief media preventive intervention, especially for the participants in this study who were within the normal mental health range.

From the perspective of the Theory of Reasoned Action and Planned Behavior (TRA/PB), the results of this study implied that the influence of a one-time brief media preventive intervention was limited and could not significantly change the participants' belief (e.g., cultural belief or bias) about help-seeking behaviors. If the participants' belief could not be adjusted, one would not expect there was any significant change on the help-seeking attitudes of the participants. When the attitudes toward seeking help from mental health professionals remained the same, it is anticipated that there will be no change on the intention of seeking help and the actual help-seeking behaviors.

Finally, in terms of application, television broadcasting has been used as a major platform for the media intervention. However, with the improvement of technology, the influence of the television broadcasting may not effectively affect the help-seeking attitudes of the youth. It is suggested that further study can adopt a more intensive media preventive intervention using Internet-based or smartphone-based platforms (e.g., Facebook and Whatsapp) because these are the most popular platforms used by the youth nowadays.

In conclusion, this study did not find solid evidence to support the effectiveness of a one-time brief media preventive intervention on the attitudes toward seeking help from mental health professionals among college students in Hong Kong. We attempted to explain the insignificant findings from the theoretical, methodological, and cultural perspectives. Although some of our explanations are somewhat speculative, future studies should further investigate the effect of brief media preventive intervention on the help-seeking attitudes. From a practical perspective, simply using media intervention may not be sufficient to change the receiver's beliefs and attitudes toward help-seeking. Instead, we recommend that the content of the media preventive message should be cultural relevant, age specific, and group specific in order to remove some belief barriers. In addition, the media intervention should be delivered through multiple platforms (e.g., mental health workshops at school, self-help toolbox at school intranet, online resources on Facebook, self-help apps, etc.) with repeated exposures for a period of time to enhance its effectiveness.

References

Ajzen, I., & Fishbein, M. (1980). *Understanding attitudes and predicting social behavior*. Englewood Cliffs: Prentice Hall.

Caldwell, M. A., & Miaskowski, C. (2002). Mass media interventions to reduce help-seeking delay in people with symptoms of acute myocardial infraction: Time for a new approach? *Patient Education and Counseling, 46*(1), 1–9.

Chan, K., & Fang, W. (2007). Use of the internet and traditional media among young people. *Young Consumers: Insight and Ideas for Responsible Marketers, 8*(4), 244–256.

Demyan, A. L., & Anderson, T. (2012). Effects of a brief media intervention on expectations, attitudes, and intentions of mental health help seeking. *Journal of Counseling Psychology, 59*(2), 222–229.

Elhai, J. D., Schweinle, W., & Anderson, S. M. (2008). Reliability and validity of the attitudes toward seeking professional psychological help scale – Short form. *Psychiatry Research, 159*, 320–329.

Fischer, E. H., & Farina, A. (1995). Attitudes toward seeking professional psychological help: A shortened form and considerations for research. *Journal of College Student Development, 36*(4), 368–373.

Hung-Bin, S., & Sedlacek, W. E. (2004). An exploratory study of help-seeking attitudes and coping strategies among college students by race and gender. *Measurement & Evaluation in Counseling & Development (American Counseling Association), 37*(3), 130–143.

Kung, W. W. (2003). Chinese Americans' help seeking for emotional distress. *The Social Service Review, 77*(1), 110–134.

Lin, T. Y., Tardiff, K., Donetz, G., & Goresky, W. (1978). Ethnicity and patterns of help-seeking. *Culture, Medicine and Psychiatry, 2*(1), 3–13.

Sing Tao Daily. (2011, June 26). *The youth suicide rate increased 58 % in 6 years*. Retrieved from http://la.stgloballink.com/hk/201106/t20110626_1601889.html

Social Indicators of Hong Kong. (2011). *Youth suicide rate*. Retrieved from http://www.socialindicators.org.hk/en/indicators/youth/30.4

Sun, C. T. L. (2013). *Themes in Chinese psychology*. Singapore: Cengage.
The Samaritan Befrienders Hong Kong. (2006). *2005 annual report*. Retrieved from http://www.sbhk.org.hk/annual/2005.pdf
The Samaritan Befrienders Hong Kong. (2007). *2006 annual report*. Retrieved from http://www.sbhk.org.hk/annual/2006.pdf
The Samaritan Befrienders Hong Kong. (2008). *2007 annual report*. Retrieved from http://www.sbhk.org.hk/annual/sbhk_report_2007.pdf
The Samaritan Befrienders Hong Kong. (2009). *2008 annual report*. Retrieved from http://www.sbhk.org.hk/annual/sbhk_report_2008.pdf
The Samaritan Befrienders Hong Kong. (2010). *2009 annual report*. Retrieved from http://www.sbhk.org.hk/annual/sbhk_report_2009.pdf
The Samaritan Befrienders Hong Kong. (2011). *2010 annual report*. Retrieved from http://www.sbhk.org.hk/annual/sbhk_report_2010.pdf
The Samaritan Befrienders Hong Kong. (2012). *2011 annual report*. Retrieved from http://www.sbhk.org.hk/annual/sbhk_report_2011.pdf
Vogel, D. L., Wester, S. R., Wei, M., & Boysen, G. A. (2005). The role of outcome expectations and attitudes on decisions to seek professional help. *Journal of Counseling Psychology, 52*(4), 459–470.

Chapter 5
Understanding the Obstacles of Using Tablet as a Learning Tool in Primary Schools from Teachers' Perceptions

Xiaolei Li, Allan H.K. Yuen, and Wenting Zou

Abstract With the development of using tablets instead of traditional (nontouch screen) notebook computer in the classrooms, it is raised concern in education how to enhance the effectiveness of using tablets in teaching and learning. In this study, it provides a significant framework included four main obstacles of using tablet as a learning tool related to schools, teachers, parents, and students that are studied with grounded theory. Furthermore, the purpose of this study is to explore teachers' perceptions of teaching and students' engagement that occurs as a result of using tablet as a learning tool in the classrooms.

Keywords Tablet • Learning tool • Obstacles • Teachers' perceptions • Primary schools

5.1 Introduction

5.1.1 Problem Statement

Today's children in many countries, whose entire lives have been immersed in the twenty-first century media culture, are referred to as "digital natives". They literally live in the world via the filter of computing devices: the mobile phone, handheld gaming devices, tablets, and laptops they can take everywhere. As mobile information and communication technologies has become one of the most popular learning tools in

X. Li (✉) • A.H.K. Yuen
The University of Hong Kong, Hong Kong, China
e-mail: xiaolei1990@hotmail.com; hkyuen@hku.hk

W. Zou
CCC Heep Woh Primary School, Kowloon, Hong Kong
e-mail: ellenzou2012@gmail.com

© Springer Science+Business Media Singapore 2015

W.W.K. Ma et al. (eds.), *New Media, Knowledge Practices and Multiliteracies*,
DOI 10.1007/978-981-287-209-8_5

education recently, it also "will feature prominently in the future of learning and classroom environments", however, "these devices also carry the potential to distract learners and create frustration in the classroom" (Rossing et al. 2012) in universities. Therefore, an increasing concern arises: for primary school students, are they suitable to use tablet as a learning tool to enhance their effectiveness of learning in classrooms since "digital natives" may contact with mobile learning early even in their primary schools. Furthermore, it is important and necessary to pay attention to children using tablets and understand the obstacles of tablet as a learning tool in the digital age.

5.1.2 Purpose of the Study and Research Questions

The main purpose of this study is to explore teachers' perceptions of teaching and students' engagement that occurs as a result of using tablet as a learning tool in the classroom. And the research questions are display as below:

- How do the teachers perceive tablet as a learning tool for students in primary schools?
- What are the obstacles of teaching with tablet as a learning tool in classroom from teachers' perceptions?

5.2 Literature Review

5.2.1 Potential Benefits of Using Tablet as a Learning Tool

Tablets, one kind of portable devices, supported the "mobile learning" which is "perhaps the fastest growth area in the whole field of ICTs in education" (Pegrum et al. 2013). Apart from its convenience and portable use, tablets are also used in education to enhance handwriting and input use friendly for children according to Newhouse (2006) study. Furthermore, tablets "offers all the functionality of a common desktop computer at nearly the price of desktop computers and light enough for children to carry" (Newhouse 2006). The study shows, "students preferred tablet PCs to netbooks and also indicated greater self-confidence in expressing their ideas with the tablet's digital ink and paper technology than with the netbooks' traditional vertical screen and keyboard arrangement" (Alvarez et al. 2011). Additionally, Alvarez et al. (2011) indicated that tablet PCs could strengthen students' collective discourse capabilities and facilitate a richer and more natural body language.

5.2.2 Teachers' Perceptions as a Factor in Implementation of Using Tablet as a Learning Tool

According to Hativa (1986), teacher is the most crucial factor in implementing and maintaining an innovation. And teachers' perceptions may influence to the efficiency of the implementation of tablet as a learning tool in classrooms. Dundar and Akcayir

(2012) also pointed out that applications of tablet PCs for students could also be examined based on the opinions of teachers. Therefore, it is feasible and reliable to understand the obstacles of using tablet as a learning tool in classrooms by examining teachers' perceptions.

5.2.3 Factors Affecting the Effectiveness Using of Tablets as a Learning Tool

Although there are multiple potential benefits to using tablets in classrooms, there are also documented factors that affect the effectiveness using of tablet as a learning tool that should be considered. For example, the fear of change, lack of training, modeling, personal use, and motivation, as well as knowledge, teaching beliefs, self-efficacy, and school culture are included as a number of barriers to technology integration (Bitner and Bitner 2002; Ertmer and Ottenbreit-Leftwich 2010). These are few factors may affect using tablet as a learning tool in classroom. And there is research to suggest that obstacles does influence tablets used in classrooms as a learning tool, but it is mixed and few research doing of it.

5.3 Research Methodologies

5.3.1 Research Design/Approach

In order to address the research questions fully, this study employed a case study with concurrent qualitative method of interviews. A qualitative data are obtained to gain a rich and informative evaluation with the ground theory.

5.3.2 Participants

Participants in the study are six teachers sampled from different subjects, registered in two primary schools in Hong Kong. And these two primary schools are already integrated tablets into their classrooms.

5.3.3 Procedures

It is widely acknowledged that the new technology integration in classroom should be supplemented with some in-depth interviews constructed to probe teachers thinking on their use of that technology (Painter 2001). Hence, six primary school teachers were invited to participate in in-depth interviews. And because of the small

Table 5.1 Teachers' information

School	Teacher	Position
School A	Teacher A	IT manager and Chinese teacher
	Teacher B	English teacher
	Teacher C	IT teacher assistant
School B	Teacher D	Chinese teacher
	Teacher E	English teacher
	Teacher F	Mathematics and IT teacher

sample size, a case study approach was used. It is widely accepted that the case study approach provides an opportunity for an individual researcher to study one aspect of a problem in depth within a limited time scale. Also, a case study allows the researcher to create insights and understanding rather than to generalize to a large population (Alamaki 1999).

5.3.4 *Data Collection*

In this study, interviews were conducted with six experienced teachers from two primary schools in Hong Kong (see Table 5.1). And semistructured questions use for the interview with teachers. Furthermore, the semistructured interviews begin with an open-ended question to allow ideas to suggest the use of tablet in learning and teaching. It is well-known fact that the strength of the open-ended question is flexible and provides an opportunity to obtain unusual response in in-depth interviews (Burroughs 1975). Interviews were conducted to explore the teachers' perception of impact of tablets as a learning tool in classrooms and whether any factors that affect the effective use of tablet in learning and teaching.

5.3.5 *Data Analysis*

According to Glesne and Peshkin (1992), "data analysis done simultaneously with data collection enables you to focus and shape the study as it goes". And the data were triangulated with information gathered from semistructured interviews and school documental data.

First, school A and school B in ICT education were selected as a sample through theoretical sampling. Since these two schools have introduced mobile technology into classrooms in recent years, there are enough tablets for teachers and students used for teaching and learning. Then, the concepts and categories generated from case interviews would be revised and improved constantly according to grounded theory, until the concepts and the relationship between categories are well accepted.

Data analysis procedure by using grounded theory can be divided into three steps: open coding, axial coding, and selective coding. In this process, the efficiency of coding was improved by using mind-mapping software Xmind 2013.

5.3.5.1 Open Coding

According to Glaser (1978) as well as Strauss and Corbin (1990), open coding is the initial step into the coding process with grounded theory. Moreover, open coding means to generate the original data after data collection and involves describing the overall obstacles of using tablet as a learning tool under the study. And it is necessary and significant to compare each piece of data with the codes already identified to determine its distinct characteristic on any relevant scale before forming the categories and concepts. Additionally, the concepts and categories naming should reflect the reality adequately with multiple sources including the literature, the interview record, and the result from the discussion. During open coding, it may be open minded and necessary to code each sentence from interview records, without any assumptions.

Thus, data from teacher interview were transcribed from the audio records and coded after consideration and negotiation from the authors. And part of the open coding from the records of School A and School B is illustrated in Table 5.2. With the reference of a variety of relevant literatures, 20 concepts and 8 subcategories were finally acquired (see Table 5.3).

Eight subcategories were abstracted as follows: school-related management, school-related service received, teacher-related service provided, teacher-related management, teacher-related service received, student-related management, student-related service received, and parent-related management.

5.3.5.2 Axial Coding

Axial coding is to select one open coding category and places it at the center as the central phenomenon and then relates all other categories to it (Strauss and Corbin 1998).

With the comparison between concepts and categories in the open coding repeatedly, four main categories were acquired from comprehensive consideration of relationship between categories. Finally, the four main categories were acquired with the paradigm model are school-related, teacher-related, student-related, and parent-related obstacles of using tablet as a learning tool which are illustrated in Table 5.3 as below.

5.3.5.3 Selective Coding

Selective coding is to write a theory based on the interrelationship of the categories from axial coding (Strauss and Corbin 1998).

Table 5.2 Examples of open coding analysis from the records of schools A and B

The records of teachers	Open coding Coding	Conceptualization	Categorization
Teacher C: Availability of a good platform, for example, we are temporarily using Modern Publishing platform provided homework for students, "welnet" enable students study online on their own at home, browsing article and practice excise. There is a lot of room to improve platforms	Availability of a good platform for students to study on line on their own	Platform selection and management by teachers	Teacher-related management; student-related service received
Teacher D: The most problem is battery flat, or damaged, it can be charged or repaired or use spare machine in the classroom, otherwise call the IT department for help. It normally won't disrupt the class	There is spare machine in the classroom for unexpected needs	Risk management of tablets in classroom	School-related management
Student D: Some student may forget their password so that they cannot get into the e platform. While some may remember not only their own password but others as well so that they can use others account to get into the platform for not good	Forget password or remember others password may lead them to do something not related to study	It may provide an opportunity for children to disrupt classroom order because of their lack of self-control	Student-related management
Teacher E: It is easier and more convenience to use desktop with mouse than iPad	Teachers may familiar or use to using mouse	Habits sometimes may become obstacle to technology integration	Teacher-related service received
Teacher E: I have asked my class how many of you have tablets at home (such as iPad)? There are 29 out of 31 raise hands, but only few of them that are not allow them to use at home because they use it to play games	Parents not allow their children to use tablets because of their lack of self-discipline	Children are lack of self-discipline to use tablets	Parent-related management; student-related management
Teacher F: Obstacle is parents will not give their children to use tablets because of their lack of self-discipline. For example, the teacher asks them to search some information online for homework, but they play games instead of homework			

Table 5.3 Concepts and subcategories from open coding

Concept	Subcategory
Teachers are lack of capability and experience	School-related management
Lack of risk management in classroom	
Platform selection and management not suitable and inconvenience for teachers and students to use	
Lack of chance for teachers to exchange and share knowledge with IT department	
Poor Internet connection	School-related service provide
Lack of workshop training in IT education amount teachers	
Teachers are lack of capability and experience	Teacher-related management
Scaffolding instruction is not suitable for students	
Platform selection and management not suitable and inconvenience for students	
Platform selection and management not suitable and inconvenience for teachers to use	Teacher-related service received
Poor Internet connection	
Habits sometimes may become obstacle to technology integration	
The apps in tablets not user friendly	
Teaching instruction with tablets is not easy for student to follow	Teacher-related service provided
Students' lack of care using tablets	Student-related management
Students may not catch up with or not follow the teaching steps to disrupt the classroom order because of their lack of self-control	
Students are lack of self-discipline to use tablets	
Platform selection and management not suitable and inconvenience for students to use	Student-related service received
The apps in tablets not use friendly	
Students may not familiar with the apps in tablets	
Students inexperienced on tablets because of lack of parental education on it	Parent-related management

After aggregated all categories from the open coding and axial coding, it is generally accepted to verify their relationship, and further generate the categories that were not well conceptualized. It is well proven that the core category "the obstacles of using tablet as a learning tool" can analyze other categories through the interactive comparison, discussion, and analysis of the original record with 20 concepts. Furthermore, the 8 subcategories, which are generated from 20 concepts, finally are summarized into 4 main categories shown as Table 5.4 adapted from Yuen et al. (2010).

5.3.5.4 Theory Construction

With the emphasis of the implied relationship between the core category, the main category, and subcategory, the obstacles of using tablet as a learning tool model was constructed with grounded theory shown as Fig. 5.1. After coding and analyzing the

Table 5.4 Axial coding analysis

Subcategory	Main subcategory
School-related service provide	School-related obstacles of using tablet as a learning tool
School-related management	
Teacher-related service provide	Teacher-related obstacles of using tablet as a learning tool
Teacher-related management	
Teacher-related service receive	
Student-related management	Student-related obstacles of using tablet as a learning tool
Student-related service receive	
Parent-related management	Parent-related obstacles of using tablet as a learning tool

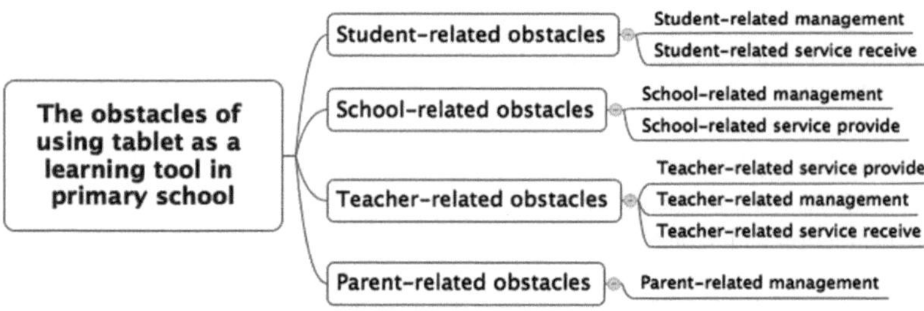

Fig. 5.1 The obstacles of using tablet as a learning tool in primary schools

two sample schools again, there is no new category and relationship was found. Therefore, the theoretical model about understanding the obstacles of using tablet as a learning tool is shown as below.

5.4 Discussions and Conclusions

With the advance of technology and society, it is necessary to improve students using tablet as a learning tool to enhance effectiveness of learning in primary schools. In addition, it is commonly believed that there are some obstacles with the new technology integration. Therefore, to understand the obstacles of using tablets as a learning tool deserves educators' attention.

In this study, the obstacles of using tablet as a learning tool was studied with grounded theory. There are 20 kinds of obstacles that were identified from interviews and categorized into 8 subcategories. Eventually, the four main obstacles from 8 subcategories are respectively related to schools, teachers, and parents as well as students themselves. Although this study only selected a small sample size, it provides a summary and significant framework for future work to understand obstacles of using tablet as a learning tool in primary schools.

Acknowledgments This study is a part of the public policy research project entitled '*Digital Divide in Education: An Experiential Understanding*' (HKU7032-PPR-12) funded by the Research Grants Council (RGC) of the Hong Kong SAR Government. The research team would like to thank the participating students, teachers, school principals, and parents for their valuable contribution.

References

Alamaki, A. (1999). Technology education in the Finnish primary schools. *Journal of Technology Education, 11*(1).

Alvarez, C., Brown, C., & Nussbaum, M. (2011). Comparative study of netbooks and tablet PCs for fostering face-to-face collaborative learning. *Computers in Human Behavior, 27*(2), 834–844.

Bitner, N., & Bitner, J. (2002). Integrating technology into the classroom: Eight keys to success. *Journal of Technology and Teacher Education, 10*(1), 95–100.

Burroughs, G. E. R. (1975). *Design and analysis in educational research.* Birmingham: University of Birmingham.

Dundar, H., & Akcayir, M. (2012). Tablet vs. paper: The effect on learners' reading performance. *International Electronic Journal of Elementary Education, 4*(3), 441–450.

Ertmer, P. A., & Ottenbreit-Lefwich, A. T. (2010). Teacher technology change: How knowledge, beliefs, and culture intersect. *Journal of Research on Technology in Education, 42*, 255–284.

Glaser, B. G. (1978). *Theoretical sensitivity: Advances in methodology of grounded theory.* Mill Valley: Sociological Press.

Glesne, C., & Peshkin, A. (1992). *Becoming qualitative researchers: An introduction.* White Plains: Longman.

Hativa, N. (1986). Computer guided teaching: The microcomputer revolution. *Journal of Educational Computing Research, 2*(3), 307–325.

Newhouse, C. (2006). *Using a Tablet PC with young children.* Canberra: Australian Council for Computers in Education.

Painter, S. R. (2001). Issues in the observation and evaluation of technology integration in K12 classrooms. *Journal of Computing in Teacher Education, 17*(4), 21–25.

Pegrum, M., Oakley, G., & Faulkner, R. (2013). Schools going mobile: A study of the adoption of mobile handheld technologies in Western Australian independent schools. *Australasian Journal of Educational Technology, 29*(1), 66–81.

Rossing, J. P., Miller, W. M., Cecil, A. K., & Stamper, S. E. (2012). iLearning: The future of higher education? Student perceptions on learning with mobile tablets. *Journal of the Scholarship of Teaching and Learning, 12*(2), 1–26.

Straus, A., & Corbin, J. M. (1990). *Basics of qualitative research: Grounded theory procedures and techniques.* Newbury Park: Sage Publications Inc.

Strauss, A., & Corbin, J. (1998). *Basics of qualitative research: Techniques and procedures for developing grounded theory* (2nd ed.). Thousand Oaks: Sage.

Yuen, A. H. K., Law, N., Lee, M. W., & Lee, Y. (2010). *The changing face of education in Hong Kong. Transition into the 21st century.* Hong Kong: Centre for Information Technology in Education (CITE), Faculty of Education, University of Hong Kong.

Chapter 6
"Whistleblower or Leaker?" Examining the Portrayal and Characterization of Edward Snowden in USA, UK, and HK Posts

Amy Wu, Will W.K. Ma, and Wendy W.L. Chan

Abstract This study evolved from the question of how whistleblowers are portrayed and characterized by the news media. A primary objective of this study is to specifically examine how Snowden was characterized and portrayed in *The Guardian* and *The Washington Post* as well as a control comparison with a Hong Kong newspaper, *South China Morning Post* (SCMP) as Snowden had been stayed in Hong Kong. To this end, a comparative textual analysis of news articles was performed—by tracking the keywords—from the period of June 10, 2013 (when Snowden first disclosed the information to the newspapers) through October 31, 2013. This study concludes that keywords may be critically important in the portrayal and characterization of individuals such as Snowden, and that portrayal of that individual can change over a selected time frame. Since this study is based on limited analysis of selected news coverage to date, its conclusions must be viewed as preliminary in need of future data as the Snowden coverage continues.

Keywords Whistleblower • Leaker • Contextual analysis • News

A. Wu
Philip Merrill College of Journalism, University of Maryland, College Park, MD, USA
e-mail: amy.h.wu@gmail.com

W.W.K. Ma (✉)
Online Communication Research Centre, Department of Journalism and Communication, Hong Kong Shue Yan University, Hong Kong, China
e-mail: wkma@hksyu.edu

W.W.L. Chan
School of Communication, Hong Kong Baptist University, Hong Kong, China
e-mail: chanwinglamwendy@gmail.com

© Springer Science+Business Media Singapore 2015
W.W.K. Ma et al. (eds.), *New Media, Knowledge Practices and Multiliteracies*,
DOI 10.1007/978-981-287-209-8_6

6.1 Introduction

This study evolved from the question of how whistleblowers are portrayed and characterized by the news media. The study was prompted by the press coverage of former National Security Agency (NSA) contractor Edward Snowden's disclosure of top-secret NSA materials to news media namely *The Guardian (London)* and *The Washington Post* and the *South China Morning Post*. Snowden is a case study on portrayal of whistleblowers by the news media; his story was extensively covered by worldwide press and had direct implications on areas, such as, national security, domestic surveillance practices, privacy issues, and above all foreign policy matters impacting on U.S. relations with other nations. A primary objective of this study is to specifically examine how Snowden was characterized and portrayed in *The Guardian*, *The Washington Post*, and the *South China Morning Post*.

The authors used the British newspaper *The Guardian* and U.S. newspaper *The Washington Post* as primary sources in this qualitative study as they broken Snowden's story in May 2013. Both newspapers consistently covered the story in the months to follow. Subsequently in May 2014 The Guardian won a Pulitzer Prize for Public Service—one of the highest accolades in journalism—for their coverage of the Snowden story. The *South China Morning Post's* coverage was included and analyzed to examine a local perspective of an international story. The *Post*, the major daily English language daily in Hong Kong, was at the forefront of breaking news about Snowden as he stopped in Hong Kong in mid-May and requested asylum. The *Post's* reporters also attained exclusive in-person interviews with Snowden.

While this study uses the definition of whistleblower per the Government Accountability Project (GAP), the origin of the word "whistleblower" derives from referees who used whistles to signal foul play (Miceli and Near 1992). Other scholars have suggested the word comes from a cartoon of a "bulbous-cheeked English bobby wheezing away on his whistle when the maiden cries 'stop thief (Branch 1979, p. 237),'" or can be traced back further to the "puffy-cheeked bobbies of Victorian England, who blew whistles when they witnessed crimes to warn the public of potential danger" (Hackett 2013). Still others suggest other criteria in defining whistleblowers (1) a person who intentionally makes information public; (2) the information is conveyed to parties outside of their organization who then make it public and a part of the public record; (3) the information is related to or about a possible wrongdoing within the organization; and (4) and that person is a member of the organization (Elliston 1985, pp. 3–15). Beginning of the 1930s, the word "whistleblower" transformed from something positive to a negative description associated with "snitch." According to an April 15, 1960 United Press International article, Paul Hall, president of the maritime trades department of the AFL-CIO, accused Teamsters Union President Jimmy Hoffa a "notorious fink," a "whistle blower," and an "opportunist," and ruled out any AFL-CIO participation in Hoffa's proposed National Conference of Transportation Unions. In the decade that followed, there were signs of the words shifting from negative to positive. The journalist and activist Ralph Nader (1972) legitimized the term through his writing in the 1970s by including it in the title of his 1972 book "*Whistleblowing: The Report of the Conference on Professional Responsibility*." Nader, a consumer activist, was seeking a "label that could fit these responsible, civic-minded people working in corporations or government who would step up and report fraud or negligence," said Ben Zimmer a linguist and language columnist for *The Wall Street Journal* (Time Magazine, Katy Steinmetz, 7/10/2013).

The types of whistleblowers can vary widely from corporate whistleblowers to government whistleblowers, and there is a long list of prominent whistleblowers who have been actively covered in the news media including Karen Silkwood, Erin Brokovitch, Daniel Ellsberg, Bradley Manning, W. Mark Felt, and Linda Tripp. These individuals can and have served as case studies in scholarly journals to examine a variety of topics from journalistic and professional norms such as objectivity in relation to sourcing to legal aspects such as the First Amendment; a 1974 journal article by Charles E. Goodell (1974), a counsel to Ellsberg, examined the limits of advocacy in public service related to Ellsberg who disclosed information about the Pentagon Papers to *The New York Times* in 1969. Snowden's case shares similarities to the individuals listed above in that the case has implications on national security, and there is the ultimate question or gray area as to whether the individual should be characterized as a hero or traitor. Under a positive light, the whistleblower is portrayed as heroic, and courageous, while the latter are labeled as traitors, informers, spies, and snitches (Nader et al. 1972).

Matt Carlson's article (2010) on the portrayal of Mark Felt, an analysis of 515 articles looking at patterns of language use and interpretations of Felt, shows that Felt as "Deep Throat" received a positive portrayal of the best of watchdog journalism. "Deep Throat became a symbol of the need for unnamed sources, even if his provision of background information to help the reporters' investigation differs from a common form of anonymity driven by a need for access" (p. 240). At the same time, Felt himself has been portrayed somewhat negatively by media. After the 2005 *Vanity Fair* article (2005) revealing Deep Throat as Felt was published and Woodward and Bernstein confirmed Felt's identity, critics questioned Felt's motives, which media columnist Robert Novak pegged as "reasons that were not necessarily noble or patriotic" in the June 1, 2005 column in the *Chicago Sunday Times* and June 2, 2005 column in *Townhall.com* (2005).

To be sure, cursory review of articles including those outside the nonscholarly realm suggests that the word "whistleblower" may have as more positive to neutral connotations as opposed to negative connotation, but this is dependent on the context that it is used. Specifically within news coverage factors include publication, the description of whistleblower can be used as either a positive or negative light, and the overall accuracy and preciseness of that characterization. NPR Dana Farrington's column, "What is Meant by the Term Whistle-Blower?" (June 10, 2013) examines the various ways that Snowden had been portrayed by media and questions the accuracy of the using whistleblower to describe Snowden. "Is the term (whistleblower) a misnomer?" Farrington asks in her piece. Is there a clear definition of what a whistleblower is?

James Fallows (June 9, 2013) of *The Atlantic* wrote the following of Edward Snowden's leak on the NSA's infiltration and tapping of others countries, "these programs are legal—unlike the Nixon 'Plumbers' operation, unlike various CIA assassination programs, unlike other objects of various whistle-blower revelations over the years—is the most important fact about them. They're being carried out in 'our' name, ours as Americans, even though most of us have had no idea of what they entailed. The debate on the limits of the security-state is long overdue, and Edward Snowden has played an important role in hastening its onset."

Erik Wemple (June 10, 2013) in an article in *The Washington Post* entitled "Edward Snowden: 'Leaker,' 'source' or 'whistleblower'?" concluded that *The Guardian* from the start of its coverage on June 10, 2013 characterized Snowden as "whistleblower." In an article in the early part of the coverage *The Guardian* wrote of Snowden, "Snowden will go down in history as one of America's most consequential whistleblowers, alongside Daniel Ellsberg and Bradley Manning. He is responsible for handing over material from one of the world's most secretive organisations-the NSA." Wemple has pointed out that *The Washington Post* has consistently portrayed Snowden as the "source" when Snowden came out, and *The New York Times* described Snowden as a "leaker," as per one of the early stories about Snowden, "…the leaker is a relatively low-level employee of a giant government contractor, Booz Allen Hamilton…" The writer concluded that news organizations hedge in using the description "whistleblower," based on the existing definitions including the definition from The Free Dictionary as, "an informant who exposes wrongdoing within an organization in the hope of stopping it." Based on the definition by the Government Accountability Project (GAP) (2014), *The Guardian's* portrayal of Snowden makes sense. When Glenn Greenwald the journalist at *The Guardian* who Snowden leaked to was asked if a whistleblower must identify illegal activity or misconduct Greenwald's response was, "I don't think 'whistleblower' requires revelation of illegal conduct. Dan Ellsberg is considered the classic whistleblower for exposing the systematic lying about the Vietnam War, and that lying wasn't illegal."

The Associated Press explained why they characterized Snowden as "the leaker," and reissued their internal guidelines when writing about Snowden. "A whistleblower is a person who exposes wrongdoing. It's not a person who simply asserts that what he has uncovered is illegal or immoral. Whether the actions exposed by Snowden and Manning constitute wrongdoing is hotly contested, so we should not call them whistleblowers on our own at this point." In some cases, says the AP, answers as to whether a given person is a whistleblower surface, "only after the revelations have sunk in, depending on what wrongdoing is confirmed or how public opinion eventually develops."

Paul Vallely (2013, August 25) in the British newspaper "*The Independent*" in an article "Heroes and villains—a modern definition; Whistleblowers are vilified or intimidated while the wrongs and the wrongdoers that they expose go uninvestigated," compared the portrayals of Bradley Manning with Edward Snowden and concluded that the line between definitions lies in the moral context of their act.

Manning's sentence of 35 years and prison was not justified as "much of what Manning did was a global public service," Vallely, a visiting professor of public ethics and media at the University of Chester, writes "…(Manning) felt the higher moral duty to protest against abuses by the army of which she was part. Snowden's motives look altogether murkier, and journalists exploiting them have a duty to take additional care in handling the material he is leaking."

Outside of the news media, there appears to be differences in portrayal/ characterization of Snowden too. The Hill, a publication that focuses on covering the U.S. Congress, concluded that lawmakers struggled with how to define Snowden as they wrestled with whether Snowden should be defined as hero or traitor based on the information he leaked. Senator Chuck Grassley (Iowa), a Republican with a history for supporting protection for whistleblowers, said that Snowden should be penalized for the leaks and is not a hero, whereas other lawmakers remained uncommitted, Republican Raul Grijalva (D-Ariz) said, "I don't think it's raised to the level of sedition, treason, defector…or (traitor)…Is there a culpability on his part? Yes. But does it raise to that level? I don't think so (Lillis 2013)."

In an article "Edward Snowden: The New Brand of Whistleblower" published in the September 2013 edition of "Quill Magazine," Kara Hackett (2013) suggests that the word "whistleblower" can be used as a negative, positive, or neutral description based on the individual written about; thus, the word is malleable. Snowden's specific case makes the word even more challenging as he engaged in specific behavior that does not conform entirely with GAP's definition of whistleblower such as not initially consulting with the higher ups at Booz Allen Hamilton where he worked, and already having a plane ticket prepared to leave the country. Nonetheless, the author cites specific examples of where Snowden falls into the definition of "whistleblower," specifically in that the information he disclosed is of "whistleblowing material" (Hackett 2013). Notably, he is not the first individual to accuse the NSA of violating the Fourth Amendment against unreasonable search and seizure. "Whistleblower" as a positive term can be seen in a Quinnipiac University poll conducted July 28–31 that shows 55 % of Americans support Snowden as a whistleblower and 34 % call him a traitor. The Merriam-Webster dictionary defines "traitor" as "a person who is not loyal to his or her own country, friends, etc.; a person who betrays a country or group of people by helping or supporting an enemy."

The concept of whistleblower may be viewed very differently by other authorities outside of the news media, and dependent on the type of material leaked. Colman McCarthy writes in his column "Samuel Morison: A Leaker, Not a Thief" in *The Washington Post* (11/17/1985), Morison was a naval intelligence analyst who was prosecuted in the U.S. District Court and sentenced to 2 years in prison for providing the classified satellite photographs of a Soviet aircraft under construction to a British magazine "Jane's Defence Weekly." "A federal classifier decides a harmless picture of a Soviet ship is relevant to national security, and the teeth of espionage clamp the neck of a luckless bureaucrat," McCarthy writes.

6.2 Methodology

The following methodology was used in this study. A search in Lexis/Nexis between June 10, 2013 and October 31, 2013 with the key words "Edward Snowden," within *The Guardian* and *The Washington Post* and retrieved 217 articles under *The Guardian* and 257 articles under *The Washington Post*. Similarly, 145 articles were retrieved under *South China Morning Post* (SCMP, the most popular English newspaper at Hong Kong), using WiseNews online database. The time frame used for this study started on June 10 from the time that Snowden leaked the documents and information to columnist Glenn Greenwald at *The Guardian* and *Barton Gellman* a reporter at *The Washington Post*. Since the beginning of June, Gellman was reporting the classified intelligence documents provided to him by Snowden. The research time frame ends on October 31 as the majority of news stories about the aftermath of Snowden's leaked documents were published in late October, and soon after diminished in coverage.

This comparative textual analysis solely focused on news articles, and eliminated op-eds, letters to the editor, editorials, and blogs. The study identified the first description of Snowden on first reference in all stories and tabulated the number of times the keyword was used to identify Snowden on first reference.

Second, the study also included a search of how many times the reporters Greenwald and Gellman covered Snowden's stories and third the number of appearance of the most commonly detected keyword.

The articles were organized chronologically. In total, 217 articles in *The Guardian,* 257 from *The Washington Post,* and 191 from *SCMP* were reviewed and specifically used the keyword used in first reference of Snowden. The keyword was identified and highlighted, and each one counted. In addition, changes and shifts in Snowden's portrayal based on shifts in keywords were examined. In summary, the basic unit for analysis was the news item with keywords and any changes in those keywords within the same publication.

6.3 Findings

6.3.1 *The Guardian*

The study found that *The Guardian* most commonly used "whistleblower" to portray Snowden, from the very start of the coverage and used the word whistleblower 137 times out of 217 articles to describe Snowden on first reference. The newspaper used the word leaker or the context of leaked 11 times. The Guardian used variations of whistleblower including NSA Whistleblower, US whistleblower, American whistleblower, prominent whistleblower, intelligence whistleblower, and surveillance whistleblower. In significantly less number the newspapers used the key descriptors of former US National Security Agency contractor, US intelligence analyst, and American whistleblower, one of America's most consequential whistleblowers, a very modern spy, and man of mystery, and US analyst who revealed himself as the source of *The Guardian* expose. Based on the definition of whistleblower and leaker as presented above, *The Guardian's* use of whistleblower portrays Snowden in the higher ground to neutral as opposed to leaker, which is defined as lower ground or in some cases a negative. The study also tabulated the number of stories written by Glenn Greenwald and found that a total of 14 articles included Greenwald's byline. Greenwald also contributed two editorials about Snowden, one editorial about Snowden published June 15, 2013 "Comment: Thankfully, Snowden's worst fear has not been realised: The NSA whistleblower's only concern was that his disclosures would be met with apathy. Instead, they are leading to real reform.Z," and another column *The Guardian (London)* August 10, 2013, "What would Google do?: Lavabit, the encrypted email service, has closed rather than betray users. Others should do so too."

As mentioned, in the early coverage the articles characterized Snowden using descriptors such as 'man of mystery' and 'one of America's most consequential whistleblowers.' Adjectives such as 'spy' seem to be used in a positive context most of the time. For example, a June 10 article describes Snowden as "a very modern spy—neither gun-blazingly dashing nor cat-strokingly sinister. He is young, tech-savvy, quietly articulate and intensely interested in human rights." One of the earliest articles in the Snowden story was headlined, "The whistleblower: I can't allow the US government to destroy privacy and basic liberties: Edward Snowden, 29, emerges from hiding in Hong Kong: IT contractor says his concerns were ignored and he had to go public." Based on the headline alone, Snowden is characterized as an individual who wants to go public with wrongdoing in almost a David vs. Goliath kind of tale. To be sure, the keyword most frequently used to portray him was "whistleblower," and within that variations such as "U.S. whistleblower" and "prominent whistleblower." In addition, Snowden is portrayed as an asset to the media as described in a June 11 story as "the whistleblower for *The Guardian* and *The Washington Post*." A June 14 news story describes Snowden as "the US analyst who revealed himself as the source of *The Guardian* expose." Thus, the descriptors characterize Snowden as a reliable and important source for the press.

The tone of *The Guardian's* coverage toward Snowden remains steady at positive and neutral, with the U.S. government portrayed in perhaps a more negative light. For example, a July 2 front page story is headlined "Obama scrambles to limit crisis amid EU outrage over bugging: Merkel and Hollande want answers: Fugitive applies for asylum in Russia." An extended study would have a model that specifically addresses how the U.S. government was portrayed by the news media within the Snowden case. A day later, the newspaper once again publishes a rather positive profile of Snowden headlined, "Edward Snowden: A whistleblower, not a spy." *The Guardian*, similar to *The Washington Post*, examines its own coverage of the Snowden story in later coverage, specifically on October 11, when the newspaper published insight and comments from editors at various news outlets after it received criticism from its competitor *The Daily Mail*. The piece is headlined "The Snowden files: Yesterday, the Daily Mail described the Guardian as 'The paper that helps Britain's enemies'. We showed that article to many of the world's leading editors. This is what they said."

Over the course of 4 months, *The Guardian's* coverage shifted steadily from portrayal of Snowden as an individual and as a "whistleblower," an individual who carries about an air of mystery, a modern day spy, to the information that Snowden leaked about the NSA, the reaction from countries such as Germany and France. The spotlight thus moved from Snowden as whistleblower to Snowden as a source. The Guardian consistently characterized Snowden as a "whistleblower" within their coverage, even in latter coverage. For example, an October 22 piece entitled "Front: Obama tries to calm French fury over mass surveillance" focused on the French government's reaction to the publication of French newspaper Le Monde's response to the materials that Snowden disclosed and describes Snowden as "NSA whistleblower."

6.3.2 The Washington Post

The Washington Post's portrayal of Snowden differs from *The Guardian's* in that the primary keyword on first reference used to describe Snowden is leaker, which does not appear in *The Guardian's* stories. In a review of all 257 stories, the word "leaker" or reference to "leaked" appeared 103 times. *The Washington Post* on the other hand most frequently used the keyword leaker on first reference to describe Snowden in different variations including NSA leaker, 29-year-old leaker, the National Security Agency leaker, admitted leaker, and contractor-turned-fugitive.

The word "whistleblower" or "whistleblowing," appeared once in the context of the front page article "Another effort at nuclear cuts," where the article included a paragraph at the end as follows "Now it's whether Edward Snowden is a whistle-blowing hero or a traitor for exposing the National Security Agency's program that collects and stores Americans' phone numbers to be searched when a suspected foreign terrorist link is established." Analysis suggests that *The Post* proceeded cautiously when describing Snowden in its initial coverage and does not have a key word or descriptor for Snowden in the first several stories. *The Post's* June 10 story describes Snowden simply as "the 29-year-old Edward Snowden who identified himself Sunday as the main source behind recent disclosures of sweeping government surveillance programs" and seemed to take a more conservative approach to portraying him. Snowden is simply described as the NSA contractor, and *The Post* portrays Snowden as someone quite separate from the news media rather than a confidential or reliable source, which comes through in *The Guardian's* stories.

A June 16, 2,697 word profile of Snowden describes him as "the skinny kid from suburban Maryland who took it upon himself to expose-and, officials say, severely compromise—classified U.S. government surveillance programs, loved role-playing games, leaned libertarian, worked out hard and dabbled in modeling." While not proving anything, it is yet another portrayal by the news media of someone highly controversial in what he did and illustrates *The Post's* decision to describe Snowden through facts including his personal history and politics. Findings showed that Barton Gellman's byline appeared 17 times within the 257 news articles included in this study. For example Gellman's byline was included along with Aaron Blake and Gregory Miller in the June 10 story entitled "Man who leaked NSA secrets steps forward," the first one about Snowden.

The Post's coverage of the Snowden story shifted over time, as the analysis showed that coverage beginning June 10 focused primarily on Snowden as an individual as opposed to the information about the NSA he disclosed. Starting in late July the coverage shifted personal and professional background of Snowden to, stories about the NSA, with Snowden now portrayed as more of a news source. The August 10 front page article "President seeks to raise scrutiny of NSA programs," focuses on President Obama's sharing of potential reforms on government surveillance programs. An August 16 story entitled "Audit: NSA repeatedly broke privacy rules," by Barton Gellman zeroed in on the classified information that Snowden shared with the reporter. During this time period, the coverage is extended to the specific information that Snowden disclosed. Snowden, who in June and July, was often the focus of coverage takes a backstage as the information is disclosed is spotlighted and he is referred to as the source of information. An August 17 front page story headlined, "Lawmakers call for more control of NSA programs," focuses on the problems with the NSA disclosed through the top-secret documents. *The Post* places itself as the forefront of the story as seen in the following paragraph that is part of the lead. "The contrasting reactions came after *The Washington Post* reported that the NSA broke rules or overstepped its legal authority thousands of times in recent years, and the chief judge of the special federal surveillance court that oversees NSA spy programs said the court's ability to provide oversight is limited." The first reference to Snowden appears in the fourth paragraph as "The violations were recorded in top-secret documents, including an NSA internal audit, provided to The Post this summer by former agency contractor Edward Snowden." An analysis of *The Post's* coverage suggests that when the classified information is the main focus of the story, Snowden is no longer referenced as a "leaker," but rather a source of the story.

An August 30 front page story headlined, "NSA pays firms large sums for network access," begins describing Snowden as the provider of documents as opposed to leaking the documents. "Voluntary cooperation from the 'backbone' providers of global communications dates to the 1970s under the cover name Blarney, according to documents provided by former NSA contractor Edward Snowden. These relationships long predate the PRISM program disclosed in June, under which American technology companies hand over customer data after receiving orders from the Foreign Intelligence Surveillance Court." At this time *The Post* also introduces the word "provided by" as opposed to "leaked." As focus moves to the NSA program and the fallout from the leaked materials including response from countries such as Germany and France, Snowden is increasingly described in stories as "a former National Security Agency contractor who leaked highly classified documents about U.S. surveillance programs." In summary, the study suggests that whistleblowers and their implications may change over time depending on evolving knowledge, especially in the case of Snowden.

6.3.3 SCMP

As a comparison of the two main posts, the study also underwent a keyword search on "Edward Snowden" in the most popular English Post in Hong Kong, *South China Morning Post*, from the period of June 10, 2013 through October 31, 2013. This post was not going to be examined in-depth. It was treated like a control in order to note any irregularities. The data therefore would be only listed below for reference.

There were in total 145 relevant news articles. A number of descriptors were identified to describe Snowden. Among them, most commonly used terms included *leaker*, *spy*, and *whistle blower*. Specifically, 71 news articles used *whistle blower*; 8 of them used *spy*; whereas *leaker* was used only for one time in the period; and the phrase *former US National Security Agency* appeared only once.

It seemed that after August 27, the term *leaker* no longer appeared while referring to Snowden. The term *leaker* appeared in various forms, including *leaker*, *US data leaker*, and *NSA leaker*. For example, one headline wrote, "*Cybersecurity queries surge in wake of Snowden claim*" in which the security matter that linked up closely with the word *leaker*. The first paragraph of that news quoted the comment from a consultant at an international conference on cybercrime and computer forensics. This reflected how readers perceived Snowden as a *leaker* of the US confidential information. However, since August 21, 2013 the reporters as well as some columnists started to use *spy* to describe Snowden. The term *spy* appeared at the earlier news, too. For example, in one news story appeared on August 4, it said, "*Snowden, a former American spy, escaped the clutches of US justice because Hong Kong was a stickler for the absolute letter of the law*."

However, we discovered that at the later stage, the term *spy* is often used with the other term *whistle blower*. There are some variations in the use of *spy*, for example, *the criminality of the spy agencies*, *spy-cum whistle blower*, *former American spy*, *cyberspying whistle blower*, *a traitor and a Chinese spy*, and *US cyberspying whistle blower*. One of the news articles stated that, "*The drama that has unfolded since spy-cum-whistle blower Edward Snowden arrived in Hong Kong in June continues to create shock waves around the world*." The news articles connected *cyber and whistle blower* with the term *spy*. These have been more neutral in reporting in which Snowden is considered a spy over the Internet and his identity is more inclined to revealing what the USA done to their citizens as well as to the world. His identity is described as *whistle blower* in the later reporting. According to one article that employed the term *whistle blower*, it said, "*According to a report on privacy breaches by the US National Security Agency, leaked by whistle-blower Edward Snowden and published by The Washington Post yesterday, an 11 per cent rise in "roamer" incidents in the first quarter of last year may have been caused by the annual Chinese holiday*" where the headline entitled, "*Glimpse into scale of US spying on Chinese visitors*". Again, his motive to disclose the information was portrayed as *whistle blower* with the content he disclosed to the world for the benefits of the people.

The term *whistle blower* appeared frequently throughout the news articles though it appeared in various forms, for example, *national security agency whistle blower*,

US whistle blower, NSA whistle blower and *fugitive American secret surveillance whistle-blower*, etc. As the phrase *former US National Security Agency* appeared once and was the only one associated with the term *whistle blower*. From the data collected, *whistle blower* was not widely associated with the phrase *US former agency*.

6.4 Discussion

Based on this study of 217 articles in *The Guardian* and 257 in *The Washington Post,* we have a reasonable qualitative answer to the research question as to how Edward Snowden was portrayed and characterized by two separate newspapers, and whether the portrayal was positive, negative, and neutral, and whether they were different or similar. Based on an analysis of keywords, *The Guardian's* portrayal of Snowden was relatively positive to neutral and primarily described Snowden as a "whistleblower." *The Guardian's* portrayal of Snowden remained relatively consistent with a significant amount of coverage about Snowden as the main subject of the subject from the time he disclosed the NSA documents (June 10, 2013). Nonetheless, findings show that while Snowden's portrayal as "whistleblower" remained relatively consistent, there is evidence that there is a slight shift at the tail end of the coverage in late November when newspaper's coverage extended to focus on NSA materials that Snowden disclosed. Still Snowden is prominently included in these articles as a source. An October 31 article headlined, "Snowden leaks: Spanish intelligence services 'helped NSA surveillance operations in Spain': Papers suggest France swapped data with US: German delegation vents anger over Merkel bugging," not only includes Snowden in the headline, but also for the first time in 4 months of coverage there is the emergence of the keyword "leaked." An extended study would examine the factors and reasons behind this.

This study's findings show that *The Washington Post's* coverage characterized Snowden cautiously at the very start when the Snowden story first emerged sticking with relatively objective descriptors such as "29-year-old Snowden." This shifted to a more negative portrayal of Snowden as seen by the number of times Snowden is described as a "leaker" and ultimately as a "fugitive." Notably, an extended study of this chapter would include a definition of fugitive by authorities and demonstrate whether fugitive is a positive, negative, or neutral word. A June 11 news article reads, "Edward Snowden, the leaker, did the honorable thing in revealing his identity; it would be more honorable if he would turn himself in and face the consequences for his law-breaking." The findings, particularly those from *The Washington Post's* coverage, are on similar lines to Jessica Roberts' study on the news media's commentary of WikiLeaks. Roberts' study was limited to U.S. media, but based on this study the coverage of whistleblowers in U.S. newspapers (*The Washington Post*) appears to fall in the more critical spectrum as opposed to the British newspaper (*The Guardian*).

An overall analysis of the portrayal of Snowden in all three newspapers concludes that there is a similar pattern amongst them, specifically which the adjectives and descriptors of Snowden morph over the course of coverage. Second, the word "whistleblower" overall is most commonly used to describe Snowden in *The Guardian* and *The South China Morning Post*, whereas NSA leaker is most prevalently used in *The Washington Post*.

The study's findings in SCMP show that there is altogether 191 news coverage. Besides *Leaker, Spy,* and *Whistle Blower*, there are still some other descriptions towards Snowden. For example, *World's most-wanted man breaks cover in Hong Kong, Snowden conjures up the ghosts of our long-lost spooks,* or even *Public Eye*, these descriptions have also caught the attention of the public toward this incident.

On the other hand, as Snowden has left Hong Kong, therefore, most of the headlines did not mention Snowden his name or association of him in the headlines. Instead, we could see *Russia ties grow amid U.S. pivot to Asia*, *US bill could come back to bite HK,* these examples actually imply that Snowden has become an international issue and people did not just put focus on him, but how he affected the international relationship.

Conclusion

In conclusion, this study set out to explore how three newspapers, specifically one that the whistleblower leaked to, portrayed the whistleblower, in this case Edward Snowden. The further study should narrow the scope of analysis with the objective of making a more convincing case. The study was conducted after reviewing an array of literature about whistleblowers in books, scholarly journals, and mainstream media. This study analyzed news coverage in two newspapers by a model adopted by a previous study that examined portrayal of a specific category of people through a comparative textual analysis of the first keyword used to describe Snowden in every article. This study concluded that keywords are significant in the portrayal of individuals such as Snowden as positive, negative, or neutral, and findings suggest that portrayal can shift either slightly or dramatically with the change of news events under the umbrella of the story.

This study aims to contribute to a much broader area of study on how the news media characterize whistleblowers. As stated earlier, due to the limited scope of this study, this analysis of the Snowden case should be viewed as preliminary rather than definitive; concrete conclusions must await future data unraveled by further coverage of Snowden and information disclosed therein. It is hoped

(continued)

that the textual analysis utilized in this study could be extended into a more comprehensive project giving insights on the news media's portrayal of individuals who have willingly revealed otherwise privileged information that may significantly impact various dimensions of the human society and global intercountry harmony, cooperation, and communication.

As a study, the materials for this chapter were limited in scope, specifically its sole focus was on identifying the initial keyword in each article used to describe Snowden. Analysis was also limited to two newspapers—chosen as they were the ones that Snowden leaked to. An extended study would include an additional British newspaper such as *The Independent* and U.S. newspaper such as *The New York Times*, which would offer additional perspective as to whether the portrayal follows the patterns of *The Guardian* and *The Washington Post*. An additional limitation was the confined time frame of analysis from June 10, 2013 to October 31, 2013. By extending the time frame of analysis, the objective is detecting additional patterns of coverage, which includes the aftermath of his disclosures notably the continuing debate by top government officials versus advocates of transparency, and the debate that Snowden ignited over the NSA's surveillance methods (Face the Nation, December 29, 2013).

Additionally, this study does not identify the reasons behind the findings. Why was the characterization different in these newspapers? How do American newspapers and British newspapers characterize whistleblowers differently? How did *The Guardian* and *The Washington Post* previously portray whistleblowers? How much of the characterization was due to the fact that Snowden leaked information related to national security? Is there a pattern or characterization of whistleblowers by the newspaper that the whistleblower leaks to? An extended study would continue to examine the relationship between whistleblowers and the newspapers that they leaked to. Does the newspaper or the whistleblower become at the forefront of the backend of attention and spotlight? This more ambitious study would involve looking at major cases in journalism history and view what the metanews coverage was and how these sources have been viewed. An extended study would analyze more newspapers, which would give a clearer and more comprehensive picture of whether portrayal is dependent upon the kind of newspapers (mainstream vs. tabloid), American vs. British (does the style of tradition of journalism impact portrayal or on a deeper level does the political system. For example, how did the Chinese press portray Snowden?), or the kind of information leaked (how is portrayal of Snowden different than say Julian Assange), and then there is the issue of gender (how does portrayal of a male whistleblower differ from a female whistleblower?).

References

Branch, T. (1979). Courage without esteem: Profiles in whistleblowing. In C. Peters & M. Nelson (Eds.), *Culture of bureaucracy*. New York: Holt, Rinehart, and Winston.

Carlson, M. (2010). Embodying deep throat: Mark felt and the collective memory of Watergate. *Critical Studies in Media Communication, 27*(3), 235–250.

Elliston, F. (1985). *Whistleblowing research: Methodological and moral issues*. New York: Praeger.

Fallows, J. (2013, June 9). *Edward Snowden in Hong Kong*. Retrieved from http://www.theatlantic.com/china/archive/2013/06/edward-snowden-in-hong-kong/276692/

Farrington, D. (2013, June 10). *What is meant by the term 'whistle-blower'?* Retrieved from http://www.npr.org/blogs/thetwo-way/2013/06/10/190380255/what-we-mean-when-we-say-whistleblower

Goodell, C. E. (1974). Limits of advocacy: Government. *Public Relations Quarterly, 18*(3), 13–25.

Government Accountability Project (GAP). (2014). *The origins of the American whistleblower tour*. Retrieved from http://www.whistleblower.org/origins-american-whistleblower-tour. Accessed 15 May 2014.

Hackett, K. (2013, September/October). Edward Snowden: The New Brand Of Whistle-Blower? *Quill Magazine*. Retrieved from http://digitaleditions.walsworthprintgroup.com/article/EDWARD+SNOWDEN%3A+THE+NEW+BRAND+OF+WHISTLEBLOWER%3F/1515492/0/article.html

Lillis, M. (2013, June 13). *Lawmakers see Edward Snowden as a leaker, not as a hero*. Retrieved from http://thehill.com/homenews/house/305245-lawmakers-see-snowden-as-a-leaker-not-as-a-hero

Miceli, M. P., & Near, J. P. (1992). *Blowing the whistle: The organizational and legal implications for companies and employees*. New York: Lexington Books.

Nader, R., Petkas, P. J., & Blackwell, K. (1972). *Whistle blowing: The report of the conference on professional responsibility*. Viking Pr.

Novak, R. (2005, June 2). *Felt's motivation might not have been so noble*. Retrieved from http://townhall.com/columnists/robertnovak/2005/06/02/felts_motivation_might_not_have_been_so_noble/page/full

Vallely, P. (2013, August 25). *Heroes and villains – A modern definition*. Retrieved from http://www.independent.co.uk/voices/comment/heroes-and-villain---modern-definition-8783592.html

Wemple, E. (2013, June 10). *Edward Snowden: 'Leaker,' 'source' or 'whistleblower'?* Retrieved from http://www.washingtonpost.com/blogs/erik-wemple/wp/2013/06/10/edward-snowden-leaker-source-or-whistleblower/

Chapter 7
"Destuckification": Use of Social Media for Enhancing Design Practices

Yun Yi Tan and Allan H.K. Yuen

Abstract This study sets out to explore the potential of social media in facilitating designers to progress and enhance their professional development. This study starts with a review on the use of social media and current practices of designers. We then attempted to link the intersections between the design practices and how it may be enhanced with the help of social media technology. The aim of the study is twofold. First, we conducted case studies to explore the functionalities that may accommodate the strategies and design practices in two existing social media platforms that are developed specifically for the design community. Then we attempted to compare and evaluate the functionalities that could motivate the designers to progress.

Keywords Social media • Design practices • Professional development

7.1 Introduction

The word 'de-stuck-ification' is a word inherited from Havi Brooks, an Internet writer who writes a series of post in her website (http://www.fluentself.com/), on how to get unstuck and get going over failed progress. This process of getting unstuck may also be associated with the design process of designers. It is very common for designers to get stuck in their designer block at some point when they ran out of ideas on how to progress their works. Hence, staying inspired and creating designs could be one of the most challenging elements about being a professional designer. The advent of Internet is revolutionizing the design practices of the designers. When designers get stuck, they may find ways to dissolve the 'stucknesses' by feeding themselves with sources that could be found on the Internet. This could also be known as a 'destuckification' process for designers. The growth and emergence

Y.Y. Tan (✉)
Division of Information and Technology Studies, Faculty of Education, The University of Hong Kong, Hong Kong, China
e-mail: yunyi.tan@connect.hku.hk

A.H.K. Yuen
The University of Hong Kong, Hong Kong, China
e-mail: hkyuen@hku.hk

© Springer Science+Business Media Singapore 2015

W.W.K. Ma et al. (eds.), *New Media, Knowledge Practices and Multiliteracies*,
DOI 10.1007/978-981-287-209-8_7

of social media technology has enhanced the experience in using the Internet. With the help of technology offered by social media, designers may now easily look for worked examples and tutorials, share their ideas, and gain supports and feedbacks for improvisation beyond their immediate sphere of experience, while working behind their desk all day. For these reasons, it is beneficial to consider the use of social media for supplementing the design process of the designers.

In this chapter, we are particularly interested in understanding the social phenomena and design learning experiences of the designers that took place in the social media platforms. For this study, the term social media platform (SMP) refers to the web-based or mobile application that could be utilized to integrate or facilitate a community by using social media features such as content creation, social interactions, and networking. We present studies on the designer uses of social media in two separate sections. The first section discusses the potential of social media based on the literature reviews and how it may intersect with the nature of designing. The second section focuses on how two SMPs (namely Deviantart and Behance) are being used by designers as learning spaces for solving their design problems and professional development. We also attempted to explore the potential of design creation on the SMPs by disseminating how creativity is being communicated and conveyed among the online community of designers.

7.2 Social Media and Design Practices

Social media is generally known as a medium for linking and enabling social interactions among its users through multiway communication in a digital environment such as blogs, content communities, and social networking sites (Kaplan and Haenlein 2010). Over the years, social media technology has opened various possibilities to improve the way people learn from the Internet and interact with each other. Social media users no longer need to rely on mediators to enable interactions among people they know or even strangers. Besides that, social media has also influenced the way Internet is being utilized. Contents are no longer individually created but instead, through collaboration where all users may gather, evaluate and continuously modify the information. Furthermore, the information that can be disseminated on the social media is far beyond just text. They may consist of multiple forms of media such as audio, video, and images. Users could also discover and share hyperlinks that lead to other online resources.

Researchers in the field have conducted various studies to demonstrate the uses of social media technologies. For instance, Facebook is currently one of the latest phenomena in supporting online interaction (Boyd 2007; Boyd and Ellison 2007; Ellison et al. 2007; Kaplan and Haenlein 2010). It is an online social networking site that creates opportunities for its users to connect with their friends, publish and share contents such as photos and videos, and keep in touch with them via asynchronous and synchronous messaging. In other words, users could also generate their own content instead of being just information consumers. They could also create and join groups of interests or follow and subscribe to fan pages. This contributes to the notion of collective intelligence as such social software tools enable users to participate in a networked society where the knowledge creation process can be performed collaboratively.

The process of designing involves thinking processes that are made up of creative activities (Lawson and Dorst 2009). Generally, designing is defined as a process of creating an artifact by transforming its functional description into physical description. For example, a designer may begin the design process by first having the idea of how the artifact is supposed to look like. The idea is then being transformed into a tangible outcome such as products, or intangible outcome such as design services. On the other hand, Eder (1999) describes designing as a process of developing a simple or a more complex artifact with an intended purpose. Hence, designing is a conscious effort done by designers to provide the best solution and idea to a certain problem. This responsibility of "making things better for people" is placed in the hands of creative individuals (Seymour 2008).

The study of design is often related to the strong sense of social nature. According to Engeström (1987), creativity emerges out of activities that involve interactions among individuals and their sociocultural context. Schön (1987) asserts that designers should first obtain in-depth understanding of a certain phenomena through repetition of active engagements and critical reflections on the tasks performed before providing the best solution to solve design problems. Interactions and communicative activities in the design process help designers to decipher design worlds of other individuals (Schön 1992). A number of researchers have also pointed out that creativity is a social phenomenon. For instance, Perry-Smith (2006) suggests that creativity could be facilitated through different types of social interactions or relationships. Other examples include social impact on the creative outcomes (Watson 2007) and the role of social networks as the enabler for attaining creative results (Cattani and Ferriani 2008).

At this age, the social media technology has created new practices of producing and sharing design outcomes. The technology has also changed the speed and ways of sharing information where design processes can be easily discovered in social media sites. Indeed, a number of social media platforms have been developed specifically for the design community, such as Dribbble (http://www.dribbble.com), Behance (http://www.behance.net), Coroflot (http://www.coroflot.com), and DeviantART (http://www.deviantart.com). These SMPs are developed to support the activities and practices of creative individuals across various creative fields. The SMPs are also known as 'showcasing' platforms that enable designers to upload their artworks onto the network for feedbacks and idea sharing. All users of the specific platform could gain access to view the design work published in the platforms and provide feedbacks regardless of their geographical locations at any point of time. In addition, the SMPs encourage users to learn from each other through active engagement as it highly emphasizes on participation and social interactions. Moreover, social media creates new opportunities to facilitate experiential knowledge sharing of experts (Panahi et al. 2012) and encourage the growth of collaborative art projects (Harrison and Barthel 2009). For instance, social media sites, such as Digg, Tumblr, and Pinterest, enable users to generate and share their own original contents. Hence, users do not only appear as readers but also contributors

(Mcloughlin and Lee 2007). Applications that allow user-generated content also attract wider and diverse range of active audiences and encourage the creation of collaborative creative design as the users are motivated by the expressive and aesthetic experiences offered by the technology.

Therefore, we argue that social media technologies have great potentials to enhance and support the designing processes due to the intersections of social aspects in design practices of the designers (Buchanan 1992) and the social media technologies. The potential of the SMPs in supporting design practices and helping the designers to progress is illustrated and discussed in the next section.

7.3 Design Practices in Social Media Platforms

In this section, we discuss about the design practices in two SMPs. We began by conducting searches about SMPs that are developed specifically for the design community via the web search engine (i.e., Google and Yahoo), focusing on the popular online platforms or popular portfolio sites for designers. The SMPs are selected based on the recommendations from top-ranked websites that provide professional advice and highlight importance issues to the design community such as Smashing Magazine, Hongkiat, Speckyboy Design Magazine, and Vitamin T.

We screened through the recommended SMPs and selected two platforms, namely DeviantART and Behance. The selection criteria were (1) the SMP must host a creative community that actively exhibit user-created design works and promote design-related discussions; (2) the SMP must be open to the public with free account registration; and (3) the SMP must have existed and being used by the design community for at least 5 years. However, it is important to note that these platforms are not intended to be representatives of other platforms, but to provide a further understanding on the social media phenomenon in the context of design learning. The two selected SMPs may have similar features and functionalities, yet are used by users from contrasting backgrounds. Based on our observations, users of DeviantART are usually newcomers or enthusiasts who are interested in design. On the other hand, users of Behance tend to be professionals from the industry.

7.3.1 DeviantART and Behance

DeviantART (dA) was launched in August 2000. It is an online platform that forms one of the largest online art communities, which helps to connect and inspire people. Through this art community, users are able to showcase, share, promote, and sell their original works. As of May 2014, the platform consists of over 31 million registered members, receives over 160,000 daily uploads, and attracts 65 million unique visitors per month. In order to join the community, the user must first register an account with their chosen username. This platform is open to everyone, free of

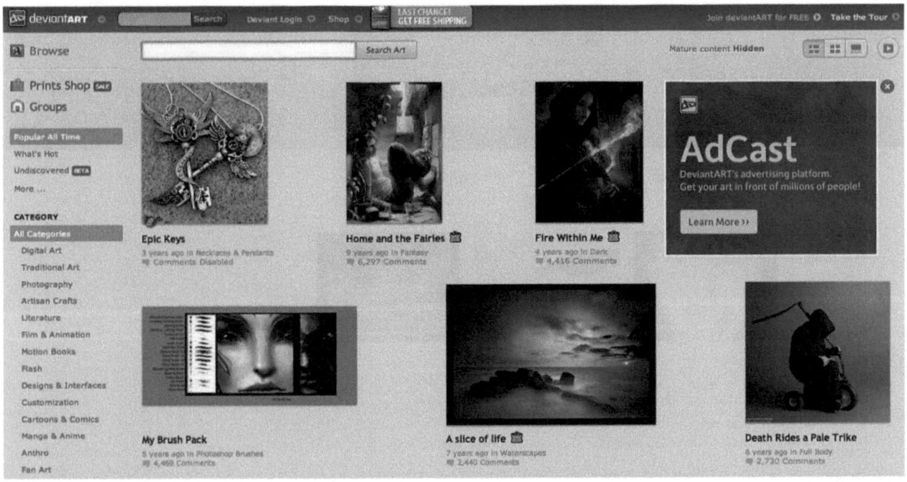

Fig. 7.1 Sample screenshot of deviantART website (http://www.deviantart.com)

charge. Free accounts are equipped with all the basic functionalities. However, users may opt to upgrade their accounts to Premium Membership for a fee if they are interested in using the advanced features such as message center and critique functions. All registered users in the dA community will then be known as 'Deviant'. Besides being able to search for design inspirations, users can leave feedbacks, publish journals, organize contests, and events and also create groups according to their own interests (Fig. 7.1).

Another social media platform which is often used by designers is Behance. Launched in 2006, Behance is developed as an online site that offers free portfolio services to creative individuals and also companies from creative fields. Behance is aimed to reduce the barriers between talents and opportunities. Instead of being designers who are required to work under restrictions of bureaucratic agencies, they should be encouraged to produce creative works according to their passion and talents. Therefore, Behance is seen as a medium for connecting the talented designers to the best opportunities. In December 2012, Adobe acquired Behance as part of their social strategy in creating a collaborative creative community. Behance consists of various users such as individual professionals, freelancers, design agencies, design schools, creative organizations, and corporate companies (Fig. 7.2).

7.3.1.1 Showcase Artwork

Both SMPs allow their users to create and organize their own portfolio online. Designers may publish unlimited number of their original works for public viewing, which could be organized according to the types of works and creative fields. dA allows their users to publish their works in different formats, such as photographs, illustrations, videos, literatures, or even works made in Flash. On the other hand,

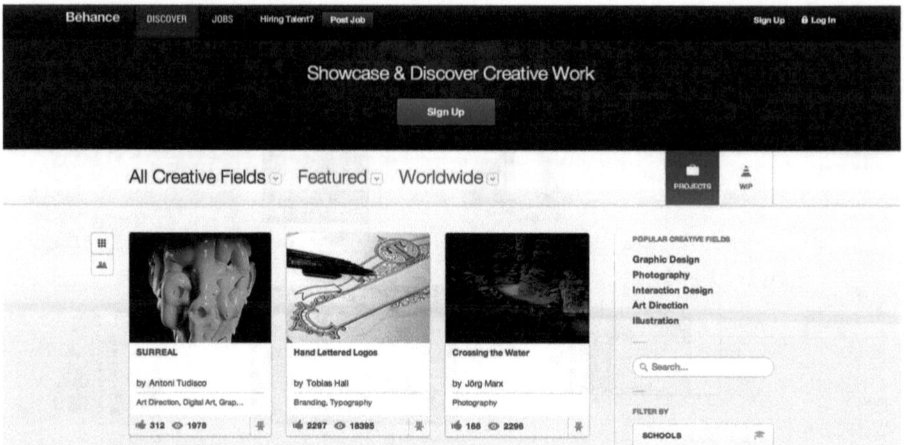

Fig. 7.2 Sample screenshot of Behance website (http://www.behance.net)

Behance has some limitations to the file formats that can be uploaded onto the platform. However, users can include embeds from third-party sites such as Vimeo, YouTube, Veoh, and Soundcloud if they want to include video or audio files into their project posts. The online portfolio also acts as a venue that helps the designers to showcase their artwork and build up their reputation by presenting to the public what they are capable of doing. A good portfolio could attract potential clients and secure better work opportunities. In the SMPs, the user community determines the value of the work published through actions enabled by the platform such as comments and ratings. Traditionally, artists and designers would exhibit their works in art galleries, museums, or art markets for evaluation. Now, with the help of social media technology, newcomers and professionals could easily exhibit their best works and solicit useful feedbacks from a wider and diverse audience across the globe.

7.3.1.2 Create and Share Resources

The SMPs are also seen as a potential tool for helping the designers learn informally. Besides showcasing personal works on the platform, users could also share their knowledge and skills with the community. Usually users would create posts and share contents that they find interesting and helpful. For example, users may share some guidance or instructions on how to produce a certain outcome based on his experiences. The types of resources that are published are slightly different in both platforms. Tutorials posted in dA tend to be more suitable for new designers unlike Behance, which seems to be more focused on professional works. Behance users often show their work in progress development with less detail on the "how-to" perspectives. In contrast, dA allocates a category for open source and free resources where anyone could download and reuse them to enhance their outcome. The free resources include templates, stock images, and even customized application plugins. In return, the users are only required to leave a comment and show the reuse outcome under the resources shared. dA also provides a category for tutorials where users could post and search for step-by-step guidance in producing creative works. This may be a great support especially for newcomers who are able to get direct help on real-time and improve further following the tutorials given.

7.3.1.3 Social Networking

Each user may interact with other users via different features using synchronous or asynchronous technologies that enable conversations and social interactions. For example, users may post questions in the commenting spaces and learn more from the experienced users when they have difficulties in progressing their design works. The social media technology has enlarged the pool of community where people can learn better from the expanded access. Through this casual way of interaction, users may also engage themselves in informal professional learning development. Instead of just browsing on the static portfolio sites, users may also participate in discussions with professionals and create networking. They may follow new people they met on the SMP or connect with the people of existing relationship by getting regular updates of their activities on the SMP. dA has a more laid back learning environment, compared to Behance. Users in the community of Behance mainly focus on serious discussions aimed to improve their creative works to fulfill the industry demand while dA seems to be more welcoming toward works of newcomers. Nevertheless, both SMPs may encourage successful collaborations and enhance the creation of collaborative artworks. Based on the loops of feedbacks and comments between the designer and other users, the designer may negotiate an improved new form of creation.

7.3.1.4 Find Work Opportunities

The SMPs have changed the way designers look for work opportunities in the creative field and also the way employers recruit talents. Designers tend to engage in the SMP to build their own reputation and increase their chances of getting hired. Exposing themselves to the limelight enhances their online presence and 'searchability'. Talented designers who are actively engaged in Behance tend to have a greater chance of being discovered by professional agencies, compared to dA which provides a list of job vacancies too but only advertises job openings for joining the team. Behance provides a job listing page to enable potential employers advertise job vacancies according to their location and creative field. Behance has also partnered with several organizations such as Adweek, Cooper-Hewitt, and National Design Museum and runs online portfolio galleries for art and design institutions such as Rhode Island School of Design and Art Center Gallery. This could encourage crowdsourcing, as job and portfolios posted on Behance are viewed by millions of users across the globe every month. Besides that, the profiling and showcasing features help the employers to seek suitable candidates. Therefore, the use of SMPs may not only benefit employers, but also designers by providing opportunities to engage with new clients and freelance works.

Conclusions

The social media age has indeed altered the design practices of the designers. The capabilities of technology have offered new opportunities and flexibilities for developing creativity, disseminating knowledge, and accessing information. Particularly, it supports interactivity and socially rich environment, which plays a central role in the design learning community. In this study, we have attempted to illustrate the use of social media platforms in facilitating the designers to 'destuck' themselves from the creative block and how they may motivate the professional development of the designers. In tracing the various structures of the SMPs, this study has also highlighted the comparison between dA and Behance where both SMPs are developed to fulfill different needs of the target audiences. However, this study is limited and only provides the surface of the potential of the SMPs. Although these SMPs seem to be promising for the development of designers, external considerations such cultural aspects should also be taken into account. Therefore, our future goal is to expand this study and provide further understanding on the potential of social media platforms. We hope to gain better insights from various perspectives, especially in the context of design education in higher learning institutions.

References

Boyd, D. (2007). Why youth (heart) social network sites: The role of networked publics in teenage social life. In B. David (Ed.), *MacArthur foundation series on digital learning–Youth, identity, and digital media volume* (pp. 119–142). Cambridge, MA: MIT Press.

Boyd, D. M., & Ellison, N. B. (2007). Social network sites: Definition, history, and scholarship. *Journal of Computer-Mediated Communication, 13*(1), 210–230.

Buchanan, R. (1992). Wicked problems in design thinking. *Design Issues, 8*(2), 5–21.

Cattani, G., & Ferriani, S. (2008). A core-periphery perspective on individual creative performance: Social networks and cinematic achievements in the Hollywood film industry. *Organization Science, 19*(6), 824–844.

Eder, W. E. (1999). Designing as an educational discipline. *International Journal of Engineering Education, 15*(1), 32–40.

Ellison, N. B., Steinfield, C., & Lampe, C. (2007). The benefits of Facebook "friends": Social capital and college students' use of online social network sites. *Journal of Computer-Mediated Communication, 12*(4), 1143–1168.

Engeström, Y. (1987). *Learning by expanding: An activity-theoretical approach to developmental research*. Helsinki: Orienta-Konsultit.

Harrison, T. M., & Barthel, B. (2009). Wielding new media in Web 2.0: Exploring the history of engagement with the collaborative construction of media products. *New Media and Society, 11*(1–2), 155–178.

Kaplan, A. M., & Haenlein, M. (2010). Users of the world, unite! The challenges and opportunities of Social Media. *Business Horizons, 53*(1), 59–68.

Lawson, B., & Dorst, K. (2009). *Design expertise*. Oxford: Elsevier Ltd.

McLoughlin, C., & Lee, M. J. W. (2007). Social software and participatory learning: Pedagogical choices with technology affordances in the Web 2.0 era. In *ICT: Providing choices for learners and learning. Proceedings ascilite Singapore 2007.*

Panahi, S., Watson, J., & Partridge, H. (2012). Social media and tacit knowledge sharing: Developing a conceptual model. *World Academy of Science, Engineering and Technology, 64*, 1095–1102.

Perry-Smith, J. E. (2006). Social yet creative: The role of social relationships in facilitating individual creativity. *Academy of Management Journal, 49*(1), 85–101.

Schön, D. A. (1987). *Educating the reflective practitioner.* San Francisco: Jossey-Bass Publishers.

Schön, D. A. (1992). Designing as reflective conversation with the materials of a design situation. *Knowledge-Based Systems, 5*(1), 3–14.

Seymour, R. (2008). Designing demand: Richard Seymour. *The Design Council.* Retrieved August 20, 2013, from http://www.designcouncil.org.uk/our-work/support/designing-demand/what-is-designing-demand/audio-about-designing-demand/richard-seymour/

Watson, E. (2007). Who or what creates? A conceptual framework for social creativity. *Human Resource Development Review, 6*(4), 419–441.

Chapter 8
News Reading Habits of Young University Students in Hong Kong in the Age of New Media

Alvin C.M. Kwan, Ivy C.T. Cheng, and Joie H.Y. Wong

Abstract A number of recent studies indicated a rapid increase in the use of mobile devices and apps worldwide. Nevertheless, little research has been done on how the new media affect young adults' reading habits. The current study addresses this research gap by studying the news reading habits of 118 young university students in Hong Kong in the Internet era. Selected key findings of the study, mainly obtained through analyzing the quantitative data from an online survey, are as follows: (1) smart phone apps were students' most favorite news source; (2) ease of access was students' key concern when selecting news sources; (3) students of both genders had a clear preference to local news, followed by international and China news; (4) students' news reading habits had little to do with their personal income or their parents' education level; (5) students read news more often and for a longer time if their families had a habit of buying printed newspaper; and (6) students spend less time in news reading when compared to the past. The study also reveals a clear uprising of new media for news access, threatening the role of traditional news sources such as printed newspapers and radio.

Keywords New media • News reading • Habits • Information behavior

A.C.M. Kwan (✉)
The University of Hong Kong, Hong Kong, China
e-mail: cmkwan@hku.hk

I.C.T. Cheng
PCCW Limited, Hong Kong, China
e-mail: ivyivy916@hotmail.com

J.H.Y. Wong
Ogilvy & Mather Marketing Communications Limited, Hong Kong, China
e-mail: joiewonghoyee@gmail.com

© Springer Science+Business Media Singapore 2015
W.W.K. Ma et al. (eds.), *New Media, Knowledge Practices and Multiliteracies*,
DOI 10.1007/978-981-287-209-8_8

8.1 Introduction

With the support of high-speed Internet access and mobile technologies, the amount of time that people spend on the Internet keeps rising. In USA, the total amount of time that people spent on mobile apps and mobile web increased 120 % and 22 %, respectively, from July 2011 to July 2012 (Nielsen Holdings N.V. 2012). Among those who can access the Internet via mobile phones in Hong Kong, 86 % of them have ever downloaded an app to their phones (Nielsen Holdings N.V. 2011a). However, students' news reading habits in light of the proliferation of mobile apps and mobile web are not well studied. To address this research gap, a study about the news reading habits of young university students in Hong Kong was conducted in 2013. The key research question is what kinds of changes to the news reading behaviors of young university students that the age of new media has brought forth. Results of the current study can shed light to the news industry to cater for the emergent needs of new generation readership. The current study collected and analyzed data from an online survey in which 118 valid questionnaires were received. Interviews were also arranged with selected respondents in order to learn more about the rationales behind their choices in the questionnaires. This chapter reports key quantitative results of the study.

8.2 Literature Review

Akanda and Haque (2013) reported that the main purposes of newspaper reading of 150 sampled Bangladesh postgraduates were to get information (11.85 %), to broaden the horizon of general knowledge (11.39 %), for educational purpose (11.12 %), for searching new jobs (10.94 %), and to keep abreast with the current affairs of the world (10.48 %). The key news types the students preferred to read were international (12.96 %), political (12.66 %), editorial (12.06 %), sports (11.96 %), and education news (11.47 %). They were much less concerned with entertainment news (6.98 %). Fifty-five percentage of the respondents spent more than an hour daily on news reading. More than half of the respondents read online news. Majumder and Hasan (2013) conducted a similar study in another university in Bangladesh on both undergraduates and postgraduates ($n = 200$). The respondents preferred to read sports news (29 %) and entertainment news (24.5 %), followed by political news (9.5 %). Almost half of the respondents spent more than an hour per day on news reading. When compared to undergraduates, postgraduates tended to spend more time in reading newspapers.

Newspaper reading habits of 292 postgraduates of an Indian university was reported in (Kumar et al. 2011). The respondents' key preferred news types in descending order were sports news, sensational news, editorial, and political news. About 80 % of the respondents read news at least one hour daily.

Research on news reading habits of university students in Hong Kong is scarce. Lingnan University (2006) reported that in a survey involving its 556 students, the respondents generally preferred reading news of entertainment and leisure.

Leung (2003) conducted a survey participated by 866 secondary 1–3 students in two schools, with an average age of 14, in 2003 regarding factors that might affect their newspaper reading habits. Such factors include students' age, gender, academic performance, and parent's socioeconomic status, etc. The study revealed that 82.5 % of the respondents had a habit of reading newspaper reading. Three-three and forty percentage of the respondents read newspapers every day and more than once a week respectively. On average, each reading session lasted for 23 min. About 18 % of the respondents read news from the Internet. Less than 3 % of the respondents read news in transportation. Regarding content preference, their favorites were entertainment news and local news which attracted 29 % and 15 % of the votes of the respondents, respectively. It is important to note that the participants of this study and the current study are of the same generation. A comparison of the results of the two studies may reveal some interesting changes in the news reading behaviors of those youngsters who were born between late 1980s and early 1990s from the year of 2003–2013.

It is worth noting that all the aforesaid studies have paid little attention to the potential impact of new media to the news reading behavior of university students.

8.3 Methodology

8.3.1 Subjects

Invitations to an online survey were sent to 140 people through the second and third coauthors' personal networks in April–May 2013. One hundred and eighteen university students with an average age of 21.7, mostly undergraduates in the age of 20–23, joined the study. Table 8.1 gives demographic information of the respondents.

Table 8.1 Demographic information of respondents ($n=118$)

Attribute	Value	Number (%)
Gender	Male	62 (52.5 %)
	Female	56 (47.5 %)
Age	17–25	118 (100 %)
Degree	Undergraduate	113 (95.8 %)
	Postgraduate	5 (4.2 %)
Parents' education level	Primary	5 (4.2 %)
	Secondary	61 (51.7 %)
	Postsecondary	17 (14.4 %)
	Undergraduate	26 (22.0 %)
	Postgraduate	9 (7.6 %)
Personal income (in HK$)	Less than 4,000	71 (60.2 %)
	4,000–8,999	28 (23.7 %)
	9,000–14,999	11 (9.3 %)
	More than 15,000	8 (6.8 %)

Table 8.2 Factors considered in preparing questionnaire

Factor	Concerned information
Background	Gender
	Personal income
	Education level
Personal relevance	Habitual news reading time
	Purpose of news reading
Environmental	Parents' education level
	Whether any family member has a habit of buying newspaper

8.3.2 Study Procedure

8.3.2.1 Survey

A questionnaire of 23 questions was used in the survey. The background and personal relevance factors from the information seeking model proposed by Johnson and Meischke (1993) and the environmental influences of the social learning theory (Bandura 1997) were considered when preparing the survey questions (see Table 8.2). The questionnaire also collected data about the news reading habits of the respondents such as how often they read news, how much time they spend on reading news each day, their preferences on different news sources and how often they read news from those sources, their favorite news sources and reasons for their choices, their purposes of news reading and preferred news types, etc. A pilot test was done with two university students and revisions were made to the questionnaire before the survey was launched in April 2013. Results of the pilot test were not used for data analysis.

8.3.2.2 Interview

Based on the survey results, six participants who preferred to read news from different sources were individually interviewed for 45–60 min so as to get an in-depth understanding of the factors contributing to the formation of their reading habits. For example, participants who opted for accessing news with new media were asked for the reasons that supported their decisions. Their answers may hint at an explanation to certain quantitative results. Due to the page limit, a discussion of the qualitative results is beyond the scope of the current chapter.

8.3.2.3 Statistical Analysis

Since the nature of the collected quantitative data was mainly categorical or ordinal and their distributions were usually nonnormal, nonparametric statistics were used to analyze those data in most cases. For Kruskal–Wallis and Mann–Whitney *U* tests, we set the hypotheses as follows:

H_0: The concerned distributions in terms of ranked data are the same.
H_1: The concerned distributions in terms of ranked data are different.

For Chi-square and Fisher's exact tests, the corresponding hypotheses are:

H_0: The occurrence of outcomes for the concerned groups is equal.
H_1: The occurrence of outcomes for the concerned groups is different.

The 95 % level of confidence, i.e., alpha being 0.05, was used. Whenever a result was found statistically significant, its effect size was also computed except for the Kruskal–Wallis test as its overall effect size is not particularly useful.

8.4 Results and Analysis

8.4.1 News Reading Frequency and Duration

As shown in Fig. 8.1, 40 % of respondents read daily. The corresponding figure for a group of junior secondary students in Hong Kong was 32.7 % (Leung 2003). Regarding reading duration, only 11 % of the respondents spent more than 25 min in news reading each day. This figure is much smaller than the corresponding figure reported in Lingnan University (2006) in which 49 % of its students were reported to spend at least 3 h reading newspapers in a week (or about 26 min per day).

8.4.2 Habitual News Reading Time

Forty-seven and thirty-three percentage of the respondents typically read news in transportation and spare time, respectively. Eleven percentage of the respondents preferred reading news during breakfast, whereas 9 % preferred dinner time. These results differ from the junior secondary students' practices reported in Leung (2003) as less than 3 % of them read news in transportation. Reading news

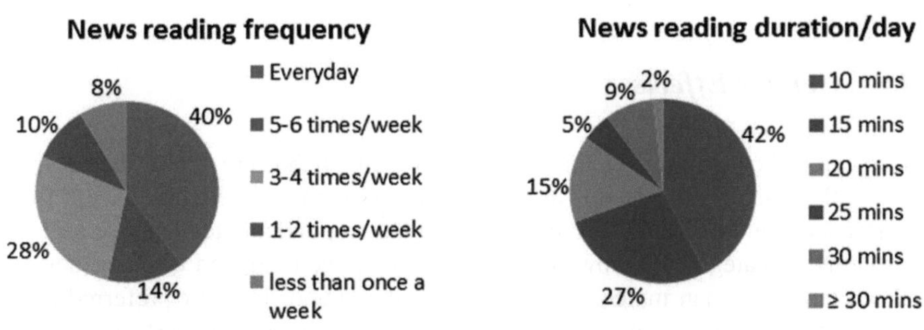

Fig. 8.1 Respondents' news reading frequency and duration per day ($n = 118$)

Table 8.3 Reasons for respondents' choice on favorite news sources ($n=115$)

News source	Mean	Std. deviation	Mean rank
Ease of access	3.58	0.546	4.61
Rich news coverage	3.09	0.732	3.52
Cost	3.04	0.831	3.55
Good use of language	3.01	0.800	3.38
Well-defined news types	2.89	0.792	3.14
Well structure of layout with less advertising	2.75	0.836	2.80

in transportation is more convenient nowadays than a decade ago due to advances in wireless and mobile technologies.

8.4.3 Favorite News Sources and Reasons for Choices

Respondents had a strong preference toward smart phone apps (44 %), free e-newspapers (31 %), and television (14 %) when selecting their favorite news sources. Results of Wilcoxon signed-rank test confirm that smart phone apps is the clear winner when compared to free e-newspapers which is the second most popular choice [$n=118$, $p=0.000$, effect size=0.362 (medium)]. The same test also confirms that free e-newspaper is the first runner-up [$n=118$, $p=0.000$, effect size=0.485 (high medium)]. Six reasons for supporting the choice of favorite news source were presented to the respondents for rating. Respondents were asked to rate each reason in a Likert scale of 1–4, representing "strong disagree (1)", "disagree (2)", "agree (3)", and "strong agree (4)". The results are tabulated in Table 8.3.

When compared to *rich news coverage*, the second most popular choice, the results of Wilcoxon signed-rank test indicate that *ease of access* is the winner [$n=116$, $p=0.000$, effect size=0.486 (high medium)]. This partly explains why smart phone apps and free e-newspapers, both of them being highly accessible, were the respondents' top two favorite news sources.

8.4.4 Gender Effects

Past research showed little evidence that news reading habits are gender stereotyped (Leung 2003, p. 22). Our results are largely in line with past research except for a few aspects (see Table 8.4). For instance, female respondents tended to care how news items are categorized, how news contents are structured, and whether they are well written more than male respondents did when choosing their preferred news sources. Female respondents tended to rank editorials higher and sports news lower than male respondents did (see Table 8.5).

Table 8.4 Gender effects on reading habits ($n = 118$)

News reading habit/feature	Test used	p-value	Effect size
Why the preferred news source—Well-defined news types	Mann–Whitney U	0.012*	0.230 (small)
Why the preferred news source—Good layout with little advertising	Mann–Whitney U	0.029*	0.201 (small)
Why the preferred news source—Good use of language	Mann–Whitney U	0.006**	0.254 (small)
Preferred news type—Sports news	Mann–Whitney U	0.000**	0.343 (medium)
Preferred news type—Editorial	Mann–Whitney U	0.004**	0.264 (small)

*$p < 0.05$; **$p < 0.01$

Table 8.5 Mean ranks (in 1–10 scale) of preferred news types by gender

News category	Male (rank)	Female (rank)	All
Local news	2.32 (1)	2.39 (1)	2.36 (1)
International news	3.63 (2)	3.73 (2)	3.68 (2)
China news	4.55 (4)	4.11 (3)	4.34 (3)
Entertainment	5.08 (5)	4.54 (4)	4.82 (4)
Sports	4.45 (3)	6.54 (9)	5.44 (5)
Supplement	6.15 (6)	5.27 (5)	5.73 (6)
Finance	6.16 (7)	6.36 (7)	6.25 (7)
Editorial	7.37 (10)	5.79 (6)	6.62 (8)
Property	6.65 (8)	6.68 (10)	6.66 (9)
Education	6.85 (9)	6.48 (8)	6.68 (10)

Both genders had a clear preference to local news, followed by international, China, and entertainment news. These results are different from the findings of Lingnan University (2006) and Leung (2003), which indicated that a students' preference towards news about entertainment and leisure.

8.4.5 Personal Income

Students' personal income seems to have little effect to their reading habits except for a few cases (see Table 8.6). No comparison of the results with other local studies can be done as the potential effect of students' personal income has never been investigated in those local studies.

Our results are different from the survey results of American Press Institute (API 2014) in which higher income groups were reported to be more likely to receive news from traditional news sources such as newspapers and radios. However, it is important to point out that the institute's survey covered 1,492 adults of 18+ years old with a much diverse range of background.

Table 8.6 Effects of students' personal income on reading habits ($n = 118$)

News reading habit/feature	Test used	p-value
Preferred news type—Local news	Kruskal–Wallis	0.050*
Preferred news type—Financial news	Kruskal–Wallis	0.031*
Preferred news type—Entertainment news	Kruskal–Wallis	0.037*
Access frequency—Radio	Kruskal–Wallis	0.045*

*$p < 0.05$

Table 8.7 Favorite news sources of different income groups

	Monthly income (in HK$)				
News source	≤4,000	4,000–9,000	9,000–14,999	≥15,000	Total (%)
Smart phone apps	32	10	6	4	52 (44.1 %)
Free e-newspaper	23	10	1	3	37 (31.4 %)
Television	11	3	2	1	17 (14.4 %)
Paid newspaper	2	3	0	0	5 (4.2 %)
Free newspaper	1	1	2	0	4 (3.4 %)
Social Network	1	1	0	0	2 (1.7 %)
Paid online news	1	0	0	0	1 (0.8 %)
Radio	0	0	0	0	0

According to the survey results, students' with higher incomes tended to pay more attention to financial news when compared to students with less income. However, no clear trend regarding how income level affects university students' readership in local news and entertainment news types can be identified.

Radio was the respondents' least preferred news source. It was also least popular among young adults when compared to adults of other ages in (API 2014). However, respondents with low income seemed to be more willing to use radio to get news. Regardless of their income, no respondents considered radio their favorite news source and new media channels such as smart phone apps and free e-newspapers were preferred (see Table 8.7). Such a preference to new media was confirmed by one-sample chi-square test ($n = 118$; $p < 0.001$) with a large effect size (0.559). In contrast to the results reported by Clark et al. (2004) that television (44 %), the Internet (21 %), and newspaper (20 %) were the preferred news and information sources among 1,500 respondents between 18 and 34, our survey results indicated that traditional media had been overtaken by new media.

8.4.6 *Family Influence*

The potential influences of parents' education level and family members' newspaper reading habits to university students' own reading habits were studied. Leung (2003) claimed that socioeconomic status reflected by a student's father's income, mother's income, father's education level, and mother's education level could affect the student's newspaper reading habits such as content preferences. However, a comparison of Leung's results with those of the current study cannot be drawn as the latter study did not collect those socioeconomic data.

Statistical results of the current study failed to reveal any link between parents' education level to respondents' reading habits and preferences except that respondents with more educated parents tended to read news from television more often than respondents with less educated parents did ($n = 118$; $p = 0.003$). This may be linked to a finding reported in API (2014, p. 45), indicating that "*more highly educated Americans being more likely than those with lower levels of education to receive news from both traditional news sources such as newspapers and radios and online and emerging sources*." Due to the crowded living conditions in Hong Kong, the respondents might have watched news programs on television with their more educated parents since they were small. Getting news from television may have been developed as one of the respondents' news reading habits.

For those respondents whose families had a habit of buying newspapers, referred to as Group A, their reading habits seemed to be different from those whose families did not, referred to as Group B, in various aspects (see Table 8.8).

Group A respondents read more often than Group B respondents did. Fifty-six percentage of them read news every day, whereas only 35 % of Group B respondents did the same. While 56 % of Group A respondents spent at least 25 min a day on news reading, only 3 % of Group B respondents did the same. Besides, Group A respondents (89 %) were much more willing to pay for news than Group B (29 %) did. Seventy-four percentage of Group A and 12 % of Group B respondents were willing to buy newspapers. Group A respondents also tended to read from newspapers and paid e-newspapers more often than Group B did. These findings confirm that family newspaper literacy practices are the strongest predictor of later newspaper reading habits as reported in (Wilson 2007).

Table 8.8 Influences of family habit of buying newspapers on respondents' reading habits ($n = 118$)

News reading habit/feature	Test used	p-value	Effect size
Reading frequency	Mann–Whitney U	0.040*	0.189 (small)
Reading duration per day	Mann–Whitney U	0.000**	0.645 (large)
Willing to pay for news	Fisher's exact[a]	0.000**	0.511 (large)
Willing to pay for newspapers	Fisher's exact[a]	0.000**	0.589 (large)
Access frequency—Paid printed newspapers	Mann–Whitney U	0.001**	0.299 (close to medium)
Access frequency—Paid e-news	Mann–Whitney U	0.022*	0.211 (small)

*$p < 0.05$; **$p < 0.01$

[a]Computed with the online calculator at http://www.quantitativeskills.com/sisa/statistics/fiveby2.htm as SPSS does not support Fisher's exact test for non-2×2 tables

Table 8.9 Respondents' purposes of news reading ($n=115$)

Purpose	Mean	Std. deviation	Mean rank
To improve language proficiency	2.99	1.090	2.96
For leisure	2.78	1.055	2.81
To acquire knowledge, e.g., finance and sports	2.41	1.056	2.34
To be aware of current issues	1.94	1.303	1.89

8.4.7 *Purpose of News Reading*

Four purposes of news reading were presented to the respondents for rating. Respondents rated the relevance of each of them from their own perspective in a Likert scale of 1–5, varying from "most relevant" to "least relevant".

As shown in Table 8.9, respondents considered keeping themselves aware of current issues the most relevant purpose of reading news. Knowledge acquisition was second, whereas reading for leisure and language improvement was less relevant to the respondents.

Conclusion

The drop of readership of daily printed newspapers is a worldwide phenomenon. This may sound worrying as news reading is believed to have an impact to the success of continuous personal development in terms of common sense and civil responsibility in one's development process (Leung 2003, p. 2). However, the number of people reading news may not decrease in reality due to a rapid increase of people reading news via the Internet and mobile devices. According to Nielsen Holdings N.V. (2011b), accessing news with mobile devices increased almost three times from July 2009 to June 2011. While the infiltration rate of smart phones in Hong Kong was only about 35 % in 2013 (BBG 2013), the rate among young university students is believed to be much higher. Besides, university students can access online news through other forms of new media channels conveniently at home or at university. These factors have facilitated the formation of new news reading habits among young university students in Hong Kong.

Despite its small scale and weakness in the sampling method, the current study has revealed that the rising popularity of new media and the declining use of traditional media for getting news among university students in Hong Kong. Accessibility was our respondents' major concern in the selection of news source. This concurs with the view of Costera Meijer (2007) that young people want their need be satisfied instantly. While new media can offer easy access to up-to-date news, its use is not problem-free. New media users tend to spend less time on news reading when compared to paid newspaper readers. Further research is needed to look into this phenomenon.

References

Akanda, A. M. E. A., & Haque, M. A. (2013). Newspaper reading habits of university graduate students in Bangladesh: A case study. *International Journal of Research in Applied, Natural and Social Sciences (IMPACT: IJRANSS), 1*(3), 1–8.

API. (2014, March 17). *Social and demographic differences in news habits and attitudes*. The Media Insight Project. American Press Institute and Associated Press-NORC Center for Public Affairs Research. Retrieved May 12, 2014 from http://www.americanpressinstitute.org/publications/reports/survey-research/social-demographic-differences-news-habits-attitudes/

Bandura, A. (1997). *Self-efficacy: The exercise of control*. New York: Freeman.

BBG. (2013, November 8). *The smartphone infiltration around the world*. BBG Communications. Retrieved May 8, 2014 from http://www.bbgcommunicationunitedstates.com/advancements-in-mobile-phones/article/37.php

Clark, Martire, & Bartolomeo. (2004). *Growing lifelong readers: A study of the impact of student involvement with newspapers on adult readership*. Unpublished study prepared for the Newspaper Association of America Foundation. Retrieved May 13, 2014 from http://www.nieworld.com/lifelongreaders.htm

Costera Meijer, I. (2007). The paradox of popularity: How young people experience the news. *Journalism Studies, 8*(1), 96–116.

Johnson, J. D., & Meischke, H. (1993). A comprehensive model of cancer-related information seeking applied to magazines. *Human Communications Research, 19*, 343–367.

Kumar, D., Singh, R., & Siddiqui, J. A. (2011, January). Newspaper reading habits of university students: A case study of Chaudhary Charan Singh University, India. *Library Philosophy and Practice*. Retrieved May 8, 2014 from http://www.webpages.uidaho.edu/~mbolin/devendrakumar-singh-siddiqui.pdf

Leung, H. H. M. (2003). *Newspaper reading habits of secondary students in Hong Kong*. Unpublished master dissertation, Department of Social Work and Social Administration, University of Hong Kong, Hong Kong.

Lingnan University. (2006, December 20). Reading habits of Lingnan students. *Learning Matters at Lingnan*, Teaching Learning Center, Lingnan University.

Majumder, D., & Hasan, M. M. (2013). Newspaper reading habits of private university students: A case study on World University of Bangladesh. *IOSR Journal of Business and Management, 12*(1), 87–91.

Nielsen Holdings N.V. (2011a). *Hong Kong digital behaviour insights report*. Retrieved July 7, 2014, from https://www.yumpu.com/en/document/view/5262740/hk-digital-behavior-insights-report-final-nielsen

Nielsen Holdings N.V. (2011b). *Free newspaper and new media squeeze paid newspaper market*. Retrieved May 10, 2014, from http://hk.nielsen.com/news/20111113.shtml

Nielsen Holdings N.V. (2012). *State of the media: The social media report 2012*. Retrieved May 10, 2014, from http://cn.en.nielsen.com/site/documents/NielsenSocialMediaReport2012_FINAL.PDF

Wilson, B. (2007). *Factors that predict newspaper reading habits in college students*. Paper presented at the annual meeting of the Association for Education in Journalism and Mass Communication. The Renaissance, Washington, DC. Retrieved May 10, 2014, from http://citation.allacademic.com/meta/p202904_index.html

References

Part III
Knowledge Practices

Chapter 9
An Exploration of Online Viewing on an Individual's Dating Attitude and Love Style

Hilda Yuet-hang Kho

Abstract In recent years, viewing online has become popular due to the rise of social media and video sharing platforms. Internet users can access to a variety of programs online easily, they can comment on the videos, or even share the videos to other online platforms as they wish. Nowadays, the younger generations are choosing to watch TV shows online rather than on a television. Therefore, it is necessary to know the influence of online viewing to viewers. With reference to Cultivation Theory, this study explores the effect of online viewing to viewers' attitude and behavior, particularly in the love aspect. The results showed that active online viewing and perceived realism had a significant and positive relationship with one's dating attitude. The implications of these findings are discussed.

Keywords Online viewing • Cultivation theory • Perceived realism • Dating attitude • Love style

9.1 Introduction

In recent years, with the advancement of technology and the rising of social media, viewing online becomes very popular. A current study (Mashable.com 2010) showed that 83 % of young adults aged under 25 watched some, most or all of their TV programming online. As the new generation no longer sees television as their major media, it is necessary to know what effects will online viewing brings to viewers. Previous studies have done a lot of research on the effects of watching TV to viewers, among which the Cultivation Theory was the most authoritative theory in explaining the phenomenon. However, few studies have explored the effect of

H.Y.-h. Kho (✉)
Online Communication Research Centre, Department of Journalism and Communication, Hong Kong Shue Yan University, Hong Kong, China
e-mail: hildakho521@gmail.com

© Springer Science+Business Media Singapore 2015

W.W.K. Ma et al. (eds.), *New Media, Knowledge Practices and Multiliteracies*,
DOI 10.1007/978-981-287-209-8_9

watching online videos to viewers, we would like to know if Cultivation Theory also applies on online viewing. Hence, the objective of this research was to study the influence of viewing online on the attitude and behavior of viewers.

9.2 Literature Review

9.2.1 Cultivation Theory

Cultivation Theory, developed by Gerbner et al. (1986), examined the long-term effects of television viewing and stated that TV could cultivates or creates a worldview that becomes the reality as the viewers believe it to be and would base their judgments about their own everyday worlds on that reality. The "level of cultivation" also hinges on the frequency of viewing TV as well as the social status of the audience. Scholars had done different researches regarding the influences of television viewing to viewers' attitude and behaviors. Ferris et al. (2007) found out that viewers with higher average viewing scores of reality dating shows would be more likely to endorse the dating attitudes and behaviors found in the programs. Furthermore, Ward and Friedman (2006) pointed that more frequent viewing of talk shows and "sexy" prime-time programs were associated with greater endorsement of sexual stereotypes as well as levels of sexual experience. Hetsroni and Tukachinsky (2006) developed a model on the relationship between TV viewing and the estimation of TV-world and real world. The model suggested five groups of viewers, namely, simple cultivation, over cultivation, double distortion, simple no cultivation, and distorted no cultivation. Another research by Woo and Dominick (2003) also stated the relationship between daytime TV talk show viewing and viewers' beliefs about social reality.

9.2.2 Viewing TV Programs Online

Due to the advancement of technology, the medium for watching TV programs cease to confine within the television set. According to Bondad-Brown et al. (2012), viewers are increasingly accessing television and video content via the Internet on computers, mobile phones, and other devices. Mashable.com (2010) posted a study conducted by Retrevo, a consumer electronics shopping site, and the survey showed that "more of us than ever before are choosing to watch TV shows on website rather than on a tv". This study concluded that "online TV viewership is on the rise". In a research conducted by Haridakis and Hanson (2009), results suggested that there was a distinctly social aspect to YouTube use that reflects its social networking characteristics, while people watch videos on YouTube for some of the same reasons identified in studies of TV viewing. They stated that participants viewed videos for information seeking, co-viewing and social interaction.

9.2.3 Viewing Motives

However, as compared to previous discussions on Cultivation Theory, Tiggemann (2005) pointed that television watching did have an impact on young people's sense of body image, but the critical aspects was not the total amount of television watched. His study found that the critical aspects were the type of material as well as the motivations for watching. Ward and Friedman (2006) also found that viewing motive was a significant factor for adolescent's sexual attitudes and behavior. Their research suggested that viewing TV in a friend/companion motive, which meant watching TV more intently for companionship, was associated with greater endorsement of sexual stereotypes. Furthermore, a research by Minnebo and Eggermont (2012) indicated that with regard to television, viewing motives in particular had net effects that hamper or benefit the recovery process of crime victims. These suggest that viewers' viewing motivations might be influential to their attitudes.

9.2.4 Content Type

Gerbner's et al. Cultivation Theory (1986) stated the long-term effects of watching TV but focused only on the "quantity" (how much people watch TV) instead of the "quality" (what is shown on TV) of TV programs. And as stated by Tiggemann (2005), the type of material shown on TV was a critical aspect that influences young people's sense of body image. The research by Ferris et al (2007) examined the content of reality dating shows and its relationship with viewer's actual dating attitudes and behaviors.

9.2.5 Dating Attitude

Regarding one's perception of dating, Ferris et al. (2007) examined the relationship between content of reality dating shows and viewer's actual dating attitudes and behaviors. Results showed that male viewers, who perceived higher realism in the shows, were more likely to endorse attitudes found in the programs.

To sum up, four hypotheses are proposed to study the factors affecting viewers' dating attitude in online viewing. The hypotheses are as follow:

***H*1**: Viewing programs online has a positive effect on an individual's dating attitude.

***H*2**: Viewer's motivations for watching online videos have a positive effect on their dating attitude.

***H*3**: The content of online programs has a positive effect on an individual's dating attitude.

***H*4**: Viewer's perceived realism of online programs has a positive effect on their dating attitude.

9.3 Methodology

9.3.1 *Background*

These days, viewing online is very popular, including a lot of platforms which are free of charge to audience to a mass collection of TV programs. For example, YouTube allows billions of people to discover, watch, and share originally created videos. It provides a forum for people to connect, inform, and inspire others across the globe and acts as a distribution platform for original content creators (YouTube.com 2013). Similarly, there are a number of video sharing sites, such as Hulu, Vimeo, Tudou, Youku, and PPS, where they share similar functions.

9.3.2 *Subjects and Data Collection*

This study targeted universities students as the subject, because they are the Internet native generation and are heavy users of Internet. Therefore, they could represent people who are using the Internet as their platform or medium to watch TV programs. Printed questionnaires were distributed to 250 universities students at assemblies, canteens, and libraries of universities. Two hundred and sixteen were completed and collected where they spent not more than 15 min on the questionnaires.

9.3.3 *Measurements*

The questionnaire included two parts. First, subjects were asked to self-report their viewing habit both on TV and on online from a number of passive and active categories of activities, ranged from 1 (*never*) to 10 (*many times* and *every day*). The second part was designed to collect subjects' opinion. Three items of viewing motives (Ward and Friedman 2006; Tiggemann 2005), two items of perceived realism (Ferris et al. 2007) and three items of dating attitudes (Ferris et al. 2007) were adopted from previous validated scales, see Appendix for the whole instrument. All of these were measured in Likert scale, ranged from 1 (*strongly disagree*) to 7 (*strongly agree*).

9.4 Findings

9.4.1 *Descriptive Statistics of Respondents and Variables*

The 216 subjects in the sample included 53 male (24.5 %) and 163 female (75.5 %), with a mean age of 20.8 years old. The most popular program genre was love dramas, 51 respondents loved to watch it; and the most popular online platform was YouTube,

Table 9.1 Descriptive statistics of constructs ($n=216$)

	Min.	Max.	*M*	S.D.	α
Viewing motives (View)					
View1	3	7	5.61	0.954	0.805
View2	1	7	5.58	1.046	
View3	1	7	5.64	0.985	
Perceived realism (Real)					
Real1	1	7	3.97	1.348	0.606
Real2	1	7	4.08	1.315	
Dating attitude (Attitude)					
Attitude1	1	7	4.40	1.348	0.755
Attitude2	1	7	3.23	1.435	
Attitude3	1	7	3.03	1.502	
Passive online viewing habits (Passive)					
Passive1	1	10	7.03	2.186	0.792
Passive2	1	10	5.22	2.489	
Passive3	1	10	4.73	2.419	
Passive4	1	10	3.26	2.433	
Active online viewing habits (Active)					
Active1	1	8	1.71	1.635	0.846
Active2	1	9	1.82	1.657	
Active3	1	10	2.59	1.998	

179 respondents' most often visited online viewing platform. The descriptive statistics of the variables were shown in the table (see Table 9.1).

9.4.2 Instrument Validation

Internal consistency was tested by reliability Cronbach's α-value where values greater than 0.7 is considered reliable (Nunnally and Bernstein 1994). The alpha values for viewing motives, perceived realism, dating attitude, passive online viewing habits, and active online viewing habits were 0.805, 0.606, 0.755, 0.792, and 0.846, respectively. Except perceived realism which is 0.606, all the constructs were reliable and internal consistent. However, it is not uncommon for researchers to characterize reliabilities in the 0.6 and 0.7 range as good or adequate (Clark and Watson 1995, p. 315). Therefore, the instrument is considered reliable and exhibited internal consistency.

Five components were extracted by Principal Components, Varimax Rotation factor analysis. The Eigen values were 3.806, 2.695, 1.904, 1.301, and 1.007 where the percentage of total variance explained was 71.426 %. The constructs exhibited convergent validity if "*the items that are indicators of a specific construct converge or share a high proportion of variance in common*" (Hair et al.

Table 9.2 Factor analysis validity test

	Component				
	1	2	3	4	5
View1			0.752		
View2			0.865		
View3			0.851		
Real1					0.804
Real2					0.812
Attitude1				0.729	
Attitude2				0.858	
Attitude3				0.807	
Passive1	0.763				
Passive2	0.844				
Passive3	0.838				
Passive4	0.612				
Active1		0.801			
Active2		0.852			
Active3		0.864			
Eigen Values	3.806	2.695	1.904	1.301	1.007
% of Variance	25.376 %	17.965 %	12.695 %	8.673 %	6.717 %

Table 9.3 Descriptive of summed mean score of constructs

	Min.	Max.	*M*	S.D.
View	3	7	5.61	0.845
Real	1	6.5	4.03	1.130
Passive	1	10	5.06	1.872
Active	1	8	2.04	1.549

2010, p. 709). As a good rule of thumb, the standardized factor loading estimates should be 0.5 or higher, and ideally 0.7 or higher (p. 709). From the table, except passive4 is 0.612 (>0.5), all factor loadings are greater than 0.7, showing an acceptable value for convergent validity of the instrument. At the same time, the constructs were all distinct without any significant cross-loadings, exhibited discriminant validity (Table 9.2). Therefore, overall, the instrument was both reliable and valid. Summed mean score would be computed for each construct and for regression analysis of their relationship test (Table 9.3).

A manipulation check was conducted. Using 2-sample independent *t*-test, male and female were not found any significant differences in the three different love attitudes, passive usage. However, there was significant higher means of male in active usage (2.49) than their female counterpart (1.89) at significant level $p = 0.014$ (<0.05).

Table 9.4 Linear regression model and hypotheses testing for dating attitude

	Model summary					ANOVA	
Dating attitude	Model	R	R^2	Adjusted R^2	Std. Error of the Estimate	F	Sig.
Att1	1	0.325	0.105	0.088	1.292	6.071	0.000
Att2	1	0.302	0.091	0.073	1.384	5.162	0.001
Att3	1	0.329	0.108	0.091	1.433	6.193	0.000

9.4.3 Dating Attitude

We used linear multiple regression to test the model and paths for the effect of viewing motives, perceived realism and online viewing habits on dating attitude.

For all three attitude models, they were significant ($p<0.05$) and the R^2 was 0.105, 0.091, and 0.108 for Att1 ("Men are sex-driven"), Att2 ("Dating is a game"), and Att3 ("Women are sexual objects"), respectively. That means, the models explained 10.5 %, 9.1 %, and 10.8 % of the variance of Att1, Att2, and Att3, respectively (Table 9.4).

For H1, it was supported. We found that the path was significant and the standardized coefficient was 0.169 (unstandardized coefficients 0.167, std. error 0.075, $p<0.05$) for the active online viewing habits (Active) to attitude3 (Att3: "Women are sexual objects"). That is, for every standardized unit of active online viewing habits increased, there would be 0.169 standardized unit of Att3 increased. The higher they engaged in active online viewing habits, the tendency for them to possess the attitude "Women are sexual object" would be higher. For H2, it was not supported. There was no significant relationship between viewing motivations and dating attitude. For H4, it was supported. We found that the path was significant and the standardized coefficient was 0.317 (unstandardized coefficients 0.378, std. error 0.082, $p<0.001$), 0.152 (unstandardized coefficients 0.196, std. error 0.089, $p<0.05$), and 0.160 (unstandardized coefficients 0.213, std. error 0.091, $p<0.05$) for attitude1, attitude2, and attitude3, respectively. That is, for every standardized unit of perceived realism increased, there would be 0.317 standardized unit of Att1 increased; for every standardized unit of perceived realism increased, there would be 0.152 standardized unit of Att2 increased; and every standardized unit of perceived realism increased, there would be 0.160 standardized unit of Att3 increased. The higher realism an individual perceive, the tendency for them to possess the three dating attitudes, namely "Men are sex-driven", "Dating is a game," and "Women are sexual object" would be higher (Table 9.5).

9.4.4 Online Programs Viewing

We further analyzed the effect of favorite online program and TV program to respondents' love attitude. *Favorite online program*: Independent-samples *t*-tests were conducted to compare respondents' dating attitude in their favorite online program.

Table 9.5 Linear regression model and coefficients for the three dating attitudes

Dating attitudes	Factors	Unstandardized Coefficients		Standardized coefficients		
		B	Std. Error	Beta	*t*	Sig.
Att1	Constant	2.927	0.714		4.097	0.000
	View	−0.012	0.116	−0.007	−0.101	0.920
	Real	0.378	0.082	0.317	4.606	0.000
	Usage1	−0.011	0.052	−0.016	−0.216	0.829
	Usage2	0.033	0.067	0.038	0.496	0.621
Att2	Constant	2.610	0.769		3.393	0.001
	View	−0.160	0.123	−0.094	−1.300	0.195
	Real	0.196	0.089	0.152	2.199	0.029
	Usage1	0.099	0.056	0.130	1.783	0.076
	Usage2	0.106	0.071	0.115	1.483	0.139
Att3	(Constant)	2.651	0.798		3.323	0.001
	View	−0.208	0.129	−0.115	−1.610	0.109
	Real	0.213	0.091	0.160	2.329	0.021
	Usage1	0.067	0.057	0.084	1.164	0.246
	Usage2	0.167	0.075	0.169	2.226	0.027

Results show that there were no significant difference in watching "Running Man" and other programs ($p>0.05$). These results suggest that the online programs content do not have any effect on dating attitudes. *TV program*: The respondents listed their favorite TV programs in total of 216, including "Running Man" (36, 16.7 %); "Bounty Lady" (20, 9.3 %); "Come Home Love" (12, 5.6 %); and others (148, 68.5 %). A one-way ANOVA was used to test for favorite TV programs among four groups of programs. Results showed that there was no significant difference between watching different TV programs at $p<0.05$ level ($p=0.821>0.05$). That means, watching different TV programs have no significant relationship with an individual's dating attitude. Hence, H3 was not supported. The content type on programs viewers watched has no effect on their dating attitude.

9.5 Discussion

9.5.1 Online Viewing and Dating Attitude

The results suggest that certain online viewing habits do pose an effect on one's dating attitude. Active viewing habits, including uploading videos, commenting on others' videos, and sharing videos to other platforms, are correlated to the "women are sexual objects" attitude, which emphasize on the physical beauty of women. This type of user is usually very much engaged in the online world. With the rise of online bullying directed against people's appearance, and also the rise of pretty online "youtubers", bloggers, etc., those heavy Internet users might have a higher probability to focus on the physical appearance of women.

9.5.2 Viewing Motives and Dating Attitude

Results show that there were no correlation between viewing motivations and dating attitudes. According to the study of Ward and Friedman (2006), watching TV for companionship (i.e., in a friend/companion motive) was associated with a greater endorsement of sexual stereotype, in which the "sexual stereotypes" in the context were the same as "dating attitudes" used in this study. As there are a wide range of content available online, users can access a lot more information in the Internet than that in TV. This probably creates the "gap" between watching TV and watching online; since what are provided on TV is fixed, but users can choose what to watch online. Hence, viewing online became a more "personal" experience that the companion motive ceased to be the reason for them to watch certain content; and although viewers might watch videos for an enjoyment or relaxation motive, it could no longer affect their attitudes.

9.5.3 Content and Dating Attitude

There were also no significant difference between the content of online programs and dating attitude. This is probably because the range of types of programs is wide in the online world; users are receiving a lot of information from the Internet. The wide range of content generated may not be specific enough to influence one's attitude.

9.5.4 Perceived Realism and Dating Attitude

The results reveal that perceived realism of an individual has a positive effect on his/her dating attitude. This is consistent with the study by Ferris et al (2007) that viewers perceiving TV programs are realistic would have a higher tendency to endorse attitudes found within the programs. Videos that are available online often provide alternative concepts or views about love to viewers. In TV programs, romantic plot are usually being touched on slightly due to certain regulations; but for online videos, they could be bolder on its idea and could feature more undisguised content. As viewers have a higher chance to receive this kind of content and perceive that is the reality, they are more likely to believe in the dating attitude featured in the videos.

9.5.5 Limitations and Future Studies

There were a number of limitations in this study and they offer opportunities for future research. Although it is believed that university students are a good proxy for the general Internet users as they are the Internet native generation, further studies are needed to determine the representativeness of the results. The sample in future studies should involve a wider range of respondents, for instance, in terms of age, dating experience, and relationship status, so as to obtain a more generalized result.

Conclusion
The most important finding of this study is the correlation between an individual's perceived realism and their dating attitude. The results provide evidence that a higher perceived realism in online videos would lead to a higher tendency for an individual to endorse the dating attitudes shown in the videos. This outcome shows that Gerbner's et al. cultivation theory (1986) would still hold even when the medium of the communication channel has changed from television to the Internet. People would still be "cultivated" by the content, especially when they perceive that the substance of the videos is the reality, they would be much more likely to endorse the attitude conveyed. The worldview in online videos could be instilled to viewers.

Appendix: Measurement Items Used in the Study

Construct	Measurement items
Viewing motives (View)	
View1	I watch videos online because they are entertaining and enjoyable
View2	I watch videos online for enjoyment
View3	I watch videos online for relaxation
Perceived realism (Real)	
Real1	The same things that happen to people in online videos happen to people in my neighborhood
Real2	People in online videos are just like people in the real world
Passive online viewing habits (Passive)—"there" refers to respondents' most often visited online viewing platform, ranged from 1 (*never*) to 10 (*many times, every day*)	
Passive1	In the last week, how often did you visit there?
Passive2	In the last week, how often did you watch the "popular videos" there?
Passive3	In the last week, how often did you watch the "recommended videos" there?
Passive4	In the last week, how often did you add/edit playlist(s) there?

(continued)

Construct	Measurement items
Active online viewing habits (Active)—"there" refers to respondents' most often visited online viewing platform, ranged from 1 (*never*) to 10 (*many times, every day*)	
Active1	In the last week, how often did you upload video(s) there?
Active2	In the last week, how often did you make comment(s) there?
Active3	In the last week, how often did you share video(s) from there?
Three dating attitudes (Att)	
Att1	Men are sex driven
Att2	Dating is a game
Att3	Women are sexual objects

References

About YouTube. (2013). *YouTube*. Retrieved November 18, 2013, from http://www.youtube.com/yt/about/index.html

Bondad-Brown, B. A., Rice, R. E., & Pearce, K. E. (2012). Influences on TV viewing and online user-shared video use: Demographics, generations, contextual age, media use, motivations, and audience activity. *Journal of Broadcasting & Electronic Media, 56*(4), 471–493.

Clark, L. A., & Watson, D. (1995). Constructing validity: Basic issues in objective scale development. *Psychological Assessment, 7*(3), 309–319.

Ferris, A. L., Smith, S. W., Greenberg, B. S., & Smith, S. L. (2007). The content of reality dating shows and viewer perceptions of dating. *Journal of Communication, 57*(3), 490–510.

Gerbner, G., Gross, L., Morgan, M., & Signorielli, N. (1986). Living with television: The dynamics of the cultivation process. In *Perspectives on media effects* (pp. 17–40). Hillsdale: Lawrence Erlbaum Associates.

Hair, J. F., Black, B., Babin, B., & Anderson, R. E. (2010). *Multivariate data analysis: A global perspective* (7th ed.). Upper Saddle River: Pearson.

Haridakis, P., & Hanson, G. (2009). Social interaction and co-viewing with YouTube: Blending mass communication reception and social connection. *Journal of Broadcasting & Electronic Media, 53*(2), 317–335.

Hetsroni, A., & Tukachinsky, R. H. (2006). Television-World estimates, real-world estimates, and television viewing: A new scheme for cultivation. *Journal of Communication, 56*(1), 133–156.

Mashable. (2010). *Mashable*. Retrieved November 1, 2013, from http://mashable.com/2010/04/12/tv-online/

Minnebo, J., & Eggermont, S. (2012). Trauma recovery in victims of crime: The role of television viewing motives and television exposure. *Journal of Loss & Trauma, 17*(1), 73–97.

Nunnally, J. C., & Bernstein, I. H. (1994). *Psychometric theory*. New York: McGraw-Hill.

Tiggemann, M. (2005). Television and adolescent body image: The role of program content and viewing motivation. *Journal of Social & Clinical Psychology, 24*(3), 361–381.

Ward, L., & Friedman, K. (2006). Using TV as a guide: Associations between television viewing and adolescents' sexual attitudes and behavior. *Journal of Research on Adolescence, 16*(1), 133–156.

Woo, H. J., & Dominick, J. R. (2003). Acculturation, cultivation, and daytime TV talk shows. *Journalism & Mass Communication Quarterly, 80*(1), 109–127.

Chapter 10
The Restriction of Degree: Reform of Public School Management Models

Kongzhen Li and Jingjing Zhang

Abstract Since the reform and opening up policy in China, according to different social demands, the reform of public school management models has experienced different periods. Through the educational policy document analysis and interview study of the two periods of the reform of school management models in the city of Beijing, it is discovered that, during 1985–2005, the reform is characterized by "decentralization and public school system transformation", introducing market mechanism, and since 2006, the reform has been featured by "cross-school organization," aiming to achieve the equity of educational opportunities. It also found that in the future, while the local governments conduct the reform of public school management model, more attention should be paid to the timely policy adjust, the limits of expanding school running autonomy, and the balance between responsibility and power.

Keywords Public school • Management models • School autonomy

10.1 Introduction

China's reform of public school management models is under the influence of the economic development and social demands, and profoundly affects the school development, reflecting pursuits of the value of educational policies.

The purpose of this chapter is to examine the restriction of educational reform degrees through educational policy document analysis and interview study of the reform of public school management models in Beijing and draw some enlightenment from this reform. Nowadays, most countries are delivering some kinds of educational reform, sometimes the reforms can get the results that the policy makers expect, sometimes it is very difficult to achieve the reform goals, even though the

K. Li (✉)
College of Education, Capital Normal University, Beijing, China
e-mail: Kzhli08@163.com

J. Zhang
Faculty of Education, Beijing Normal University, Beijing, China
e-mail: jingjing.zhang@bnu.edu.cn

© Springer Science+Business Media Singapore 2015

W.W.K. Ma et al. (eds.), *New Media, Knowledge Practices and Multiliteracies*,
DOI 10.1007/978-981-287-209-8_10

reform policy makers think that they have made the policy by a scientific way and have thought of all the difficulties that policy implementation may encounter and the measures to overcome the difficulties. This study is to find the restriction of educational reform degrees and the factors that the local governments should think of while making and implementing educational policies. The specific research questions that guided this study are as follows:

What are the characteristics of China's reform of school management models in different periods?

In what ways can the reform of school management models be restricted to a suitable degree to achieve better results from the perspectives of school principals?

This chapter begins with a background to the context. Following this the chapter introduces data collection and the case study in Beijing. Then the researchers discuss different characteristics of the reform of public school management models in different periods since the Chinese reform and opening up policy. In the conclusion, the chapter summarizes the main enlightenments that will help the educational reform not go too far and be restricted to a suitable degree.

10.2 Background

During the time of 1950s to the beginning of twenty-first century, there were two kinds of public schools, key schools and ordinary schools, in primary schools and middle schools in China. Key schools were established to cultivate urgently needed talents, so the government would allocate them more funding and give more advanced teaching equipment to them. Compared with ordinary schools, these schools usually have better teachers and more famous school principals. Before 1990s, all the pupils graduated from primary schools would have to take a city unified entrance test to compete to the key junior middle schools. The competition was so fierce that the pupils had too heavy academic burden, then in 1990s, the junior middle school entrance examination was canceled. In the 1990s, with the market-oriented reform in economy and some people getting more and more rich, there appeared system transformational schools, including private school with governmental support or public school with private sponsors in order for the schools can draw extra money from the society. A large part of this system transformational schools were previously key schools, other system transformational schools also have more advantages than ordinary schools because they have the chance to draw money from society. Because every family hope their children to have a chance to study in key schools and system transformational schools, the parents began to think of other ways, such as donating more money to the key school, to let their children to get into key schools, but the people who were not so rich would lose such chances, which aroused equity concern in the academic field and society. In 2002, Beijing established model senior middle school system to replace key school system in senior middle schools. Model senior middle school is an honorary title given to the senior middle school that has good reputation. Usually students who graduate from these schools have a higher university enrollment rate. In 2006, in all the basic education, the name of "key schools" is not allowed to exist, and the system transformational schools also began to be banned. The government put more efforts to balance the resources between schools and give more support to ordinary schools in recent years, but people still think that those previous key schools are better than ordinary schools. Pilot schools are the schools to which government give more autonomy and more resources to permit them do experiment in school management or teaching methods, usually these schools are also very good schools which people compete to let their children to get in.

10.3 Method

This research carried an interview study in Beijing. The data were collected through interviews and document collection and the effort was to explore how school principals understood and viewed the reforms of public school management models and their opinions on the ways to restrict the degree of the reforms of public school management models. Public school principals play an important role in the actual effects of school reform. School principals in different kinds of schools may have different experiences and see different facts. And the school principals who are appointed to the position of school principals earlier usually have more knowledge about the reforms. So school principals were selected on this basis. From March to May in 2014, the researchers interviewed 16 school principals in primary and middle schools with semistructured questions, these schools including 8 previous key schools, 8 ordinary schools, in which 6 are junior middle schools, 5 are senior middle schools, and 5 are primary schools. The interviewees are 42–50 years of age, who almost have all experienced all reforms of school management models since 1985. Each interview was conducted about 1 h, most of the interviews are conducted once, and we also did 3 follow-up interviews when there was something we felt necessary to understand more. Second, a range of documents were collected from Beijing municipal government and websites. The documents were chosen through the following ways: first, three people, one was a distinguished expert in education, one was an official in Ministry of Education, and one is the author, wrote the most important educational policy documents from 1985 and second, we put the documents together to find the same ones we all chose, and these were the documents selected in this article. There were altogether 11 documents here, of which 7 were national level and 4 were provincial level from Beijing municipal government.

Finally, in efforts to ensure confidentiality the researchers have used simple pseudonyms. The interviewees were identified by two letters, P refers to primary school, J refers to junior middle school, and S refers to senior middle school. At the same time, schools also have been given the prefix letter K, O, T, and E, K refers to key school, O refers to ordinary school, T refers to system transformational school, and E refers to experimental pilot school. So the letters denote an association with a specific school. School principals KJ, for example, is a school principal interviewee from a junior middle school which is also a key school.

The data is analyzed with the following qualitative method: first, the researchers read the interview transcripts and policy documents through an iterative process of constant comparison to identify relevant themes in the data. Then gaps, inconsistencies, and unanswered questions guided subsequent rounds of data collection. After that, the researchers created a research text that outlined the data according to the identified themes, which include references to quotes and notes that supported and challenged the researchers' initial understanding of the case. The researchers repeated this process until the conclusions were conceptually dense and additional data yielded no new insights. This chapter represents the final understanding.

10.4 Results

With the fast development of economics and society since the opening up policy in China, in order to satisfy the need of the society, the reform of school management models presents different characteristics in different times.

10.4.1 1985–2005 The Reform of School Management Models Characterized by "Decentralization and Public School System Transformation"

From the issue of Decision on Reform of the Educational System (Central Committee of the Chinese Communist Party and the State Council 1985), "decentralization" turns out to be an important content of the education reform. Policy makers hope to improve the status of schools through expanding school running autonomy. Then the Outline for Educational Reform and Development (Central Committee of the Chinese Communist Party and State Council 1993) pointed out that we should establish the goals that the reform of educational system adapts to the socialist market economy. Then, diverse ways and models of school running can be tried and practiced. Later, Opinions on the Implementation of the Outline for Educational Reform and Development (the State Council 1994) claimed that some local districts with certain condition can implement the model called private school with governmental support or public school with private sponsors. These schools are also called system transformational schools, which were usually junior middle schools. The purpose of it is to make the schools develop fast with extra social money. In this way, the autonomy in terms of funding and admission in these kinds of system transformational schools is a lot larger than other schools, and the charging rules, to some extent, publicly accepted the rationality of choosing schools through money.

Interviews with school principals provided some opinions that indicated that public school system transformation pursue the efficiency of education, but brought about equity problems:

> The government wanted to pursue the efficiency of education with less government money and drawing society money to make schools develop faster. (KJ school principal)
>
> System transformational schools have better teachers; parents would like to pay more money to these schools to let their children get in. In this way, some students can get to key junior middle schools through their parents donating the school more money instead of ability, which of course aroused equity problems. (OJ school principal)

In response to the national policy, from 1997, Beijing Education Commission promulgated relevant policies to take out more than 40 public junior middle schools to transform into system transformational schools. Till 2007, the number of system transformational schools has reached 47. The majority of them are previous key schools with eligible teaching staff and many ways of educational funding. Moreover, these schools can also break through the regional limits of school entrance and select their students from the whole district or the whole city. At the moment, in order to be able to receive better education, families with good financial conditions owing to the opening up policy intend to pay sponsor fees to choose this kind of schools. Thus, the phenomenon of irregular charging becomes more and more serious. In an interview about the phenomena of the reform, a school principal said:

> The ordinary school students flow to system transformational schools and with few students enrollment, the ordinary schools can only rely on government funding. (OJ school principal)

As a result, the gap between system transformational schools and ordinary schools is getting larger. "There is a dilemma between adhering to the independent school running and ensuring the public nature of schools" (Lao 2010). "The processes of decentralization and the development of a competitive educational market have left schools competing for funds and for students in efforts to secure an advantageous position in the education market place" (Liu and Dunne 2009). So, the negative effect, such as the heat of school choice, the problem of education equity, and irregular charge aroused strong resentment and discussion among the public.

In 2005, Preparation Notice to Clean up the Charges of System Transformational Schools (the National Development and Reform Commission and the Ministry of Education 2005) pointed out that some schools have problems such as unclear defined running property and high charges; these are all the deviation from the aim of school running system reform. So it is quite essential to do well in the work of cleaning up and rectifying the system transformational schools' charging. In 2007, Opinions on the Further Deepening of the Pilot Work of School System Reform (Beijing Education Commission 2007) pointed out that, "From 2007 onwards, all districts and counties shall standardize and improve more than 30 % system transformational schools every year." At the end of 2009, all the system transformational schools have completed their retransformation in Beijing. In an interview about the result of cleaning up and rectifying the system transformational schools' charging, a school principal said:

> Nowadays no one dares to start arbitrary collection of fees. And it is more and more difficult for parents to choose school for their children through denoting more money. (KJ school principal)
>
> But because of the big gap between key schools and ordinary schools, parents still hope to choose a key school for their children. And the mandatory nearby enrollment rules make parents complain that why my child must go to an ordinary school when there is no key school near us. It is unfair."(KP school principal)

From the international scope, school choice is not a problem of right or wrong. But when it is intertwined with the equity of educational opportunity, it will undoubtedly cause strong concern to the government. In face with these problems, the reform went on to a next period.

10.4.2 From 2006, the Reform of School Management Models Characterized by "Cross-School Organization"

Since the twenty-first century, there is no doubt that the pursuit of education equity has become a most important value of China's education policy. Amendments of Compulsory Education Law pointed out that we "should narrow the gap between schools in school conditions, should not divide schools into key and non-key schools" (Standing Committee of the Tenth National People's Congress 2006). The National Medium and Long-Term Program for Education Reform and Development (2010–2020) (National Medium and Long-Term Program for Education Reform and Development Working Group Office 2010) pointed out that it is essential to encourage the local government and schools to explore to promote fair education. Several Major Decisions on Deepening Reform (Central Committee of the Chinese Communist Party 2013) again put emphasis on promotion of education equity.

Beijing Middle and Long-Term Education Reform and Development Plan (2010–2020) (Beijing Municipal Government 2011) pointed out to achieve the goal of balanced development of compulsory education. In 2011, the Ministry of Education and Beijing Municipal Government signed "Memorandum" enlisting the promotion of the balanced development of compulsory education into one of the assessment indicators for the major administrators in the regional people's governments. Besides, The Beijing Municipal Government signed the "Letters of Responsibility" with district governments in Beijing, respectively, set a timetable and roadmap to promote the balanced development of compulsory education. In this process, along with dealing with arbitrary charge, to promote education equity and improve the overall quality of education has now become the city's important policy objectives.

In order to narrow the gap between schools, every administrative district of Beijing is trying their best to explore a variety of school management models according to their practical situations. For example, Dongcheng District has manipulated the model of school district management, dividing the whole area into 15 school districts, each school district is subdivided into 2–3 parts within which the previous key schools taking as a lead, carrying out the implementation of one legal person and integrated management. In 2007, Xicheng District involved 9 municipal model senior middle schools as leaders and other ordinary 37 schools to form 9 school development joint bodies, pushing the process of resource sharing. In 2012, Xicheng District further set up four education groups led by previous key schools, within the group different schools can share each other's high-quality resources in the aspects of school management, teaching and teacher training, etc. Fengtai District currently has already had four education clusters; each one is consisted of several schools. It will realize longitudinal and lateral coordination among its schools. Longitudinal coordination aims to let the stage of preschool, primary school, junior middle school, and senior middle school connect closely with each other, whereas lateral coordination is aimed to make the resources among junior middle schools, or among primary schools, complement for each other. To describe conveniently, the researchers call all the school district management, education groups, education clusters, school development joint bodies, etc., as cross school organizations.

Cross school organizations aim to promote resource sharing and common development. According to the interviews, of all the cross school organizations, some establishing close relationship among its member schools while some only maintain a loose connection, some having formal regulations while some arbitrary rules, some being formed in the support of the District Education Commission while some established because of the active joint of schools themselves.

Interviews with school principals about the policy value indicate that equity is the most important educational policy value and the way to achieve it is to promote balanced development of compulsory education:

> We have taken many measures to promote balanced development of compulsory education. We delivered standardization construction project in primary school and weak school construction project in junior middle school several years ago. Now what we do is to make the previous key schools alliance with ordinary schools to further share their resources and promote teaching quality in ordinary schools (KS school principal).

Interviews with school principals about the results of the establishment of cross school organization indicate that cross school organization has brought about positive phenomenon:

> Each semester, we will have once or twice students' activities; teachers from each joint school can listen and discuss one or two classes together. However, it is still difficult to share more resources. But anyway, there is fresh blood put into our school as for the mutual exchange of teaching ideas, new methods, and good experiences (KJ school principal).
>
> Since we formed the educational group, we have regularly invited excellent teachers from group member schools to give classes to our students; our teachers will listen to their lectures, prepare lessons with them, in this way we have improved our teachers' professional development and we can recruit better students now. As a result, now we no longer suffer from the brain drain of teachers and students which we previously suffered from (OS school principal).

But it also has something not so good. Interview with a school principal about the strategy to make the cross school organization more effective indicate that responsibility is very important:

> Some cross school organizations only organize several activities at the very beginning, then nobody cares and they rarely contact each other, the organization can't be effective, and the effects can't be obvious. Then what's the difference with having no cross school organization at all (OP school principal)?

Interviews with school principals about how to guarantee the responsibility show that some districts in Beijing have broaden the idea in school evaluation:

> There was once an external evaluation in our district, the participants in the evaluation of schools include not only the education administrative personnel but also students and parents, and even the results of telephone interview and satisfaction survey made by some commissioned company were taken into account (KJ school principal).

To conclude, in cross school organization, the improvement of ordinary schools thanks to the driving force of previous key schools in many ways, it is beneficial both to the teachers and the students in ordinary schools and is useful for the balanced development of compulsory education. But there is still something to do to strengthen the effect of cross school organizations.

10.5 Discussions and Conclusion

Based on the above analysis of the reform of public school management models, it is found that there are several following enlightening points in the restriction of the "degree" of the reform of public school management models:

10.5.1 The Policy Should Be Adjusted in the Proper Time

In 1950s, in order to foster all kinds of talents needed by the society, China carried out a key school policy, which made some schools be significantly superior to ordinary schools in teachers and facilities. There was a unified examination to enter the key junior middle schools at that time, but this kind of selection system caused too much pressure and burden for the primary students. Therefore, in 1990s, the government put forward the policy "the exemption of examination" for the primary students who intent to go to the key junior middle schools, which let the school selecting not just focus on students' academic level, primary school students should go to the nearest school to continue with junior middle school.

Then, with the appearance of system transformational schools and that the disparity between schools became bigger and bigger, many parents broke through the compulsory education's requirement on "going to the nearest school", and tried to send their children to go to key schools by paying more money under the policy permission of raising educational funds in multiple channels. The original purpose of raising educational funds in multiple channels is to help schools to absorb more social funds and encourage the development of education. However, it unexpectedly caused the chaos of the tuition fees charge and the inequity of entering schools. Thus, there appeared public school variation, and it resulted in the discontent of the public. The system transformational schools have too many priorities than the ordinary schools both in funds and admission, which gives the ordinary schools no chance to compete. This is "a non competitive system environment" (Kang 2004). Then system transformational schools were banned, and at the same time, narrowing the gap between schools is put on government agenda, so various cross school organizations leaded by the previous key schools come into being, attempting to share the resources and develop together.

It is a big turn from unified examination to the exemption of examination, and from the school system transformation to cross school organization, and during these turning points, there are a lot of anxieties on school choice and hot discussion of educational equity from the public. This process of reform indicates that a policy can be reasonable at first, but if it cannot adapt itself to the development of the society or the system environment, it will lose its rationality and bring some negative effects.

10.5.2 The Restriction of Expanding School Running Autonomy

In 1996, Notice of Beijing Municipal Education Commission on the Tuition Fees of Private Schools Supported by the Government and Public Schools Sponsored by Individuals (Beijing Municipal Education Commission 1996) pointed out that system transformational schools should charge students in accordance with the public schools tuition standard. Apparently, during the process of school system transformation, the policy provided very clear criteria to the charge of school fees. There is the policy to restrict the fee charging of system transformational schools, but another fact is that schools can collect parents' sponsorship fees and this is permitted by the policy of raising educational funds through different channels. In fact, this kind of sponsorship fees is nominally voluntarily paid, but indeed it is a must for parents who want to choose a system transformational school for their children and the number of the fees vary depending on different situations. In this way, with raising education funds through different channels, the public schools tuition standard became nothing. It can be seen that when schools apply one policy, it can bring about the expected positive results, but when schools apply several policies simultaneously, the policies work together can expand policy effect, leading the effect exceeds expectations and going to the degree of negative side, even though the policies themselves are not obviously in opposition to each other. Here, the policy of school transformation and the policy of raising educational funds through different channels work together expand the school running autonomy to a too high degree in school fees charging. One of the bottleneck problems of reform is the internal defects of the system design (Zhang 2013). The school running autonomy is not the greater the better.

Unlike the system transformational schools, at the beginning of twenty-first century, Opinions on Managing the Chaos of Educational Fees in Beijing, 2004 (Beijing Municipal Education Commission 2004) stated three restrictions: in principle, the scores of the students who select public senior middle schools should not be 20 points less than the schools' normal admission scores, the population should not be 20 % larger than schools' original plan of the enrollment, and the tuition fee of each student must be less than 30,000 yuan, and the admission scores of students to select schools, the proportion of them and the standard of tuition charge ought to be announced to the public. It is strictly forbidden to charge other kind of fees such as sponsorship fees, school construction funds, and donations from parents in the public schools. For schools that violate this rule, severe punishment will be given. These three restrictions not only gave some autonomy to the schools but also made some limits to them. Thus, this policy not only satisfied students' needs of school selection but also controlled the selection to a certain extent with no more negative effects.

In 2013, the document of Several Major Decisions on Deepening Reform (CPC Central Committee 2013) again suggested "expanding the autonomy of school running". The former reforms have already set up many examples about how the educational policies not only expand the school running autonomy and enhance their vitality but also make school running accepted by the public, that is, to expand the autonomy with some proper restrictions.

10.5.3 Balance Between Responsibility and Power

As for the cross school organizations which are established for the purposes of narrowing the gap between schools and promote the balanced development of compulsory education, the problem of how to make the previous key schools maintain their own advantages, promote the development of the ordinary schools, and share resources cannot be solved only by previous key school principals' personal consciousness, but by making provisions of responsibility, power, and profit. Only when the power and responsibility equivalent to each other, cannot the power be abused. Only when the responsibility and interests equivalent to each other, can they promote people to implement the responsibility. However, just given the responsibility in policy documents cannot make a difference, corresponding measures must be made to ensure the equivalence of responsibility, power, and interests.

Making provisions of responsibility is the precondition of all the other problems. The external evaluation is one of the guarantees of promoting the implementation of responsibility. Several Major Decisions on Deepening Reform (CPC Central Committee 2013) proposed to "further promote the separation of management, funding and evaluation". Hence, with an urge to expand the autonomy in running schools, the external evaluation has become an important tool to implement the responsibility. Educational administrative personnel, students, parents, and satisfaction survey involved in the external evaluation is a very good try, but it is still not the common phenomena. This kind of external evaluation will effectively promote the implementation of school responsibility and help the application of the power to be restricted on the right track.

Peggy E. Johnson and Janet H. Chrispeels (2010) studied the linkages between a central office and its schools served as administrative controls in America and found that "the structural linkage was the primary vehicle used by the district to exert control, complete organizational tasks, and enforce desired changes" (p. 739). Now, there is still no suitable operation mechanism between the local departments of education administration and schools which can let the local education administrative departments have sufficient grasp of details about the school internal operation. Although there are Parents Committees in many schools in Beijing, parents have very limited effect on decision making through Parents Committee, the interests of parents were not clearly expressed. One of the reasons why there was abuse of power in the past reform is that the distribution of power among the school and the local education administrative departments and the parents were not perfect. Therefore, to establish the mechanism of decision-making structure, which involves the local education administrative departments and parents, will help to realize the balance between responsibility and power.

In conclusion, from the reform of public school management models in different periods in China, it can be seen that, educational reform should be restricted to a certain degree, not the greater the better. There are three ways to restrict the public school management model reform degree: to adjust the policy in the proper time, to give certain restriction of expanding school running autonomy, and to hold the balance between responsibility and power.

The implication of the study indicates that there are many other significant research topics to study, such as, how and when to adjust policy to achieve expected results? To what extent do cross school organizations cooperate and share resources each other so that each school in the cross school organization can develop well? To what extent can schools have their running autonomy from local government's decentralization?

Acknowledgments This study was supported by the Project to Improve Innovation Ability in Colleges and Universities Responsible to Beijing Municipal Education Committee (TJSHS201310028001).

We would like to thank the HKAECT 2014 International Program Committee reviewers for their suggestions in strengthening this article.

References

Beijing Municipal Education Commission. (1996). *Beijingshi jiaoyu weiyuanhui guanyu zhuanfa minbangongzhu gongbanminzhu putong zhongxiaoxue shoufei de han de tongzhi* [Notice of Beijing Municipal Education Commission on the tuition fees of private schools supported by the government and public schools sponsored by individuals]. Retrieved March 10, 2014, from http://www.eol.cn/20010101/19580.shtml

Beijing Municipal Education Commission, etc. (2004). *Opinions on managing the chaos of educational fees in Beijing*. Retrieved March 10, 2014, from http://moral.bjedu.cn/bjedu/77975178587406336/20050829/9786.shtml

Beijing Municipal Education Commission. (2007). *Guanyu jinyibu shenhua zhongxiaoxue banxuetizhi gaige shidiangongzuo yijian de tongzhi* [Opinions on the further deepening of the pilot work of school system reform]. Retrieved March 10, 2014, from http://govfile.beijing.gov.cn/Govfile/front/content/22007039_0.html

Beijing Municipal Government. (2011). *Beijing zhongchangqi jiaoyugaigehafazhan guihuagangyao 2010–2020* [Beijing Middle and Long-term Education Reform and Development Plan (2010–2020)]. Retrieved March 8, 2014, from http://www.moe.gov.cn/publicfiles/business/htmlfiles/moe/s5520/201104/117401.html

Central Committee of the Chinese Communist Party. (1985). *Guanyu jiaoyu tizhi gaige de jueding* [The decision on reform of the educational system]. Retrieved March 10, 2014, from http://www.moe.edu.cn/edoas/website18/18/info3318.htm

Central Committee of the Chinese Communist Party. (2013). *Guanyu quanmian shenhua gaige ruogan zhongda wenti de jueding* [Several major decisions on deepening reform]. Retrieved March 10, 2014, from http://news.xinhuanet.com/mrdx/2013-11/16/c_132892941.html

Central Committee of the Chinese Communist Party and State Council. (1993). *Zhongguo jiaoyu gaige he fazhan gangyao* [The outline for educational reform and development]. Retrieved March 10, 2014, from http://www.moe.edu.cn/edoas/website18/34/info3334.htm

Johnson, P. E., & Chrispeels, J. H. (2010). Linking the central office and its schools for reform. *Educational Administration Quarterly, 46*(5), 738–775.

Kang, Y. (2004). A review of research on contemporary public school system reform. *Comparative Education Research, 11*, 16–20.

Lao, K. (2010). The problem of Chinese education is the problem of public school. *Educational Research, 361*(2), 15–21.

Liu, Y., & Dunne, M. (2009). Educational reform in China: Tensions in national policy and local practice. *Comparative Education, 45*(4), 461–476.

The National Development and Reform Commission, the Ministry of Education. (2005). *Guanyu zuohao qinglizhengdun gaizhixuexiao shoufei zhunbei gongzuo de tongzhi* [Preparation notice to clean up the charges of system transformational schools]. Retrieved April 10, 2014, from http://www.moe.edu.cn/publicfiles/business/htmlfiles/moe/moe_1147/200604/14529.html

The National Medium and Long Term Program for Education Reform and Development Working Group Office. (2010). *Guojia zhongchangqi jiaoyu gaige he fazhguihua gangyao*. [The national medium and long term program for education reform and development (2010–2020)]. Retrieved April 10, 2014, from http://www.moe.gov.cn/publicfiles/business/htmlfiles/moe/A01_zcwj/201008/xxgk_93785.html

The Standing Committee of the Tenth National People's Congress. (2006). *Zhonghuarenmin gongheguo yiwujiaoyu fa* [Compulsory education law]. Retrieved April 10, 2014, from http://www.moe.gov.cn/publicfiles/business/htmlfiles/moe/moe_619/200606/15687.html

The State Council. (1994). *Guanyu zhongguo jiaoyu gaige he fazhan gangyao de shishi yijian* [Implementing opinions on "the outline for reform in education and development"]. Retrieved April 10, 2014, from http://law.lawtime.cn/d520976526070_2_p1.html

Zhang, L. (2013). The bottleneck problems and solutions to China's current reform of school system. *The Journal of Chinese Education, 4*, 14–16.

Chapter 11
Falling Through the Cracks: Undergraduate Students' Mathematics Learning Experience

Lesa M. Covington Clarkson, Forster D. Ntow, Sousada Chidthachack, and Elizabeth A. Crotty

Abstract In this chapter, we present the findings of two undergraduate students who became disinterested in studying mathematics despite initial success in high school. As a result, these students quit their science and engineering-related programs to pursue programs in the humanities. Reasons for this situation are related to how mathematics is taught at college which sometimes portrays mathematics as a subject which you are either predestined to succeed or not and a lack of teacher support.

Keywords Mathematics teaching • Mindset • Teacher support

11.1 Introduction

In its document, *Principles and Standards for School Mathematics,* the National Council of Teachers of Mathematics (NCTM) argues that individuals with mathematical understanding and ability to do mathematics are likely to have significantly improved lives (NCTM 2000). Moreover, mathematics literacy has been described as a human rights issue. Unfortunately, what makes mathematics important and a mandatory school subject seems not to be apparent to many people who have experienced school mathematics. Instead, mathematics is viewed as a gate-keeper or serves as a filter.

11.1.1 Why Mathematics?

In her book, *What's Math Got to do with It?* Boaler (2008) argues that most students see mathematics as a study of numbers and rules which bear little resemblance to the kind of mathematics mathematicians engage in or as the mathematics used in everyday life. Friere (1970) described such teaching as the "banking concept of education" (p. 257) whereby teachers are seen as depositors with students as

L.M. Covington Clarkson (✉) • F.D. Ntow • S. Chidthachack • E.A. Crotty
University of Minnesota, Minneapolis, MN, USA
e-mail: covin005@umn.edu; ntowx001@umn.edu; chid0008@umn.edu; crott050@umn.edu

© Springer Science+Business Media Singapore 2015

W.W.K. Ma et al. (eds.), *New Media, Knowledge Practices and Multiliteracies*,
DOI 10.1007/978-981-287-209-8_11

depositories. In this case, students are seen as empty receptacles with the teacher's role being to make deposits into these receptacles in a form that students can receive, memorize, and repeat at a later date. A banking approach to mathematics instruction has the tendency of depriving students of the excitement inherent in it. Furthermore, Lesh and Doerr (2003) identified some characteristics of teaching mathematics as involving learning of ideas and skills in decontextualized situations with students solving real-world problems afterward, only if time permits. Such a teaching process disengages learners with reports of students' interest in mathematics waning as they progress from the elementary level through to high school (Walker 2012).

While there is a general concern about the underachievement of many people in mathematics, the tendency has been through a *gap-gazing* approach (Gutierrez 2008), which can lead to an identity of inferiority by students perceived to be underachieving (Stinson 2013). It is argued that focus should be on how mathematics it taught and how this may influence students' learning of mathematics.

11.2 Theoretical Framework

According to Dweck (1986), an individual's motivation to achieve academically is related to two competence-related goals namely learning and performance goals. She argues that these goals determine, to a large extent, an individual's motivation to succeed based upon the individual's mindset which she classified into two: fixed or growth mindsets. People with fixed mindset see intelligence as fixed and that you are either intelligent or not while those with growth mindset believe that intelligence is malleable. An individual's mindset is believed to correlate with their level of resilience when confronted with a challenging situation. According to Dweck (2008), the impact of mindsets usually becomes evident when an individual faces challenging situations with those with fixed mindset more likely to give up.

In carrying out this study, it was believed that how participants characterized mathematics and their mathematics experiences will determine, to a large extent, their level of resiliency in pursuing the study of mathematics when faced with challenges. Using the idea of mindsets, we sought to address the following research question: How does undergraduate students' characterize their mathematics learning experience? The following subquestions were also formulated (a) What is undergraduate students' attitude toward mathematics and (b) What is the nature of undergraduate students' mathematics experience?

11.3 Methodology

A multiple case study design was adopted in carrying out this study. According to Yin (1994), the use of multiple cases allow for within-and-across case comparisons to be made. For the purpose of this chapter, we draw on interview data for two undergraduate students who were involved in a year-long mathematics tutoring and mentoring program as mentors and tutors ("mentutors"). The participants were purposively selected because they were all science and mathematics major students at the high school and started their undergraduate program in an STEM discipline but had quit their respective programs and are currently pursing humanities-related programs. The participants were all enrolled in a large public university based in the Midwest of the United States of America.

A semistructured interview was conducted with each participant to explore their mathematics learning experiences at the high school and college levels. The purpose of these interviews was to help us understand participants' mathematics learning experience and use that to understand what informed their decision to change programs. In analyzing the data, we used the ideas of constant-comparison technique suggested by Corbin and Strauss (2008) to analyze data for individual cases and also across cases for patterns across cases. The analysis involved reading though the transcripts for each individual case for codes and across cases for commonalities and also discrepancies.

11.4 Results

In presenting the results of this study, we construct cases of each participant focusing on their attitude toward mathematics, level of teacher support, and end with how these two factors shaped their mathematics experience.

11.4.1 Case 1: Tori

11.4.1.1 Attitude Toward Mathematics

Tori described her attitude toward mathematics in high school as being positive. When she was asked to describe her attitude toward mathematics she responded as follows: "I liked math in high school. It was one of my strongest points in high school so I'll say that I enjoyed it… my teachers were hit or miss but it's was fun." Despite the change in her college major, she took a class in mathematics describing her attitude toward mathematics as positive. The following excerpt typifies her attitude toward mathematics:

> I liked explorations in math … because it related math back to real world issues for me so it allowed me to understand the correlation between the two whereas those [mumbling] levels of math in high school we just kinda had to like figure out the questions to get to your end result and I knew how to do that but it didn't really click to me to relate it to real world experiences….

In Tori's response, we observe a shift in her reasons for having a positive attitude toward mathematics. At the high school, she enjoyed mathematics because it happened to be one of her "strongest points" implying success on achievement tests which could be due to her ability to "figure out the questions to get to your end result." However, at the college level, the utility value of mathematics was the hook for her positive attitude toward mathematics. Tori's characterization of her high school mathematics experience portrays how school mathematics is sometimes reduced to a game of rules with success in it being an individuals' ability to master the rules governing it. Despite Tori's success in algebra due to her mastery of procedures, she struggled through courses which appeared abstract to her. In describing her experience in geometry, her response was as follows: "…it was harder for me to like wrap my brain around geometrical equations … that class felt more arbitrary or more kinda like this could be this if this is this whereas algebra was more concrete…."

11.4.1.2 Nature of Teaching/Teacher Support

For Tori, a key feature in her mathematics success appears to be having teachers who continually challenge and support her. Such teachers were ready to provide extra support and also showed from their teaching that they cared about her learning. This group of teachers she contrasted with less supportive teachers who she described as being "hit or miss" or being "dry." Hit or miss according to her were "really bad teachers who like didn't care… and they just kinda like if you get it you get it, if you don't you don't."

This brief excerpt presents a case where mathematics is characterized as a subject where students are placed into binaries, those who are successful versus those who are not. Such binaries create a fixed mindset attitude where struggling students are likely to see themselves as those not fortunate to be born as a mathematics genius. On the contrary, a growth mindset toward mathematics teaching and learning is exemplified in the following excerpt; a teacher who has "very high expectations for me because he knew what I was capable of and so he challenged me a lot and I appreciate it in challenging me and letting me know that I could do more than what I thought I could."

While Tori had a teacher who supported her through her high school mathematics courses including other mathematics classes this teacher was not directly teaching, such support was not available to help her overcome the challenges she faced in college. Faced with a college professor whose method of teaching she described as being "dry" Tori decided to stop attending lectures. She responds as follows: "I didn't really like going to lectures I felt like it would be extremely pointless… I also feel like the professor didn't put as much effort that he should have into teaching the lecture." She rather chose to attend tutorials where she could be taught procedures which had helped her succeed as a high school student.

11.4.2 Case 2: Francis

Just like Tori, Francis had a strong mathematics background coming from high school into college having taken several Advanced Placement (AP) classes.

11.4.2.1 Attitude Toward Mathematics

Francis described his attitude toward mathematics at the high school as "a positive thing" because "I knew that learning math I will be able to go further in life because there is a lot of applications." However, his attitude toward mathematics changed at the college level with him describing his attitude toward mathematics as "negative" due to the "high risk examinations." He indicated that he felt "a lot more positive with weekly skill building and things like that versus … heading towards a goal with high risk examinations at the end of the semester, midway through the semester." Ultimately, overwhelmed with workload Francis who was taking a calculus decided he would be "dropping it."

While he explains the decision to drop calculus was due to loss of motivation in his initial desire to pursue electrical or civil engineering, the following gives a glimpse into some underlying reasons for his decision to opt out of mathematics. He explains as follows: "Statistics, I felt it was apparent, calculus wasn't for me and I didn't know the point of using limits and derivatives." This indicates that apart from the issue of workload indicating how he felt mathematics was arbitrary and its usefulness not readily apparent compared to statistics.

11.4.2.2 Nature of Teaching/Teacher Support

Although Francis appreciated that mathematics was important to move forward in life, his interest in mathematics was aroused by a teacher he described as having a really good "personality." This teacher during their first class meeting according to him "established his goal for us and then his personal goal such as becoming the greatest math teacher." He continues to describe him as providing "lots of positive reinforcement, he asked lots of questions versus telling me things so he made me use critical thinking…just overall, he was supportive and he challenged me to work more." We observe that for Francis, having a mathematics teacher who showed interest in him were crucial in his learning and success in mathematics at the high school which seemed lacking in his college mathematics experience. At the college level, his experience was a mathematics classroom where everything boiled down to one's performance on high stakes testing with little or no support in terms of skills building and weekly reviews, which he had become accustomed to at the high school.

11.5 Discussion

As was suggested by Dweck (2007), a growth mindset promotes motivation and resilience. She however cautions against the use of praise by warning of its perils since too much praise does not help students to be resilient in the face of a challenging situation.

From Tori and Francis' cases, we notice that their motivation to succeed in mathematics was not innate. It seems that their performance is contingent on favorable teacher support through encouragement, effective teaching, or extra teaching support. Having teachers who continually challenged them and supported them was very important in helping them achieve performance goals. However, at the college level, we observe that without such extrinsic sources of motivation to encourage them to meet performance goals, these students were unable to put in the needed effort to persist in the studying of mathematics. In the case of Francis, the threat of high-risk examinations was too challenging with the end result being his decision to drop out of calculus. The dropping of calculus meant, to a large extent, giving up on his initial desire of pursuing an engineering-related program since he would have had to take more mathematics classes. In the case of Tori, her epiphany moment came when she encountered a professor whose teaching strategy she described as "dry." Unable to see any reason for attending lectures, she decided to rather go for tutorials which focused on learning of procedures which she had become quite adept at from her high schools days rather than attending lectures.

Again, in both cases, we see these students characterizing their mathematics experience in terms of a fixed mindset mentality with the use of descriptors such as "hit or miss", "dry", or "high stakes" examinations. In all cases, the message being conveyed is that you are either good or not good enough.

11.6 Implication

In all, our results suggest that even with highly successful high school mathematics students, the way mathematics is taught at both high school and the college level sends different messages to them. A teaching approach, which portrays mathematics as a subject which you either "get it or you do not," has the tendency to drive students away from mathematics and other STEM disciplines. It also creates in students' minds a fixed mindset attitude such that those who are not self-motivated and resilient may give up easily in the face of challenges.

Again, the nature of students' mathematics learning experience has the likelihood of encouraging them to pursue its study or quit. For those who are struggling, teacher comments about what it takes to succeed in mathematics and the nature of mathematics portrayed can go a long way in influencing their decision. As such, if the aim is to make all citizens mathematics literate then teaching practices which portray mathematics as a subject in which you are either predestined to succeed or not should change. Additionally, there is a need to provide continual support to students and at the same time help them to develop resiliency. Furthermore, too much teacher support and praise can lead to teacher dependency such that students may not develop the ability to be resilient as demonstrated in Tori and Francis' cases.

References

Boaler, J. (2008). *What's math got to do with it? Helping children learn to love their most hated subject –and why it's important for America*. New York: Penguin Group Inc.

Corbin, J., & Strauss, A. (Eds.). (2008). *Basics of qualitative research: Techniques and procedures for developing grounded theory*. California: Sage Publications, Inc.

Dweck, C. S. (1986). Motivational processes affecting learning. *American Psychologist, 41*(10), 1040–1048.

Dweck, C. S. (2007). The perils and promises of praise. *Educational Leadership, 65*(2), 34–39.

Dweck, C. S. (2008). *Mindsets and math/science achievement*. Report prepared for the Carnegie Corporation of the New York-Institute for the Advanced St Commission on Mathematics and Science Education. New York: Carnegie Corporation of New York.

Friere, P. (1970). *Pedagogy of the oppressed*. New York: Herder and Herder.

Gutierrez, R. (2008). A 'gap-gazing' fetish in mathematics education? Problematizing research on the achievement gap. *Journal for Research in Mathematics Education, 39*(4), 357–364.

Lesh, R., & Doerr, H. M. (2003). Foundations of a models and modeling perspective on mathematics teaching, learning and problem solving. In R. Lesh & H. M. Doerr (Eds.), *Beyond constructivism: Models and modeling perspectives on mathematics problem solving, learning and teaching* (pp. 3–34). Mahwah: Lawrence Erlbaum.

National Council of Teachers of Mathematics (NCTM). (2000). *Principles and standards in school mathematics*. Reston: Author.

Stinson, D. W. (2013). Negotiating the "White male math myth": African American male students and success in school mathematics. *Journal for Research in Mathematics Education, 44*(1), 69–99.

Walker, E. N. (2012). *Building mathematics learning communities: Improving outcomes in urban high schools*. New York: Teachers College.

Yin, R. (1994). *Case study research design methods* (2nd ed.). Thousand Oaks: Sage.

References

Chapter 12
An Exploratory Study on Interactive Whiteboard Usage on Enhancing Oral English in Secondary Classrooms

Guochen Zhang and Liping Deng

Abstract This study aims to investigate two secondary school teachers' use of Interactive Whiteboard (IWB) in the facilitation of students' oral English and explore students' perceptions of the role of IWB in learning English. Through analyzing the qualitative and quantitative data, this study has found out that in spite of the similar pedagogical goals, the two teachers differed in their use of IWB. Furthermore, teachers' and students' divergent perceptions regarding IWB usage in the teaching and learning of speaking were also discovered. The teachers held positive views of the effect of IWB, yet the majority of students deemed that IWB itself would not necessarily improve their English competency. Instead, what matters most was teachers' pedagogical use of the technology.

Keywords Interactive whiteboard • Perception • Improvement • Oral English

12.1 Introduction

As acknowledged by most English teachers and learners, speaking capability is a cardinal competence in learning the language (Goh and Burns 2012). In accordance with a considerable body of research, however, Chinese students are still weak in oral English (Chen and Goh 2011), regardless of the decades of endeavor to reform English language teaching approaches (Yu 2001). Existing literature has explored the pedagogical benefits of incorporating IWB into classrooms. For instance, research has reported that using IWB could elevate students' motivation and engagement (Hall and Higgins 2005; Smith et al. 2005). In the meantime, the interactivity between teachers and students could also be improved (Glover et al. 2005, 2007).

G. Zhang
Huizhou University, Huizhou, China
e-mail: johnsonzhang11@gmail.com

L. Deng (✉)
Hong Kong Baptist University, Hong Kong, China
e-mail: lisadeng@hkbu.edu.hk

© Springer Science+Business Media Singapore 2015

W.W.K. Ma et al. (eds.), *New Media, Knowledge Practices and Multiliteracies*,
DOI 10.1007/978-981-287-209-8_12

Furthermore, an empirical study conducted by López (2010) confirmed that English Language Learners (ELLs)[1] were able to achieve academic progress when learning in the classrooms equipped with IWB.

Nonetheless, most of previous studies regarding IWB usage in English language education did not specifically stress the relations between students' enhancement of oral proficiency and teachers' IWB usage. Although Al-Saleem (2012) maintained that IWB usage in EFL classrooms could assist students in improving speaking competence, her argument was not founded on adequate empirical evidence. Besides, even though Handley's (2012) work showed that the quality of students' oral performance could be improved when students were taught with IWB, their study merely focused on the prelesson activities. This present study, on the contrary, was situated in English teaching classrooms to investigate how IWB was used throughout the whole period of a class. The results would possibly provide insights concerning teachers' use of IWB to facilitate teaching of oral English as well as students' perceptions during the process. In doing so, the study can better inform the researchers and practitioners on better harness the pedagogical potentials of IWB in language classrooms. In specific, two research questions were posed to guide the study:

1. How do teachers use IWB in class to help students develop speaking competence?
2. What are students' perceptions of teachers' IWB usage regarding improvement of speaking abilities?

12.2 Literature Review

According to Egbert and Hanson-Smith's (1999) work, the use of technology enhances interaction, provides authentic language materials and improves learner engagement. With its increasing availability in language classrooms, IWB has become an innovative representation in the research field of Computer-Assisted Language Learning (Schmid 2006, 2010).

Previous studies have argued that interactivity is one significant element of maintaining students' interest in language learning, and IWB usage in language classroom can enhance interactivity between students and teachers (Glover et al. 2007). Additionally, students' motivation and engagement in class could also be improved when studying in an IWB-supported environment, as the use of visual elements, such as video clips or texts in nontraditional paper form, facilitates students' information processing (McKendrick and Bowden 1999). These benefits brought by IWB usage are also recognized as significant to English language teaching (Liddicoat et al. 2003). Mathews-Aydinli and Elaziz (2010) find that students generally

[1] As defined by Solano-Flores (2008), English Language Learners (ELLs) refer to those whose first language is not English and are learning English in schools or other educational settings.

perceive IWB usage as useful to foster their interest and engagement. Results of the study also indicate that using IWB is helpful to facilitate the teaching, motivate students, and increase teacher–student interaction.

Nevertheless, researchers also raised a number of concerns of using IWB in classrooms, among which students' cognitive overload is a major one. Moreno (2006) reveals that when students are exposed to various kinds of multimedia materials, they are forced to process a great deal of information, which may result in cognitive overload. To study the pedagogical potential of IWB technology in English teaching, Schmid (2006) discovers that the benefits of IWB could only be enlarged when the ways in which the technology is used meet students' expectations.

To summarize, it is justifiable to argue that using IWB in language classrooms facilitates students' language learning process. Nevertheless, the ways in which IWB are used should be considered.

12.3 Methodology

12.3.1 Settings and Participants

The present study was situated at a secondary school with good reputation in Boluo, a county of Huizhou city in Guangdong Province. IWBs have been utilized to support teaching in this school since the year 2007; thus, teachers and students are familiar with functions of IWB. As to the specific participants of the study, two intact classes of students (in total $N=81$), one of which was from Grade 7 and the other one was from Grade 8, were selected. The two teachers who taught these two classes—Cindy and Catherine—also became the major informants of our study. The chosen classes were academically the best classes in each grade, and most students in the classes have been learning English in classrooms with IWB.

12.3.2 Data Collection

To obtain sufficient data, several methods have been used including observation, questionnaires, and interviews. In this study, two 40-min English lessons conducted by the investigated teachers were observed together with the other three observers. A set of close-ended questionnaire was administrated to the students ($N=81$). The design of the questions was a modified version of Xu and Moloney's (2011) study. The questionnaire consisted of 13 statements, each of which was followed by a five-point Likert scale design. The students were requested to complete the questionnaires after the classes, and all students took the questionnaire, making a 100 % response rate.

Four 20–30-min semistructured focus group interviews for students were conducted, with 2 groups from each class. Most notably, one group consisted of 4 students who are most active in English learning, whereas the second group of 4 not so active English learners. Altogether, there were 16 students participating in the interviews. With respect to the teacher interviews, semistructured interviews were conducted separately, with each one lasting approximately 40 min.

12.4 Results

Having explored the data, several themes corresponding to the research questions were determined, and they will be presented respectively.

12.4.1 Different IWB Usages

Two participating teachers both agreed that IWB could provide various language input and a more authentic English context, through which students' willingness and motivation for engaging themselves in speaking tasks could be enhanced. Notwithstanding bearing a similar notion of the affordances of IWB, their ways of using IWB in their classes differed.

Cindy described how she used IWB in class to draw students' attention. She put it in this way:

> At the beginning of the class, I will use IWB to provide my students some visual stimulation, such as videos or pictures, and then I will use IWB to display some passages and ask them to read. (Cindy)

By contrast, Catherine used IWB as a means to stimulate students' curiosity:

> When designing IWB based materials, I would like to use those updated, fancy and colorful materials. Looking at these materials, I find my students more focused and because the materials, such as the pictures or video-clips, are so interesting that they want to know more, so that they have to talk to me or they want to express their thinking, so that they have to speak in their own words. (Catherine)

In addition, they designed different tasks with IWB in their class. Cindy designed a task requiring students to use IWB to deliver their oral presentations. However, what the students did was merely reading out their notes, and they simply used IWB to present their PPTs which contain the whole speeches. As to Catherine's class, although she did not design a presentation activity, she asked her students to do exercises on the IWB and requested them to present their answers in form of an oral composition. As this task required students to cooperatively write answers on the IWB and then provide oral reports, those presenters tried very hard to interact and negotiate with their group mates. With several facets of interaction carrying on, the whole learning environment was more active and interactive as compared to Cindy's class.

12.4.2 Improvement of Interest, Motivation, and Engagement in Practicing Speaking

Regarding to what degree IWB usage has positively influenced students' improvement of speaking ability, a considerable amount of students perceived that they became more interested and motivated in English classes assisted by IWB. They also revealed that they were more willing to participate in those speaking activities organized with the help of IWB.

The questionnaire results shown in Table 12.1 has demonstrated that students' rating are generally positive with respect to whether the use of IWB enhances students' interest, motivation, engagement, and participation in learning English and practicing speaking. For instance, students endorsed that using IWB made the lessons more interesting (Question 2), with Grade 7 scoring a mean of 4.38 (SD = 0.921) and Grade 8 of 4.27 (SD = 0.672). And another salient feature shown by the data was that students generally perceived that the use of IWB could improve their attitude toward participation and interaction in class (Question 7). However, with respect to question 3, the one that directly connected the use of IWB and motivation for speaking, Grade 8 students' feedback appeared to be more conservative. And this reason might be better explained by the following excerpts:

> I don't think the use of IWB by my English teacher can further improve my motivation, because with or without it, we have to learn English and we have to be asked to speak anyway. So, I don't see any difference. (Mickey/G81#2)
>
> Well, I admit that using IWB in class can increase our interest, but the effect seems not that significant when it comes to the notion of increasing motivation for speaking. (Yvonne/G81#2)

In fact, in addition to a very small number of students who held critical opinions, the majority of students admitted that, through using IWB to present them with authentic English materials, teachers created a lively learning environment which was more conducive to practicing oral English.

Table 12.1 Students' perceptions of IWB usage in English classrooms

	Grade 7 students (*n* = 40)		Grade 8 students (*n* = 41)	
Questions	*M*	SD	*M*	SD
1. The use of IWB increases my interest in learning English	4.15	0.921	3.93	0.721
2. The use of IWB makes the content and learning more interesting	4.38	0.807	4.27	0.672
3. The use of IWB increases my motivation in speaking English during class	3.85	0.921	3.17	0.771
7. The use of IWB encourages more active participation and interaction	4.23	0.947	3.88	0.714

12.4.3 Students' Concern About Teachers' Approaches to Using IWB in Facilitation of Speaking

Overall, students accepted that IWB usages in classrooms could improve their speaking accent, facilitate their memorization of words and sentences, and provide useful materials for enhancing speaking. This can be reflected from the results of Question 4 (G7 Mean = 3.43, G8 Mean = 3.22), Question 5 (G7 Mean = 3.80, G8 Mean = 3.51), and Question 9 (G7 Mean = 3.95, G8 Mean = 3.54) (Table 12.2).

Nevertheless, students showed concern about teachers' IWB usages. For instance, in question 6, when being asked to the effect of IWB on improving fluency, students from Grade 8 (Mean = 3.58) scored fairly lower than that of from Grade 7 (Mean = 3.02). Several comments students from G8 explained this phenomenon:

> I think that if our teacher can use IWB to design some games which require us to speak English while we are playing, the effect will be better. This kind of activity is not that stressful, and it encourages me to speak more. (Jerry/G81#2)

Compared with Jerry's opinion, another girl seemed to enjoy more challenging activities.

> Our teacher always uses IWB to present us with some pictures or video-clips which arouse our different kinds of emotion, and then she asks us to express our thoughts in our own words. I like this activity a lot, because the more I speak, the more fluent I can gradually achieve. (Cherry/G81#1)

The comments above revealed students' diverse expectations of practicing speaking in class which give rise to different concerns about teachers' IWB usages. The result of question 11 yield from Grade 8 students (Mean = 3.02) revealed students' uncertainty about the direct connection between IWB usage and improvement of speaking competence. Several comments from the interviewees can further elucidate this result. For example:

Table 12.2 Students' perceptions of IWB usage regarding improvement of English learning

	Grade 7 students (n = 40)		Grade 8 students (n = 41)	
Questions	M	SD	M	SD
4. The use of IWB helps me speak English with good accent	3.43	1.035	3.22	0.852
5. The use of IWB helps me remember vocabulary and sentences better	3.80	0.992	3.51	0.870
6. The use of IWB helps me speak English more fluently	3.58	1.035	3.02	0.851
9. The use of IWB provides me with better materials for improving oral English	3.95	0.714	3.54	0.840
10. My spoken English would be weaker without being taught by IWB	2.40	0.709	2.34	0.911
11. I think the use of IWB is especially good for improving oral English	3.23	0.660	3.02	0.651

> I am not sure about the use of IWB really has a direct impact on my oral English, as it is after all only a tool used to support teaching. If our English doesn't assign speaking tasks for us, our speaking ability cannot be improved at all; even she uses IWB to teach every day. (Alex/G81#2)

The comments above not only showed students' neutral perceptions of the correlation between the incorporation of IWB in English class and the enhancement of speaking competency but also pinpointed their concerns in relation to pedagogical use of IWB. Students perceived that IWB alone did not make any difference in the cultivation of their oral proficiency. What actually matters is teachers' pedagogical approaches of utilizing IWB to facilitate their language learning.

12.5 Discussion and Conclusion

The two teachers shared the same goal of creating an input-rich language environment that is conducive to students' learning and practice of speaking. However, the ways in which they design and use IWB vary. One teacher is perceived as drilling oriented as she mainly requires students to do lots of reading aloud exercises based on those prepared materials presented via IWB. Whereas, the other teacher inclines to inspire her students to produce more meaningful utterances based on those thought-provoking pictures or videos provided by IWB. Although the latter approach to using IWB is perceived to be more innovative and promising to improve students' overall speaking abilities, it is not without drawbacks. Former literature argued that when receiving large amount of multimedia information, students have to make endeavor to process those visual or audio materials (Mayer 2001; Moreno 2006; Plass et al. 2003), which may give rise to cognitive load (Moreno 2006) and probably hinder students from organizing and producing oral utterance with quality. Furthermore, students often consider the oral presentation in a foreign language daunting (Nerlicki 2011) and face-threatening (Wen and Clement 2003) activities, those who lack confidence and oral proficiency will be reluctant to participate in the speaking tasks. With time goes by, those less self-motivated students may lose their motivation and also engagement, as they may realize the fact that IWB is merely a tool assisting in learning (Smith et al. 2005; Thompson and Flecknoe 2003). Therefore, in order to sustain students' motivation and interest, teachers are suggested to thoroughly consider the approaches to using IWB to design and present the speaking tasks. In doing so, students of different levels of speaking abilities could benefit from the diverse speaking activities.

Schmid (2010) argues that the most ideal way of integrating IWB into the language teaching that emphasizes communicative nature is to combine traditional and innovative approaches seamlessly, as a synthesis of traditional and innovative IWB usages might be able to sustain students' motivation and engagement. Thus, irrespective of being considered old-fashioned and mechanical, direct approach to teaching speaking could lay down a solid foundation for students to further strengthen their level of spoken English. An effective approach is probably the one that combines the merits of restricted speaking exercises and the open-ended ones.

From students' point of views, albeit students admit that IWB usage could enhance their motivations for taking part in speaking exercises, divergences have been found regarding students' beliefs in IWB affordances. Specifically, Cindy's students believed that the use of IWB in English class provided them with abundant additional exercises as language input, and through repeated reading aloud they could expect an increase in speaking proficiency. As to Catherine's students, they held a perspective that since those materials provided by IWB were intriguing and thought provoking, they could be inspired to discuss and express their understandings concerning the demonstrated pictures or videos. Students' perceived value of IWB usage may be affected by their learning motivations. As argued by Deci et al. (1991), "intrinsically motivated behaviors are engaged in for their own sake–for the pleasure and satisfaction derived from their performance" (p. 328).

However, a number of students concerned more about whether materials or activities organized by IWB were for the betterment of the grades in exams. In this regard, it could be assumed that once the speaking tasks could not meet their expectations, they may negatively evaluate the effect of the IWB usage, as a mismatch between students' expectation and teachers' teaching approaches may result in students' devaluation of the ways in which they are taught. This also echoes what Brown (2009) argues "for some students a mismatch in expectations for classroom teaching may result in disillusionment" (p. 46). It is argued by this chapter that in a classroom where divergent perspectives and expectations are assembled, students' variable perceptions of teachers' approaches could not be avoided.

There are several pedagogical implications of this study. First, it is necessary for teachers to gain a comprehensive understanding of the notion of being communicatively competent. The diverse conceptions of oral proficiency exist because teachers partially highlight one or two aspects, yet neglect others, among the five aspects of communicative competence. To achieve a balance, teachers are suggested to combine the direct approaches to teaching speaking and the indirect ones. Second, it is critical for teachers to constantly reflect on their approaches to the teaching of speaking. To cultivate students' high level of oral proficiency, teachers are suggested to tactically deploy the teaching strategies based on the development path of speaking competence. Third, teachers should develop their capabilities to effectively utilize IWB for purposeful teaching. It has been argued that the effect of technology integration in language classrooms is subject-to-teachers' pedagogical beliefs and their technological proficiency (Schmid 2008). That is, in hope of maximizing the advantages of IWB's pedagogical worth, it is critical for teachers to keep track of the development of educational technology.

References

Al-Saleem, B. I. A. (2012). The interactive whiteboard in English as a foreign language (EFL) classroom. *European Scientific Journal, 8*(3), 126–134.

Brown, A. V. (2009). Students' and teachers' perceptions of effective foreign language teaching: A comparison of ideals. *The Modern Language Journal, 93*(1), 46–60.

Chen, Z., & Goh, C. (2011). Teaching oral English in higher education: Challenges to EFL teachers. *Teaching in Higher Education, 16*(3), 333–345.

Deci, E., Vallerand, R., Pelletier, L., & Ryan, R. (1991). Motivation and education: The self-determination perspective. *Educational Psychologist, 26*(3), 325–346.

Egbert, J., & Hanson-Smith, E. (1999). *CALL environments: Research, practice, and critical issues*. Alexandria: Teachers of English to Speakers of Other Languages.

Glover, D., Miller, D., Averis, D., & Door, V. (2005). The interactive whiteboard: A literature survey. *Technology, Pedagogy and Education, 14*(2), 155–170.

Glover, D., Miller, D., Averis, D., & Door, V. (2007). The evolution of an effective pedagogy for teachers using the interactive whiteboard in mathematics and modern languages: An empirical analysis from the secondary sector. *Learning, Media and Technology, 32*(1), 5–20.

Goh, C. C. M., & Burns, A. (2012). *Teaching speaking: A holistic approach*. New York: Cambridge University Press.

Hall, I., & Higgins, S. (2005). Primary school students' perceptions of interactive whiteboards. *Journal of Computer Assisted Learning, 21*(2), 102–117.

Handley, Z. (2012). Investigating the use of interactive whiteboards during the pre-task phase of speaking tasks in the secondary English classroom. In *Proceedings of the CALL: Using, learning, knowing, EUROCALL conference, Gothenburg, Sweden* (pp. 111–116). Research-publishing.net.

Liddicoat, A. J., Papademetre, L., Scarino, A., & Kohler, M. (2003). *Report on intercultural language learning*. Australian Government. Department of Education Science and Training. Retrieved on May 6, 2013, from: http://www1.curriculum.edu.au/nalsas/pdf/intercultural.pdf

López, O. S. (2010). The digital learning classroom: Improving English language learners' academic success in mathematics and reading using interactive whiteboard technology. *Computers & Education, 54*(4), 901–915.

Mathews-Aydinli, J., & Elaziz, F. (2010). Turkish students' and teachers' attitudes toward the use of interactive whiteboards in EFL classrooms. *Computer Assisted Language Learning, 23*(3), 235–252.

Mayer, R. E. (2001). *Multimedia learning*. Cambridge: Cambridge University Press.

McKendrick, J. H., & Bowden, A. (1999). Something for everyone? An evaluation of the use of audio-visual resources in geographical learning in the UK. *Journal of Geography in Higher Education, 23*(1), 9–19.

Moreno, R. (2006). Learning in high-tech and multimedia environments. *Current Directions in Psychological Science, 15*(2), 63–67.

Nerlicki, K. (2011). Foreign language speaking anxiety from the perspective of Polish students of German studies. In M. Pawlak, E. Waniek-Klimczak, & J. Majer (Eds.), *Speaking and instructed foreign language acquisition* (pp. 183–199). Bristol: Multilingual Matters.

Plass, J. L., Chun, D. M., Mayer, R. E., & Leutner, D. (2003). Cognitive load in reading a foreign language text with multimedia aids and the influence of verbal and spatial abilities. *Computers in Human Behavior, 19*(2), 221–243.

Schmid, E. C. (2006). Investigating the use of interactive whiteboard technology in the English language classroom through the lens of a critical theory of technology. *Computer Assisted Language Learning, 19*(1), 47–62.

Schmid, E. C. (2008). Potential pedagogical benefits and drawbacks of multimedia use in the English language classroom equipped with interactive whiteboard technology. *Computers & Education, 51*(4), 1553–1568.
Schmid, E. C. (2010). Developing competencies for using the interactive whiteboard to implement communicative language teaching in the English as a foreign language classroom. *Technology, Pedagogy and Education, 19*(2), 159–172.
Smith, H. J., Higgins, S., Wall, K., & Miller, J. (2005). Interactive whiteboards: Boon or bandwagon? A critical review of the literature. *Journal of Computer Assisted Learning, 21*(2), 91–101.
Solano-Flores, G. (2008). English language learners. In C. Clauss-Ehlers (Ed.), *Encyclopedia of cross-cultural school psychology* (pp. 427–428). New York: Springer.
Thompson, J., & Flecknoe, M. (2003). Raising attainment with an interactive whiteboard in Key Stage 2. *Management in Education, 17*(3), 29–33.
Wen, W. P., & Clement, R. (2003). A Chinese conceptualization of willingness to communicate in ESL. *Language, Culture and Curriculum, 16*(1), 18–38.
Xu, H. L., & Moloney, R. (2011). Perceptions of interactive whiteboard pedagogy in the teaching of Chinese language. *Australasian Journal of Educational Technology, 27*(2), 307–325.
Yu, L. (2001). Communicative language teaching in China: Progress and resistance. *TESOL Quarterly, 35*(1), 194–198.

Chapter 13
Exploring Perceived Accounting Ethics of University Students on Online Knowledge Sharing

Sally M. Li

Abstract This study is to explore perceived ethics as a new dimension to an established online knowledge sharing model. The focus of this study is to examine how students' perceived ethical attitude towards multiple unethical vignettes and their attachment motives influence online knowledge sharing behavior. Since university students are prospective leaders, both training and social interactions are important to implant ethical values. Using a survey questionnaire completed by 223 undergraduate students of various majors, this study found that perceived online attachment motivation had a direct, positive, and significant effect towards online knowledge sharing behavior ($\beta = .713$, $p < .001$). Perceived ethics, however, had an inverse relationship with online knowledge sharing behavior ($\beta = -.227$, $p < .01$). The proposed online knowledge sharing model explained 35 % of the observed variance. Limitations of this study were identified with suggestion on future studies.

Keywords Perceived ethics • Attachment motivation • Knowledge sharing • Ethics education • Accounting education

13.1 Introduction

Technology has broadened our social circle. With more social interactions, ideas and values are shared implicitly. According to Prensky (2001), the digital natives are people who have grown up around and who regularly engage in new media. In particular, the recent development of mobile technology has realized the any time and any place mode of networking and social interactions. Most students are digital natives. According to Park et al. (2013), today's high school students assessed that their educational attainment and intelligence are high. What they value and behave

S.M. Li (✉)
Department of Accounting, Hong Kong Shue Yan University, Hong Kong SAR, China
e-mail: mli@hksyu.edu

© Springer Science+Business Media Singapore 2015

W.W.K. Ma et al. (eds.), *New Media, Knowledge Practices and Multiliteracies*,
DOI 10.1007/978-981-287-209-8_13

in such ways are important. Previous studies support that both a need to belong and to connect with others are significant motives for users to share or tweet in such computer-mediated relationships (Ma and Yuen 2011; Chen 2011). With tightened and anonymous connectivity, new ethical issues evolved. For example, the constant and instant connectivity to others and sharing of information in the digital media has been described as "tethering" which may adversely affect knowledge authority and users social life (Brydon 2010; Turkle 2008). Besides, a strong desire for praise and "like" to around others in social media may not be good for teens development. According to Corpus et al. (2006), both mastery and social-comparison praise can have positive or negative impact on youth's perseverance and motivation. Their findings also remind teachers to use social-comparison praise carefully as it may set a bar higher than what students expect or need to hear about their performance on future tasks.

Previous studies indicate that many relational variables influence knowledge sharing behavior. For example, trust and commitment are the prominent relational factors that have been discussed to influence individual behavior in an organization (Morgan and Hunt 1994). Both contributors and seekers can gain new perspective by exchanging views with others. Wang (2004) asserts that knowledge sharing with colleagues is work ethics. Online knowledge sharing behavior occurs when learning takes place in an online learning context (Wilson 1996). In particular, when an individual learner understands the details and implications associated with that knowledge, he or she would then be able to apply the knowledge (Ma and Yuen 2011).

Knowledge sharing is becoming increasingly complex and multi-disciplined, and researchers are interested in understanding the motives behind young people's dedicated sharing behavior within their communities. The focus of this study is to examine how students' perceived ethical attitude towards multiple unethical vignettes and their attachment motives influence online knowledge sharing behavior. This study requires students to read complex business dilemma and express their acceptability. The results provide insights to both academics and practitioners for devising better training programs to respond to their ethical awareness and acceptance.

The specific research question was as follows:

RQ: *What factors affect students' online knowledge sharing behavior* with respect to their innate need to belong and their perceived ethics?

To explore the motivation drivers influencing students' online knowledge sharing behavior, we examine the literature to find the relevant factors. An online knowledge sharing model is then proposed, and the methodology used to collect data to test the hypotheses is explained. The findings are reported and the implications discussed. We conclude by acknowledging the study's limitations and suggesting areas for further research.

13.2 Literature Review and Hypotheses Development

13.2.1 Social Interaction, Knowledge Sharing, and Interpersonal Relationship

According to Vygotsky (1978), learning is social which involves a mechanism of acquiring knowledge and representing it through sharing and social interaction with others. Knowledge includes vision, working procedures, and mutual understanding which involves an integration of an individual's prior knowledge and expectations. According to Nonaka (1994), knowledge is "justified true belief" which involves personal judgment. Through more interactions over time, trust and self-efficacy between the sharers and seekers are built which reinforce what they are being taught or seen. Webb and Palincsar (1996) explained this of the use the reciprocal teaching process to explain how knowledge sharing in social processes act as a mechanism for learning. Knowledge sharing is a reflection of the sharers' understanding of their personal values, ideas, and practices with others in particular context (Nonaka 1994). Knowledge sharing is a cognitive process in which an individual needs to evaluate what to share with whom and whether it is equitable or profitable on a transaction base or in a long-term perspective (Bouty 2000). Thus, social interaction is important for new members to integrate external standards and values to build relationship in a community.

13.2.2 Accounting Training and Knowledge Sharing

Accounting aims at providing reliable and relevant financial information for decision makers. Information and knowledge are used interchangeably at an organizational level. The ethical issues and problems of accounting stem from two characteristics of accounting information (Gaa 2004). One is that accounting information can be seen as an economic good or a public good, depending on whether and how it is disclosed to interested parties. The other is that accounting information is normally distributed asymmetrically among individuals and groups who have a stake to use or produce it in the organization. Accounting subjects have been perceived as mechanical and procedural (Li and Ma 2012). Most accounting students demonstrate a strong focus on technical competence. Accountants are being stereotyped as number crunchers who are analytic, interpersonally and socially inept, good at handling paper work, but lack creativity (Carnegie and Napier 2010). To evaluate complex business issues and ethical dilemma require wider economic and social perspectives. After the collapse of Enron and WorldCom, more stringent rules are imposed to regulate the profession. Apart from applying the conservatism and consistency principles, what to do to increase accountants' ethical sensitivity and courage to combat malpractice remains a question.

The complex business environment requires more agile and vigilant governance framework. In this regard, professional accountants need to understand the business operations in different perspectives. Thus, accountants need more interactions with wider stakeholders like suppliers, customers, bankers, regulators, and social media. Accountants can no longer be number crunchers who work on calculating profits and balancing a company's financial position. According to Carnegie and Napier (2010), accounting discipline has evolved to a social practice that need strong generic and social skills rather than technical competence especially in handling consultancy work. Thus, students should be trained to exercise professional skepticism in applying technical standards. To widen students' social perspective, teachers can adopt cooperative learning method to induce students to interact with wider peers and sharpen their social skills (Johnson and Johnson 2007; Johnson et al. 2010).

13.2.3 Perceived Online Attachment Motivation (POAM) and Online Knowledge Sharing Behavior (OKSB)

Previous studies suggest that online knowledge sharing behavior (OKSB) occurs when learning takes place in an online learning context when the individual learner understands the details and implications associated with that knowledge so that he or she can apply it through the use of online learning platforms (Ma and Yuen 2011, p. 213). OKSB refers to "the online communication of knowledge so that knowledge is learned and applied by an individual" (Ma and Yuen 2011, p. 212). They also suggest that perceived online attachment motivation (POAM) would be a determinant to online knowledge sharing (Ma and Yuen 2010, 2011). POAM refers to "the degree to which an individual believes that he or she can improve his or her social interaction and the sense of communion with others on an online learning platform" (Ma and Yuen 2011, p. 213). If an individual learner expects to have strong social interactions in an online learning community, then he or she would be more willing to develop a relationship with other members in that community. To develop a relationship, he or she would be more willing to engage in greater interaction with other members in the online learning community. In online learning communities, all learners share the common goal of learning, and thus sharing one's knowledge is a good way to develop relationships. This leads to the following hypothesis.

H1: *The perceived attachment motivation of an individual learner on an online learning platform has a positive effect on his or her knowledge sharing behavior in that context.*

13.2.4 Ethics and Knowledge Sharing: For Good or Bad?

Ethics is about relationship, whether you care about others and how you rank your personal interests. People foster relationships with others for various reasons. Apart from pecuniary rewards, Hill (1987) suggested specific social rewards like positive affect, praise, reduction of negative affect through social contact, and social comparison as driving forces to build relationship. Knowledge can be shared in both collaborative and competitive manners to promote mutual understanding and achieve synergy. Individual sharing intentions increased when employees believed that sharing knowledge with colleagues was required by the organizations (Wang 2004). To collaborate with colleagues or not will depend on organization norm and salience of his personal interests (Wang 2004).

13.2.4.1 Value of Teaching Ethics

According to Hale and the colleagues (2005), the public confidence towards the accounting profession eroded with more corporate failures. Herron and Gilbertson (2004) concluded that the respect for the integrity of the accounting profession was adversely affected since Enron and WorldCom went bankrupt. Numerous accounting scandals caused the public to question what needs to be done to resume the profession credibility. In the aftermath of these corporate failures, the profession had reexamined their ethical standards (Duska and Duska 2003). Previous studies called for the enrichment of accounting education with ethics course to improve the ethical decision-making and behavior of accountants (McPhail 2001; Mintchik and Farmer 2009). More scholars requested to include and expand ethical education in academic curricula (Dellaportas 2006; Cohen 2001). The business context is dynamic and new ethical issues evolve continuously. What is ethical is difficult to define. For example, guanxi permits an individual to help one another when the former needs something that the latter can do. Although guanxi is a legitimate practice in some countries, certain forms of guanxi can be associated with corruption and bribery (Dunfee and Warren 2001), whereas some unethical behaviors can be legal. For example, facilitating payments to foreign officials are unethical but legal under US law (Bunker and Casey 2012).

Can ethics be taught? Previous studies indicated that the effectiveness of ethical education was mixed. According to Keller et al. (2007), a university education had a positive effect on accounting students' ethical standards. Similarly, Klimek and Wenell (2011) also concluded that students who took separate ethics course did seem to have higher ethical reasoning ability than students who had only had ethics integrated into their accounting courses. To the contrary, previous studies of Evans et al. 2006 and Ritter 2006 showed little empirical support that students who took ethics courses would actually make ethical decisions. Moreover, a modern course curriculum to support diverse students is important to develop students with analytical skills and moral courage in handling global ethical dilemma (Natale et al. 2012).

13.2.4.2 Perceived Acceptability of Unethical Scenarios

From a social network perspective, Brass et al. (1998) suggested that both attributes and structures of relationship, to some extent, can foster or prevent unethical behaviors. The accounting profession has a profound reputation of competence and integrity.

Wyatt (2004) discovered that as a result of the past booming in the accounting industry, many inexperienced and unprepared professionals were attracted to the field without proper training or understanding of professional accountants' responsibilities in implementing ethical principles in their work. Ethics are a collection of values that internalized by an individual and then reflected in his or her daily context. In this study, perceived ethics (ETH) is defined as the degree of disagreement of unethical behavior, like paying bribes to improve profits or reduce competition. We test for the inverse relationship between ethical attitude and online knowledge sharing behavior. If an individual learner, who possess higher perceived ethics (perceived lower acceptability of unethical behavior), is expected to have higher integrity, then he or she would be more conscience to engage online knowledge sharing behavior in an online learning community, in order not to infringe others privacy or property right. This leads to the following hypothesis.

H2: The perceived lower acceptability of unethical behavior of an individual learner on an online learning platform has a negative effect on his or her knowledge sharing behavior in that context.

13.3 Methodology

13.3.1 Learning Management System: Interactive Learning Network (ILN)

The respondents were full-time students of various majors at a local university in Hong Kong, who used a learning management system called the Interactive Learning Network (ILN). The ILN was implemented throughout the university and all of the students had access to it. Instructors were encouraged to use it to manage their classes but it was not compulsory to do so. All of the communication tools in the ILN, including general information, calendar, announcement, resources, forum, chat room, assignment submission, course evaluation survey, contacts, etc., were available to students.

13.3.2 Subjects

The study was conducted in the 2013 spring semester. Data were collected from students who were major in accounting, economics and finance, Chinese language and literature, and counseling and psychology as vehicles to enhance our understanding of students' knowledge sharing behavior on the ILN. The students participated voluntarily and their anonymity was maintained.

13.3.3 Data Collection

Hard copies of the one-page, two-sided questionnaire were given to the instructors of the selected classes. The instructors distributed the questionnaires in class and collected them upon completion. Most of the students completed the questionnaire within 10 min and all of the data were input into SPSS for further analysis.

13.3.4 Measures

A survey instrument was used to obtain self-reported information from the respondents (Gall et al. 1996). The questionnaire was divided into three main parts. The first part asked respondents' basic personal information, including gender, age, cognitive learning style score (instrument adopted from Ma et al. 2012), department, academic results, and frequency to use social media and online games. The second part asked respondents for their opinion about their perceived acceptability of unethical scenarios and finally the perceived online knowledge sharing behavior over the use of ILN. The entire questionnaire items were adopted from prior validated scales and were measured on a 7-point Likert-type scale, ranged from 1 (*strongly disagree*) to 7 (*strongly agree*). Specifically, respondents were asked to answer 5 items each from POAM and OKSB from a validated instrument by Ma and Yuen (2011a) and 5 items from ETH by Conroy et al. (2010). The complete scale and sources were listed in the Appendix.

13.4 Findings

13.4.1 Descriptive Statistics of Respondents

The descriptive statistics of the respondents were presented in the table below (Table 13.1).

13.4.2 Descriptive Analysis of Variables

Table 13.2 presented the mean responses for the three constructs. A higher ETH score indicated that students of the department possessed higher ethical standard. Table 13.6 presented the accounting-major students, who had additionally completed a mandatory 2-credit hour professional ethics course, were the lowest (4.6) compared to the Chinese language major students were the highest (4.99).

Table 13.1 Descriptive statistics of respondents ($n = 223$)

Items	Descriptive statistics
Departments (major)	Accounting 143 (64.1 %); economics and finance 36 (16.1 %);
	Chinese lang and lit 28 (12.6 %); counseling and psy 16 (7.2 %)
Gender	Male – 73 (32.7 %); female – 150 (67.3 %)
Age	≤21–73 (32.7 %); 22–65 (29.1 %); ≥23–83 (37.2 %)
Cognitive learning style	Intuitive – 50 (22.4 %); analytical – 173 (77.6 %)
GPA (*M*, *SD*)	CGA: 2.697 (0.410); GPA: 2.675 (0.468)
Use of social media	*Mean*: 4.22; *SD*: 0.879–1 (*never*) to 5 (*always*)
Use of online gaming	*Mean*: 2.41; *SD*: 1.305–1 (*never*) to 5 (*always*)

Table 13.2 Descriptive statistics of the variables

	M	*SD*	α
Perceived online attachment motivation (POAM)			0.906
POAM1	2.71	1.392	
POAM2	2.68	1.409	
POAM3	2.77	1.365	
POAM4	2.74	1.437	
POAM5	2.90	1.502	
Online knowledge sharing behavior (OKSB)			0.950
OKSB1	3.75	1.670	
OKSB2	3.81	1.626	
OKSB3	3.78	1.694	
OKSB4	3.69	1.562	
OKSB5	3.63	1.588	
Perceived ethics (ETH)			0.790
ETH1	5.43	1.418	
ETH2	4.44	1.558	
ETH3	4.39	1.712	
ETH4	4.67	1.357	
ETH5	4.49	1.430	

13.4.3 Instrument Validation

The instrument was tested for its internal consistency and construct validity. Cronbach's alpha value was used to examine the scale's internal consistency as suggested by previous studies (Nunnally and Bernstein 1994). Cronbach's α values for POAM is .906, OKSB is .950, and perceived ethics is .790. They all have values greater than .7, the threshold value as suggested by previous studies (Nunnally and Bernstein 1994). The variables are considered as internal consistent and reliable.

Table 13.3 Pearson's correlation coefficient matrix of inter-items

	POAM1	POAM2	POAM3	POAM4	POAM5	OKSB1	OKSB2	OKSB3	OKSB4	OKSB5	ETH1	ETH2	ETH3	ETH4	ETH5
POAM1	**1**														
POAM2	**.712****	**1**													
POAM3	**.592****	**.719****	**1**												
POAM4	**.622****	**.633****	**.757****	**1**											
POAM5	**.600****	**.610****	**.638****	**.710****	**1**										
OKSB1	.430**	.416**	.415**	.452**	.516**	**1**									
OKSB2	.441**	.415**	.457**	.470**	.484**	**.850****	**1**								
OKSB3	.421**	.373**	.398**	.408**	.423**	**.786****	**.828****	**1**							
OKSB4	.483**	.448**	.462**	.474**	.484**	**.760****	**.785****	**.820****	**1**						
OKSB5	.432**	.415**	.444**	.442**	.447**	**.712****	**.743****	**.784****	**.863****	**1**					
ETH1	-0.016	0.086	0.01	0.05	0.074	-0.054	-0.056	-0.044	-0.019	-0.033	**1**				
ETH2	0.034	0.122	0.002	0.081	0.116	-0.048	-0.013	-0.051	0.001	0.005	**.393****	**1**			
ETH3	-0.055	0.056	0	0.084	0.117	-.162*	-.138*	-.183**	-.156*	-.132*	**.427****	**.451****	**1**		
ETH4	0.058	0.102	0.003	0.002	0.058	-0.09	-0.122	-0.092	-0.042	0.006	**.400****	**.387****	**.498****	**1**	
ETH5	0.045	0.102	0.043	0.002	0.057	-.175**	-0.093	-.146*	-0.105	-0.064	**.408****	**.422****	**.375****	**.581****	**1**

**$p<0.01$; *$p<0.05$, two tail

Construct validity of the instrument was examined by inter-item correlation and factor analysis. Inter-item correlation coefficient matrix shows that there was significant higher correlation among the items to their corresponding construct, exhibited convergent validity of the constructs. It was also found that the item-correlation is significantly lower across construct other than its own, exhibited discriminant validity of the constructs (Tables 13.3 and 13.4).

Therefore, the instrument is both reliable and valid. A summed average score was then calculated for each construct, including the summed mean score of POAM (5 item), OKSB (5 item), and ETH (5 item). The mean and standard deviation of the summed mean score was listed below (Table 13.5).

13.4.4 Manipulation Check

These three constructs were then examined to see if there were significant differences among the various demographic variables, including gender, cognitive style, departments, etc. Using means *t*-test and ANOVA, it was found that there weren't any significant differences among these demographic groups (Table 13.6).

Table 13.4 Exploratory factor analysis

	1	2	3
POAM1	.266	**.778**	−.001
POAM2	.219	**.832**	.107
POAM3	.226	**.849**	−.014
POAM4	.255	**.837**	.034
POAM5	.316	**.763**	.107
OKSB1	**.845**	.290	−.104
OKSB2	**.867**	.293	−.075
OKSB3	**.897**	.218	−.093
OKSB4	**.873**	.307	−.040
OKSB5	**.858**	.268	−.008
ETH1	.020	−.008	**.708**
ETH2	.029	.034	**.716**
ETH3	−.163	.071	**.728**
ETH4	−.028	.018	**.784**
ETH5	−.103	.056	**.749**
% of variance	40.976	19.456	10.279
Eigen values	6.146	2.918	1.542

Table 13.5 Descriptive statistics of summed mean scores

	M	*SD*
Perceived online attachment motivation (POAM)	2.759	1.212
Perceived ethics (ETH)	4.690	1.106
Online knowledge sharing behavior (OKSB)	3.731	1.487

Table 13.6 Means differences of ethics between demographics groups

		Ethics (*M*, *SD*)
Gender	Male ($N=73$)	4.50 (1.13)
	Female ($N=150$)	4.78 (1.09)
	2-independent t-test	$p=.080>.05$ *(n-s)*
Cognitive learning style	Intuitive ($N=50$)	4.52 (1.16)
	Analytical ($N=173$)	4.74 (1.09)
	2-independent t-test	$p=.230>.05$ *(n-s)*
Departments	Accounting	4.60 (1.17)
	Econ and finance	4.82 (1.03)
	Chin lang and lit	4.99 (0.94)
	Counseling and psy	4.63 (0.89)
	ANOVA	$F=1.179, p=.318>.05$ *(n-s)*

Note. n-s: nonsignificant

Table 13.7 Regression model summary

Model	*R*	R^2	Adjusted R^2	Std. error of the est.	ANOVA *F*	Sig.
1	.592	.350	.344	1.2045	59.249	.000

Table 13.8 Regression model coefficients

Model		Unstandardized coefficients		Standardized coefficients		
		B	Std. error	Beta	*t*	Sig.
1	(Constant)	2.829	.386		7.337	.000
	ETH	−.227	.073	−.169	−3.095	.002
	POAM	.713	.067	.581	10.650	.000

13.4.5 Hypotheses Testing

A linear multiple regression was then used to analyze the model and to test the relationships (Table 13.7).

The overall model was found significant ($p < .001$) and the R^2 was .350, showing that for every standard unit of all independent variables increase, there would be 35 % increase of the dependent variable (Table 13.8).

The coefficient table of the regression analysis showed that perceived ethics had a beta coefficient of−.227 ($p < .01$) towards OKSB. ETH had a negative and moderate effect towards OKSB and H2 was supported. The negative relationship suggested that the greater the perceived ethics, there would be a lower online knowledge sharing behavior. The table also showed that perceived online attachment motivation had a beta coefficient of .713 ($p < .001$) towards OKSB. POAM had a positive and direct significant effect towards OKSB and H1 was supported. This suggested that the greater the perceived online attachment motivation, the more the online knowledge sharing behavior.

13.5 Discussion

13.5.1 Perceived Online Attachment Motivation and Perceived Ethics

This study found that perceived online attachment motivation has a direct, positive, and significant effect towards online knowledge sharing behavior ($\beta = .713, p < .001$). Perceived ethics, however, has an inverse relationship with online knowledge sharing behavior ($\beta = -.227, p < .01$). Initially, we expect students who demonstrated higher perceived ethics (lower acceptability of unethical behavior) will engage more knowledge sharing because it is a means of establishing relationships and can be viewed as a form of social support for others. However, our results showed that the inverted relationship indicated that those students with lower perceived ethics engaged more knowledge sharing behavior. It may indicate that the students who possessed higher perceived ethics may have higher ethical awareness and are more cautious to possible consequences, like privacy or intellectual property right infringement. It may echo what Park et al. (2013) described that young people developed with more positive self-views but less individualistic in economic recession. Our results also showed that the accounting majors demonstrated a slightly higher level of acceptability to unethical issues. Indeed, both accountancy institutions and practitioners urge the teaching profession to improve their curriculum to include expanded ethical training (Dellaportas 2006). Future studies can include open-ended questions to understand students' rationale behind their choices.

13.5.2 Ethical Behavior

This study provided students an opportunity to consider business dilemma that they may encounter in the workplace. In contrast with Conroy et al.'s (2010) finding that young male auditors demonstrated higher degree of acceptability of unethical behavior, we found no significant difference among gender, cognitive learning style, and majors (Table 13.6). Teaching students' business ethics needs to integrate ethical principles to their social context (Natale et al. 2012). For good or bad, socialization can be a control mechanism or a rationalization process towards malpractice. Ethical behavior cannot be assured without internalizing to one's personal virtue and instilling as corporate culture. Knowledge sharing involves knowledge contributors and seekers who exchanged and endorsed value implicitly. Educators also play a role in providing students opportunities for the necessary interaction between them to promote each other's success (Summers and Svinicki 2007). In the digital era, it is important to inspire students to share responsibly, for examples, not to involve in cyberbully and transmitting unethical messages. Numerous corporate collapses reflected that people would accept unethical and even illegal act in order to build closer relationship. In order to fulfill an innate need to attach and to strengthen group identity, people may blindly follow or endorse some unethical act especially when they foresee personal gains like career prospects.

Ethics are important values that could not be encoded. As accountancy firms have engaged more consultancy work, more stringent control mechanism to assure higher ethical sensitivity and decision is important to safeguard public interests.

Moreover, students need more training to interpret complex business problems including ethical issues. Li and Ma (2012) suggest including a social and cultural context to educate accounting undergraduates to meet the demanding business environment. Universities can offer more elective courses in their curriculum to widen students' social perspectives. As university students are future leaders, they need to be equipped with strong ethical sensitivities and values in order to uphold social equity. Educators have to inspire business students to acknowledge a public role of professional accountants.

13.5.3 Limitations and Further Studies

Despite the usefulness of its findings, this study has several limitations. First, our research results were obtained from undergraduate students in a local university in Hong Kong. It would limit the generalizability of the results. Second, the proposed knowledge sharing model is based only on two constructs. Further studies may extend our model to the ethical and unethical dimensions that influence knowledge sharing. Other constructs such as personal value, organization commitment or social norm may be determinants of the ethical dimension that influencing knowledge sharing. Third, perceived ethics is considered as an independent variable to predict online knowledge sharing in this study. Previous studies examined that perceived ethics are determined by respondents' positive job response or employee rank (Valentine et al. 2010; Conroy et al. 2010). Thus, further studies might also consider students' positive learning experience and academic achievement to understand the ethical dimension.

Conclusion

In conclusion, our model showed a reasonably good fit with the data collected and a good prediction power to online knowledge sharing model, with 35 % explained variance. The perceived online attachment motivation was found significantly related to online knowledge sharing whereas perceived ethics had a partially inverse relationship with online knowledge sharing behavior. These results provide an alternative perspective, suggest that facilitating the formation of social bonds can promote knowledge sharing whilst perceived ethics impede online knowledge sharing behavior.

Appendix: Measurement Items Used in the Study

Perceived ethics (ETH) (Conroy et al. 2010)	
ETH1*	A company paid a $350,000 "consulting" fee to an official of a foreign country. In return, the official promised assistance in obtaining a contract that will produce $10 million profit for the contracting company.
ETH2	Sarah Jenkins, CPA, an internal auditor at Josephs Energy Company, uses the computer in her office and the company's connection to the Internet to do day trading in the stock market
ETH3	A company president found that a competitor had made an important scientific discovery that would sharply reduce the profits of his own company. He then hired a key employee of the competitor in an attempt to learn the details of the discovery.
ETH4	A highway-building contractor deplored the chaotic bidding situation and cutthroat competition in his industry. He therefore reached an understanding with the other major contractors to permit bidding which would provide them with a reasonable profit.
ETH5	A company president recognized that sending expensive Christmas gifts to purchasing agents might compromise their positions. However, he continued the policy since it was common practice and changing it might result in a loss of business.
Perceived online attachment motivation (POAM) (Ma and Yuen 2011)	
POAM1	If I feel unhappy or kind of depressed in learning the course, I usually try to be around other members using the ILN to make me feel better.
POAM2	I usually have the greatest need to have other members using the ILN around me when I feel upset in learning the course.
POAM3	I often have a strong need to be around other ILN users who are impressed with what I am like and what I do in the course
POAM4	I mainly like to be around other ILN users who think I am an important, exciting person in learning the course together.
POAM5	I often have a strong desire to get other ILN users around to notice me and appreciate what I am like in learning the course together.
Online knowledge sharing behavior (OKSB) (Ma and Yuen 2011)	
OKSB1	The advice I receive from other members using the ILN has increased my understanding of the course.
OKSB2	The advice I receive from other members using the ILN has increased my knowledge of the course.
OKSB3	The advice I receive from other members using the ILN allows me to complete similar tasks in the course more efficiently.
OKSB4	The advice I receive from other members using the ILN allows me to improve the quality of similar work in the course.
OKSB5	The advice I receive from other members using the ILN allows me to conduct similar tasks in the course with greater independence.

Note. *ETH1-5 items were reversed before analysis

References

Bouty, I. (2000). Interpersonal and interaction influences on informal resource exchanges between R&D researchers across organizational boundaries. *Academy of Management Journal, 43*(1), 50–65.

Brass, D. J., Butterfield, K. D., & Skaggs, B. C. (1998). Relationships and unethical behavior: A social network perspective. *Academy of Management Review, 23*(1), 14–31.

Brydon, D. (2010). Social media's research potential. *English Studies in Canada, 36*(4), 4–8.

Bunker, R. B., & Casey, K. M. (2012). Facilitating payments versus bribes: Are we sending conflicting ethical signals in accounting education? *International Journal of Business and Social Science, 3*(8), 47–50.

Carnegie, G. D., & Napier, C. J. (2010). Traditional accountants and business professionals: Portraying the accounting profession after Enron. *Accounting, Organizations and Society, 35*(3), 360–376.

Chen, G. M. (2011). Tweet this: A uses and gratifications perspective on how active Twitter use gratifies a need to connect with others. *Computers in Human Behavior, 27*, 755–762.

Cohen, J. (2001). Social emotional education: Core principles and practices. In J. Cohen (Ed.), *Caring classrooms/intelligent schools: The social emotional education of young children* (pp. 3–29). New York: Teachers College Press.

Conroy, S. J., Emerson, T. L. N., & Pons, F. (2010). Ethical attitudes of accounting practitioners: Are rank and ethical attitudes related? *Journal of Business Ethics, 91*, 183–194.

Corpus, J., Ogle, C., & Love-Geiger, K. (2006). The effects of social-comparison versus mastery praise on children's intrinsic motivation. *Motivation and Emotion, 30*(4), 333–343.

Dellaportas, S. (2006). Making a difference with a discrete course on accounting ethics. *Journal of Business Ethics, 65*, 391–404.

Dunfee, T. W., & Warren, D. E. (2001). Is guanxi ethical? A normative analysis of doing business in China. *Journal of Business Ethics, 32*(3), 191–204.

Duska, R., & Duska, B. (2003). *Accounting ethics*. Oxford: Blackwell Publishing.

Evans, J. M., Trevino, L. K., & Weaver, G. R. (2006). Who's in the ethics driver's seat? Factors influencing ethics in the MBA curriculum. *Academy of Management learning and Education & Training, 5*(3), 294–305.

Gaa, J. C. (2004). Accounting ethics. In R. E. Freeman & P. L. Werhane (Eds.), *Encyclopedic dictionary of business ethics* (2nd ed.). London: Blackwell.

Gall, M. D., Borg, W. R., & Gall, J. P. (1996). *Educational research* (6th ed.). White Plains: Longman.

Hale, M. W., Huston, R., & Smith, M. L. (2005). The once and future accountants: Ethics and the future outlook of the US accounting profession. *International Journal of Accounting, Auditing and Performance Evaluation, 2*(4), 426–440.

Herron, T., & Gilbertson, D. (2004). Ethical principles vs. ethical rules: The moderating effect of moral development on audit independence judgments. *Business Ethics Quarterly (Special Issue on Accounting Ethics), 14*(3), 499–523.

Hill, C. A. (1987). Affiliation motivation: People who need people, but in different ways. *Journal of Personality and Social Psychology, 52*(5), 1008–1018.

Johnson, D., & Johnson, R. (2007). Social interdependence theory and cooperative learning: The teacher's role. In R. Gillies, A. Ashman, & J. Terwel (Eds.), *The teacher's role in implementing cooperative learning in the classroom*. Dordrecht: Springer.

Johnson, D., Johnson, R., & Roseth, C. (2010). Cooperative learning in middle schools: Interrelationship of relationships and achievement. *Middle Grades Research Journal, 5*(1), 18.

Keller, A. C., Smith, K. T., & Smith, L. M. (2007). Do gender, educational level, religiosity, and work experience affect the ethical decision-making of U.S. accountants? *Critical Perspectives on Accounting, 18*, 299–314.

Klimek, J., & Wenell, K. (2011). Ethics in accounting: An indispensable course? *Academy of Educational Leadership Journal, 15*(4), 107–118.

Li, S. M., & Ma, W. W. K. (2012). Motivational factors for accounting learning – The development of a holistic framework. In S. K. S. Cheung et al. (Eds.), *ICHL 2012, LNCS 7411* (pp. 243–252). Berlin/Heidelberg: Springer.

Ma, W. W. K., & Yuen, A. H. K. (2010). Understanding online knowledge sharing: An exploratory theoretical framework. In P. Tsang et al. (Eds.), *ICHL2010, LNCS 6248* (pp. 239–248). Berlin/Heidelberg: Springer.

Ma, W. W. K., & Yuen, A. H. K. (2011). Understanding online knowledge sharing: An interpersonal relationship perspective. *Computers & Education, 56*(1), 210–219.

Ma, W. W. K., Sun, K., & Ma, J. (2012). The influence of attachment styles on knowledge sharing in social media environments. In S. K. S. Cheung et al. (Eds.), *ICHL 2012, LNCS 7411* (pp. 231–242). Berlin/Heidelberg: Springer.

McPhail, K. (2001). The other objective of ethics education: Re-humanizing the accounting profession – A study of ethics education in law, engineering, medicine, and accountancy. *Journal of Business Ethics, 34*, 279–298.

Mintchik, N., & Farmer, T. (2009). Associations between epistemological beliefs and moral reasoning: Evidence from accounting. *Journal of Business Ethics, 84*(2), 259–275.

Morgan, R. M., & Hunt, S. D. (1994). The commitment-trust theory of relationship marketing. *Journal of Marketing, 58*(3), 20–38.

Natale, S., Sora, S., & Drumheller, M. (2012). The importance of the university in the 21st century: Ethical conflicts and moral choices. *Journal of Academic Ethics, 10*(1), 1–8.

Nonaka, I. (1994). A dynamic theory of organizational knowledge creation. *Organization Science, 5*(1), 14–37.

Nunnally, J. C., & Bernstein, I. H. (1994). *Psychometric theory*. New York: McGraw-Hill.

Park, H., Twenge, J. M., & Greenfield, P. M. (2013). The great recession: Implications for adolescent values and behavior. *Social Psychological and Personality Science, 00*(0), 1–9.

Prensky, M. (2001). Digital natives, digital immigrants. *On the Horizon, 9*(5), 1–5.

Ritter, B. A. (2006). Can business ethics be trained? A study of the ethical decision-making process in business students. *Journal of Business Ethics, 68*, 153–164.

Summers, J., & Svinicki, M. (2007). Investigating classroom community in higher education. *Learning and Individual Differences, 17*(1), 55–67.

Turkle, S. (2008). Always-on/always-on-you. The tethered self. In J. Katz (Ed.), *Handbook of mobile communications and social change* (pp. 121–138). Cambridge, MA: MIT Press.

Valentine, S., Varca, P., Godkin, L., & Barnett, T. (2010). Positive job response and ethical job performance. *Journal of Business Ethics, 91*, 195–206.

Vygotsky, L. S. (1978). *Mind in society: The development of higher psychological processes*. Cambridge, MA: Harvard University Press.

Wang, C. C. (2004). The influence of ethical and self- interest concerns on knowledge sharing intentions among managers: An empirical study. *International Journal of Management, 21*, 370–381.

Webb, N. M., & Palincsar, A. S. (1996). Group processes in the classroom. In D. C. Berliner & R. C. Calfee (Eds.), *Handbook of educational psychology* (pp. 841–873). New York: Macmillan Library Reference.

Wilson, B. G. (1996). *Constructivist learning environments: Case studies in instructional design*. Englewood Cliffs: Educational Technology.

Wyatt, A. R. (2004). Accounting professionalism – They just don't get it! *Accounting Horizons, 18*, 45–53.

Chapter 14
Exploring Hong Kong Youth's Engagement with Digital Technologies Outside School

Liping Deng, Jan Connelly, Miki Lau, and Kelly Y.L. Ku

Abstract This study reports a survey study exploring Hong Kong secondary school students' engagement with digital technologies outside school. In particular, we seek to depict how the youth use mobile phone and computers in their daily life and sought to compare their use of digital tools for personal and school-related purposes. Variables including age and gender are also explored to help better understand their impact on youth's use of digital technologies. The results have shown that the Hong Kong teenagers are avid users of smartphones and computer. Although there are noted difference between their digital engagement in their daily life and for school-related work, technology especially social networking sites becomes increasingly important in their learning.

Keywords Digital technologies • Hong Kong • Informal learning • Mobile phone

14.1 Introduction

The increasing presence of digital technologies in the daily life of adolescences has given rise to a heightened need to understand the role of technologies both inside and outside school. Educational commentators have pointed out that there is a home-school mismatch in terms of access to, and engagement with, digital technologies (e.g., Clark et al. 2009; Levin and Arafeh 2002; Selwyn 2006). On the whole, there has been limited research on students' use of various technologies on their own beyond formal classroom settings. Most studies on the theme are conducted in the UK and the USA. There has been a dearth of research on young people's digital engagement outside school in Hong Kong.

The present study seeks to contribute to this line of research by exploring Hong Kong secondary school students' engagement with digital technologies outside school. In particular, we seek to depict how youth use mobile phone and computers

L. Deng (✉)
Hong Kong Baptist University, Hong Kong, China
e-mail: liping.deng@gmail.com

J. Connelly • M. Lau • K.Y.L. Ku
Department of Education Studies, Hong Kong Baptist University, Hong Kong, China

© Springer Science+Business Media Singapore 2015
W.W.K. Ma et al. (eds.), *New Media, Knowledge Practices and Multiliteracies*,
DOI 10.1007/978-981-287-209-8_14

for both personal and educational use. The use of technologies for learning purposes can include two types of learning: "formal learning, such as the use of ICT to support homework – which is structured, externally directed and usually assessed – and informal learning through the use of ICT for a variety of leisure pursuits – which is often unstructured, self-directed and exploratory" (Lewin 2004, p. 140). In light of this, we also differentiate the use of digital technologies for school-related work (e.g., assignment, group work) and personal use for other purposes (e.g., socialization, entertainment) and try to draw a comparison between the two types of uses. As such, three research questions were posed to guide the investigation:

1. How do students use mobile phone and computer outside school?
2. How do students use technologies for school-related work?
3. Do personal characteristics such as age and gender influence students' engagement with technologies?

14.2 Literature Review

14.2.1 Technologies for Learning Outside Schools

It has been widely acknowledged that digital technologies have been an integral part of daily life for young students. Against this backdrop, there is a group of researchers who are interested in to what extent technologies have been harnessed for learning outside school.

Deepwell and Malik (2008) focus on the patterns, motivations, and engagement with learning technology among university students in the UK, in particular, during self-directed study time for campus-based courses. It was found that students generally appreciated the value of Virtual Learning Environment (VLE) and showed a great degree of dependence on instructors for feedback and providing direction and assistance for their use of technology for learning. The authors concluded that more guidance on what and how to use technology for learning is needed.

A large-scale study on young people's use of digital technologies at home conducted by Furlong and Davies (2012) involved a mixed age group of young people from 8 to 21 in the UK. They contended that the boundaries between school and home, play and study, were increasingly blurred. Young people showed a wide range of informal learning practices including accessing a broad range of online and social resources and strategies such as observing experts, producing, reviewing, and sharing. Through these practices, they developed technical, networking, and collaboration skills as well as judgments that can support learning.

Another UK-based researcher, Lewin (2004), conducted another large-scale project that examined students' engagement with networked technologies at home. The study indicated that the students used the Internet for a number of pursuits among which leisure and entertainment were the most prominent. School-related work was limited yet valued by the young people. At home, the students enjoyed greater autonomy in choosing when and how to use technologies, thus they had opportunities to be deeply involved in activities with technologies.

Ben-David Kolikant (2012) explored students' perceptions and application of the Internet for schoolwork after school hours through in-depth interviews with 25 secondary school students in Israel. They revealed that although the students, in general, favored the Internet and regarded it as convenient and fun, yet they also thought of it as unreliable and not serious enough. Governed by this view, they opted to use the Internet for assignment of minor importance, while resorting to books and lesson notes for important work and exams.

14.2.2 Disconnect Between Home and School

There is also a collection of work that accentuates the "digital disconnect" between home and school. In these studies researchers seek to discern to what extent the discrepancy exist between the digital engagement in and out of school and the implication of this for students' formal and informal learning.

Clark et al. (2009) examined the UK teenagers' use of Web 2.0 tools in and out of school and reported that the social media was affording a range of activities among which social, leisure, or entertainment activities were the dominate ones. Having said this, the technologies were also employed in formal school settings; hence, the boundary between formal and informal settings became less clear. On the whole, the young students had a clear sense of the "digital dissonance" between their in- and out-of-school experiences of technologies, yet they lacked knowledge on how to deploy the tools to support their own learning.

Kent and Facer (2004) sought to answer the question whether home and school uses of ICT tools were different and how these two worlds overlapped and interrelated. They found that the two sites were reciprocal with patterns of access and use of computer at home extended to school and vice versa. The authors further challenged the dichotomy of school for formal learning and home for informal learning, and suggested there is a need to view learning as a continuum of formal and informal practices.

Levin and Arafeh (2002) conducted a qualitative study on the "digital disconnect" between net-savvy students and their schools in the USA. They reported that the net-savvy students employed the Internet for school-related work outside school in a wide range of ways. In contrast, their engagements with the Internet inside school were confined, which led to students' frustration and dissatisfaction. As a conclusion, the authors advocate that educators should create more opportunities in school to take advantage of the Internet to align with students' out-of-school practice. Following Levin and Arafeh's (2002) work, Selwyn (2006) conducted a replica study involving secondary school students in the UK. It turned out that UK schools suffered the same problem of low engagement with the Internet, mostly due to regulations and restrictions. However, although UK students in the study were aware of the problem of "digital disconnect," they treated it as a "digital inconvenience" and tried to overcome it by working around it.

14.3 Research Gap

In general, many studies on students' experiences of technologies are contextualized in classroom settings whereas there is a dearth of studies on how students use various technologies to support learning based on their own initiative and beyond formal classroom settings (Attwell 2007; Lai and Gu 2011; Vaughan et al. 2011). It follows that the tension between students' experience with technologies in and out of classrooms is not well understood, and equally misunderstood is the transferability of skills between formal and informal settings (Clark et al. 2009). Additionally, the large-scale studies that explore students' experiences with learning technologies have been primarily been conducted in the UK (e.g., Conole et al. 2006; Kirkwood and Price 2005), Australia (e.g., Kennedy et al. 2008), and North America (e.g., Smith and Caruso 2010); to our knowledge, such studies have not yet been conducted in Hong Kong.

14.4 Methods

The main purpose of our study is to explore youth's patterns of engagement with new media outside school environment. In order to achieve this, quantitative method is adopted and an online questionnaire was designed. This paper was contextualized as a large-scale research project which included six Hong Kong schools and three from the Mainland China. In this paper, we will only present data from one of the Hong Kong schools inclusive of both local and ethnic minority students. It is a coeducational private school subsided by the government. There are three classes in each grade level from form 1 to form 6. Ethnic minority students are mainly in junior levels. According to our statistics, about 40 % of the participants are living in a rented public flat and only 28 % are living in private housing. This suggests that the students of this school are mainly come from mid to lower socioeconomic backgrounds. This school was purposefully selected and recruited through the researchers' personal connections on account of its mixed demographic composition.

As shown in Table 14.1, there are totally 8 sections with 68 questions in the questionnaire. Based on the pilot testing with two colleagues and two secondary students, we expected students could finish the online survey within 40 min. The questionnaire was bilingual available in both English and traditional Chinese to cater to the needs of local and ethnic minority students. All the students were invited to participate and arrangements were made for them to complete the questionnaire during school time in school computer labs.

The data collected was imported into SPSS for statistical analysis. Other than the descriptive data on students' use of technological tools outside school, we were also interested in exploring the variables affecting students' digital engagement. In this respect, earlier research has identified several factors including gender and age (Volman and van Eck 2001). Thus, in our analysis, we compared the results across genders (males vs. females) and grade levels (junior students vs. senior students).

Table 14.1 Description of the questionnaire

Section	Description
1	Demographic information
2	General information about the use of digital devices
3	Usage of mobile phone
4	Communication with digital devices
5	Languages related to the use of digital devices
6	Creating and sharing with digital devices
7	Experience with gaming and virtual communities
8	Use of technologies in schoolworks and problem solving

14.5 Results

14.5.1 Demographic Data

In total, 480 students completed the online questionnaire. We excluded those with excessive missing responses and those whose age ranges fell outside the 11–20 years. Altogether data of 471 participants were retained for analysis.

Table 14.2 shows the demographic composition of the questionnaire respondents. We grouped the students into junior and senior levels with junior comprising of form 1 to form 3 and senior of form 4 to form 6. Altogether, there are 46 % (218) junior-level students and 54 % (253) senior-level students. The gender composition is more balanced at the senior level (54 % males and 46 % females) than it is at the junior level (male students 62 %, female students 38 %).

14.5.2 Digital Engagement Outside School

To gain a general picture of students' digital engagement, they were first asked to rate their frequency of using a range of digital devices outside school on a scale of 1–5 (from "never" to "frequently"). According to the data, smartphones were used most often (M=4.15, SD=1.10), and desktop computers rated second (M=3.37, SD=1.21). Other devices including notebooks, tablet computers, portable media players, e-book readers, and game devices were less commonly used. There is no significant gender difference noted in this respect except boys used game devices more often than girls (t (469)=4.67, $p<.01$). The senior form students reported smartphone use more frequently than their junior counterparts (t (469)=−2.48, $p<.02$).

Ninety-three percentage of our respondents own a mobile phone, among which 93 % of them have smartphones. Between genders, 84 % of boys and 90 % of girls

Table 14.2 Demographic data of questionnaire respondents ($n=471$)

	Junior		Senior	
	$n=218$	46 %	$n=253$	54 %
Genders				
Male	136	62 %	136	54 %
Female	82	38 %	117	46 %

own a smartphone but about 93 % of senior forms students have a smartphone compared to 79 % of the junior students. We also probed into what the students do with their phones. When asked to match the usage of phone and computer with a list of practices. The students often use a phone for text messaging (87 %), voice communication (81 %), and media production (e.g., photo and video taking, and sound recording) (69 %) while using computer for media production (83 %), downloading and uploading files (79 %), and document processing (71 %). For gaming, more students prefer playing on phones (68 %) than on computers (59 %).

14.5.2.1 Online Participation

In addition to computer and mobile phone, another important aspect of our investigation relates to students' engagement via the Internet. In this respect, we focused on Social Network Systems (SNS) (e.g., Facebook), forums, and online creativity work. Most respondents (83 %) acknowledged themselves as SNS users. Among SNS users, 97 % used Facebook via smartphones and 96 % via computer. To further understand students' behaviors on SNS, they were asked to choose the top three from a list of practices in relation to posting and checking information. The top three practices are checking friends' posts (74 %), updating personal information (65 %), and following posts (51 %). As to the practices in relation to sharing and commenting, the top 3 are sharing private messages (64 %), sharing personal information (62 %), and activities related to gaming (39 %).

As to online forum, close to half of our respondents (49 %) acknowledged that they visited forums. More students from senior level (55 %) have visited online forums than had junior level students (41 %). Another important aspect of online participation concerns online sharing and creativity. In this respect, 31 % of them have uploaded files for sharing on the Internet. Among these, 83 % uploaded self-created photos or graphics and 60 % for the sharing of self-created notes; 69 % have uploaded both self-created audio or video files online.

14.5.2.2 Use of Technologies for Learning

An objective of the study is to determine to what extent technologies are used for school-related work. To achieve this, we first asked the students to rate (on a 5-point scale from "never" to "frequently") their frequency of searching for information for schoolwork. Websites are ranked as the top source of information related to schoolwork (M=4.01, SD=1.08) followed by classmates (M=3.78, SD=1.20). Printed materials such as books, magazines and newspaper (M=3.41, SD=1.28), and family members (M=3.15, SD=1.37) are also common sources for information. However, the students are less likely to turn to blogs (M=2.97, SD=1.39), private tutors (M=2.89, SD=1.48), and forums (M=2.75, 1.38).

We also asked the SNS users to rate the frequency of using SNS for school-related work on a 5-point scale (same as above). The result shows that the students did not visit SNS frequently for learning purposes as the means of all the activities are below 3.0. None of the participants rated their learning-associated activities on SNS as frequent. 26 % and 31 % of the students often and sometimes discuss homework or group projects there. A similar percentage of respondents often (27 %) and sometimes (35 %) asked for help on problems through SNS. In this respect, girls tend to ask for help through SNS sites (M=2.82, SD=1.03) more than boys (M=2.51, SD=1.19) (t (363)=−2.57, p<.01). Senior form students (M=2.80, SD=1.07) are more active in seeking help on SNS sites than juniors (M=2.45, SD=1.17) (t (363)=−2.97, p<.01).

We also asked the students to rate the frequency of their use of technologies in support of group work on a 5-point scale (same as above). Among the respondents from this one school, 73 % have experienced working in group projects and they most often meet face-to-face when engaged in this practice (M=4.33, SD=1.01). Instant messaging (IM) is the second popular tool (M=3.57, SD=1.38) followed by phone calls (M=3.39, SD=1.35). Besides this, students also communicate via SNS (M=3.38, SD=1.37), and SMS (M=3.28, SD=1.42) in group works. There is no significant difference in these practices between boys and girls, but senior form students are more active in using IM for group communication (M=3.81, SD=1.17) than the lower forms (M=3.29, SD=1.54), t (342)=−3.56, p<.01.

When the students face homework problems, just over a third (37 %) meet face-to-face or turn to SNS sites for help (37 %). And a third (35 %) call someone to seek for help and just slightly less (32 %) state that they search for solutions or advice online. Fewer students use instant messaging (14 %) compared to using SNS and there is even less use of emails (4 %), SMS messaging (6 %), and leaving messages online (10 %). More girls liked to ask homework questions via IM (girls 37 %, boys 28 %) and SMS (girls 10 %, boys 3 %) than boys. When comparing students across different grade levels, more junior students prefer leaving messages online and waiting for answers than senior grade students (junior 14 %, senior 6 %).

14.6 Discussion and Conclusion

The present study explores Hong Kong secondary school students' engagement with digital devices – mobile phone and computer – in out-of-school settings and seeks to compare youth's use of digital tools for personal and school-related purposes.

14.6.1 Use of Mobile Phone and Computer Outside School

Our data, first and foremost, confirms the prevalence of digital technologies in the life of Hong Kong youth. Smartphones have become widely adopted by over 85 % of the students under study. Another trend worth noting is that the smartphone has surpassed computer as the most frequently used device outside school. Looking more closely into how the youth use mobile phone, it has been revealed that they use text messaging more often than voice-based communication. This lends support to the pervasiveness of text messaging in teenager's life reported by other studies (Lenhart 2012).

The participants in our study also reported different usage patterns for mobile phone and computers, some expected, others are not. Unsurprisingly, mobile phones were employed mostly for communication, be it through text or voice; computers were employed more for document processing tasks and file download or upload. The students' overall engagement with media processing and production was greater than expected with the majority engaged in practices using both computer and phone.

The exploration into their online behaviors shows that these Hong Kong youth are avid users of SNSs. Facebook is unquestionably the most popular SNS. On social networking platforms, students are mostly engaged in social activities such as checking friends' status and updating their information. In contrast, the students are slightly less interested in online forums of any kind. The level of participation in sharing self-created work (e.g., photos, audio/video files, and documents like notes) was even lower with around one third of students acknowledging such activities. It seems that although many students were engaged in media production, they were not keen on sharing their work online.

14.6.2 Use of Technologies for School-Related Work

Against the backdrop of the prevalence of technologies in teen's out-of-school life, we pose the question: how do students use these technologies for school-related work? Specifically, we probed into how students used technologies for searching for information, doing group work, and problem-solving when doing homework.

Considering the pivotal role of the Internet in our daily life, it is by no means surprising that websites have been the most sought-after resource for learning-related information. Looking into the extent that digital engagement was used for group work, we found that although the students are still depending on face-to-face communication the most, they are, to a considerable degree, engaging with technological tools such as IM, SNS, and SMS. Furthermore, half of all students acknowledge their use of Facebook for school-related work such as discussing homework, seeking help, and facilitating group work at least sometimes. Admittedly, their use of SNS for learning purpose might not be as extensively and frequently as for personal and social purposes. However, when there is a need to consult other students, SNS plays an equally important role as do face-to-face meetings. It is also worth noting that only 6 % of our respondents chose SMS to discuss homework problems. This posits a drastic contrast to the pervasiveness of text messaging in youth's daily life.

14.6.3 The Effects of Age and Gender on Digital Engagement

We also examined the effects of age and gender on students' engagement with mobile phone and computers. Gender seems to be the less influential one. Boys and girls show many more similarities than they do differences. The only gender difference is that boys are more engaged with gaming devices while the girls tend to use social networking site to seek help with problems related to their study.

Age appears to be an indicator of difference between students' digital engagement. More senior students have smartphones than younger students. Senior students are more active in online forums and tend to employ more digital tools for learning. They tend to use SNS to ask for help with study-related problems and are more likely to employ emails and Instant Messenger for group work than do their junior counterparts.

To sum up, the exploration of Hong Kong youth's engagement with digital devices outside school confirms our belief that youth are avid use of smartphones and computers. On the whole, although there are noted differences between digital engagement (using mobile phones and computers) related to social life practices on the one hand and school-related work on the other, our research is revealing that the importance of technology especially SNS for learning is on the rise.

Our research is deepening understandings concerning Hong Kong youth's engagement with digital technologies outside school contexts. It affords enhanced awareness, for researchers, practitioners, and policy-makers, of the problem of home-school discrepancies and informs the discussion on how to better leverage digital technologies for learning in- and out-of-school contexts.

References

Attwell, G. (2007). Personal learning environments – The future of eLearning? *eLearning Papers, 2*(1), 1–7.

Ben-David Kolikant, Y. (2012). Using ICT for school purposes: Is there a student-school disconnect? *Computers & Education, 59*(3), 907–914. doi:10.1016/j.compedu.2012.04.012.

Clark, W., Logan, K., Luckin, R., Mee, A., & Oliver, M. (2009). Beyond Web 2.0: Mapping the technology landscapes of young learners. *Journal of Computer Assisted Learning, 25*(1), 56–69. doi:10.1111/j.1365-2729.2008.00305.x.

Conole, G., de Laat, M., Dillon, T., & Darby, J. (2006). *JISC LXP: Student experiences of technologies*. Southampton: University of Southampton. Retrieved from www.jisc.ac.uk/elp_learneroutcomes.html

Deepwell, F., & Malik, S. (2008). On campus, but out of class: An investigation into students' experiences of learning technologies in their self-directed study. *ALT-J, 16*(1), 5–14. doi:10.1080/09687760701850166.

Furlong, J., & Davies, C. (2012). Young people, new technologies and learning at home: Taking context seriously. *Oxford Review of Education, 38*(1), 45–62. doi:10.1080/03054985.2011.577944.
Kennedy, G. E., Judd, T. S., Churchward, A., Gray, K., & Krause, K. (2008). First year students' experiences with technology: Are they really digital natives. *Australasian Journal of Educational Technology, 24*(1), 108–122.
Kent, N., & Facer, K. (2004). Different worlds? A comparison of young people's home and school ICT use. *Journal of Computer Assisted Learning, 20*(6), 440–455. doi:10.1111/j.1365-2729.2004.00102.x.
Kirkwood, A., & Price, L. (2005). Learners and learning in the twenty-first century: What do we know about students' attitudes towards and experiences of information and communication technologies that will help us design courses? *Studies in Higher Education, 30*(3), 257–274. doi:10.1080/03075070500095689.
Lai, C., & Gu, M. (2011). Self-regulated out-of-class language learning with technology. *Computer Assisted Language Learning, 24*(4), 317–335. doi:10.1080/09588221.2011.568417.
Lenhart, A. (2012). *Teens, smartphones & texting*. Washington, DC: Pew Internet & American Life Project.
Levin, D., & Arafeh, S. (2002). *The digital disconnect: The widening gap between Internet-savvy students and their schools*. Washington, DC: Pew Internet and American Life Project.
Lewin, C. (2004). Access and use of technologies in the home in the UK: Implications for the curriculum. *Curriculum Journal, 15*(2), 139–154. doi:10.1080/0958517042000226801.
Selwyn, N. (2006). Exploring the "digital disconnect" between net-savvy students and their schools. *Learning, Media and Technology, 31*(1), 5–17. doi:10.1080/17439880500515416.
Smith, S. D., & Caruso, J. B. (2010). *The ECAR study of undergraduate students and information technology, 2010*. Boulder: Educause.
Vaughan, N., Nickle, T., Silovs, J., & Zimmer, J. (2011). Moving to their own beat: Exploring how students use web 2.0 technologies to support group work outside of class time. *Journal of Interactive Online Learning, 10*(3), 113–127.
Volman, M., & van Eck, E. (2001). Gender equity and information technology in education: The second decade. *Review of Educational Research, 71*(4), 613–634. doi:10.3102/00346543071004613.

Chapter 15
Building up a Knowledge Repository in a School

Kai Wing Chu

Abstract In the twenty-first century, schools have to face challenges because of societal changes and education reforms. Knowledge management (KM) has been widely used to help business sectors leverage knowledge to increase their competitive advantage in such era of erratic change. KM may be the possible solutions for schools to face changes. Before the full scale of KM implementation, schools can firstly build up their knowledge repository to retain their knowledge. In this paper, the researched school has built up the Knowledge Base as its knowledge repository to retain knowledge and also facilitate knowledge sharing among teachers in the school.

Keywords Knowledge management (KM) • Information-based approach • Knowledge repository

15.1 Theoretical Foundation

In a knowledge-based society, knowledge has been recognized as a strategic intangible asset and a vital resource in any organization (Nonaka and Takeuchi 1995).

15.1.1 Knowledge Management (KM)

In this paper, the definition of KM developed by Alavi and Leidner (2001) as 'the systematic process of acquiring, organizing, and communicating the knowledge of organizational members so that others can make use of it to be more efficient and productive' (Alavi and Leidner 2001; 114). Thus, in this paper, KM is used to establish an environment to foster organizational members to create, share, learn and use knowledge together for the organizational advantages. Two approaches developed by Dalkir (2011) have been adopted to be used in this paper.

K.W. Chu (✉)
CCC Heep Woh College, Kowloon, Hong Kong
e-mail: chukw@ccchwc.edu.hk

© Springer Science+Business Media Singapore 2015

W.W.K. Ma et al. (eds.), *New Media, Knowledge Practices and Multiliteracies*,
DOI 10.1007/978-981-287-209-8_15

- Information-based approach:
  This approach established an electronic platform for knowledge storage, retrieval and sharing.
- People/interaction-based approach:
  This approach focuses on knowledge sharing interactions among organizational members to form communities of practice (CoPs).

15.1.2 KM in Schools

Schools seem to be not only lagging behind compared with that in business sectors in introducing KM as a practice and also ignoring the essence of knowledge (Sallis and Jones 2002). Teachers do not share knowledge freely with their colleagues (OECD 2004). However, educational institutions and systems should more effectively collect, disseminate and share knowledge in the school context so as to improve their services and outcomes (Petrides and Nodine 2003). KM should be widely applied in schools to foster the 'sharing of innovative practice, avoiding duplication and discouraging the loss of valuable knowledge' similar to the business organizations benefited by KM implementation (Thambi and O'Toole 2012). Thus, this paper claims that KM should be applied in the education sector for leveraging intellectual capitals in schools.

15.2 Methodology

The study attempts to explore how a knowledge repository can be established with action research methodology to examine the effectiveness of the process.

15.2.1 Action-Based Research Method

Action research (AR) can allow practitioners to examine and reflect on their practice (McNiff and Whitehead 2006) through systematic data collection and analysis and also reflection of the result. In this study, steps of 'diagnosis, action planning, intervention and reflection' (Davison et al. 2004) was adopted.

15.2.2 The Researched School

The school in this study is a secondary school in which the researcher has served as the principal. The school is a fully government-subsidized secondary school in Hong Kong with students around 1,100, number of classes (about 30), number of teachers (60–65) and number of support staff (30). The school provides integrated secondary school education including junior high school and senior high school (grades 7–12).

15.3 Diagnosis and Action Planning

In this stage, the researcher uses the result of the two pilot studies and his observation for identifying the needs of this study and formulate action plans to fulfil the needs of the school.

15.3.1 Pilot Studies

Before the core part of the study was conducted, a pilot study was performed to understand teachers' perception of the KM concept and its implementation. The pilot studies identified the problems in investigating KM implementation in a school (Chu et al. 2009, 2011). After understanding teachers' perception of KM implementation from the pilot studies, strategies for KM implementation were devised and implemented.

15.3.2 Problem Identification and Proposing Actions

From the result of the pilot study and the researcher's observation, the researcher was able to make a list of the problems in managing knowledge.

Problems Identified

- Unawareness of knowledge as a key intangible asset of schools
- Failure to equip teachers with practical knowledge by promoting knowledge sharing
- Unsystematic document management system with little functionalities in searching and retrieval

Based on the identified problems, the researcher proposes the corresponding actions to address the problems with the interventions followed.

15.4 Intervention

The aim of the information-based approach is to focus primarily on providing necessary knowledge storage to enable the sharing of knowledge among teachers by establishing a school knowledge repository. In this study, an information-based approach of KM implementation has been achieved mainly through the use of the platform, 'Knowledge Base', for building the knowledge repository.

In 2009–2010, a school-based portal called Knowledge Base was developed to share information teachers need in a single entry. At present, there are several functions: academic analysis, check mark, students' photo, teachers' notices, students' lateness, students' homework submission record, students' uniform, school documents templates, room reservation, etc.

15.4.1 Academic Analysis

The Knowledge Base compiles all the information teachers need. Teachers could choose which information to be compared and to be showed. The system can show the improvement or decline of students' academic performance individually or in class or in form and also in each subject or in all subjects (Fig. 15.1).

Analysis Result:

	Year: 2012-2013, Class: 3A	English Language - Junior 2011-2012 Class	T1	T2
1	[redacted]	2C	64.9 [86/181]	64.8 (↓0.2%) [107/181]
2		3B	56.3 [172/188]	53.7 (↓4.6%) [182/188]
3		3C	53.5 [184/188]	52.1 (↓2.6%) [185/188]
4		2A	68.7 [71/181]	72.1 (↑4.9%) [74/181]
5		2C	49.3 [165/181]	52.5 (↑6.5%) [164/181]
6		2D	57.3 [123/181]	58.7 (↑2.4%) [137/181]
7		2C	64.3 [89/181]	63.7 (↓0.9%) [109/181]
8		**2D	57.3 [123/181]	58.9 (↑2.8%) [136/181]
9		2E	67.6 [75/181]	66.9 (↓1.0%) [97/181]
10		3B	51.4 [187/188]	48.1 (↓6.4%) [188/188]
11		2E	62.8 [95/181]	71.5 (↑13.9%) [79/181]
12		2D	62.1 [99/181]	60.2 (↓3.1%) [124/181]
13		2D	47.9 [170/181]	52.3 (↑9.2%) [165/181]
14		2C	60.7 [108/181]	59.6 (↓1.8%) [128/181]
15		**2D	52.5 [153/181]	57.1 (↑8.8%) [142/181]
16		2E	58.3 [116/181]	66.8 (↑14.6%) [98/181]
17		**2E	58.1 [118/181]	59.4 (↑2.2%) [130/181]
18		2E	51.6 [157/181]	51.2 (↓0.8%) [167/181]
19		**2C	56.1 [130/181]	60.6 (↑8.0%) [122/181]
20		2D	57.6 [121/181]	56.1 (↓2.6%) [149/181]
21		**2E	65.7 [80/181]	70.4 (↑7.2%) [84/181]
22		2A	62.3 [98/181]	67.0 (↑7.5%) [96/181]
23		2D	58.7 [114/181]	57.7 (↓1.7%) [138/181]
24		2E	60.3 [110/181]	65.3 (↑8.3%) [105/181]
25		2C	58.7 [114/181]	59.6 (↑1.5%) [128/181]
26		2C	54.8 [133/181]	56.2 (↑2.6%) [148/181]
27		2D	73.4 [36/181]	77.7 (↑5.9%) [38/181]
28		2D	58.3 [116/181]	63.6 (↑9.1%) [110/181]
29		2C	61.7 [102/181]	59.0 (↓4.4%) [135/181]
30		2C	54.4 [139/181]	54.5 (↑0.2%) [156/181]
31		2D	53.1 [147/181]	47.0 (↓11.5%) [171/181]
32		2C	51.3 [158/181]	53.5 (↑4.3%) [161/181]
33		2D	61.2 [106/181]	59.1 (↓3.4%) [134/181]
34		2E	53.4 [144/181]	54.9 (↑2.8%) [154/181]

Fig. 15.1 The academic analysis function of knowledge base

15.4.2 Students' Lateness, Students' Uniform and Students' Homework Submission

Besides academic achievement, the Knowledge Base can also allow staff to access other students' data, such as students' performance in attendance, school uniform and homework submission. Teachers, especially class teachers, can trace tightly students' performance and give them help just in time (Fig. 15.2).

Similarly, students with uniform irregularities records will also be shown on the Knowledge Base (Fig. 15.3).

In recent stage of the development, the abovementioned records have been compiled into a dashboard mode to integrate with several data sources to give a comprehensive performance to class teachers, so that class teachers could conveniently obtain overall image of students' performance. If they think certain students need guidance and care, they could take action according to the data they have. Thus, teachers' intervention on students could be more evidence based with data support.

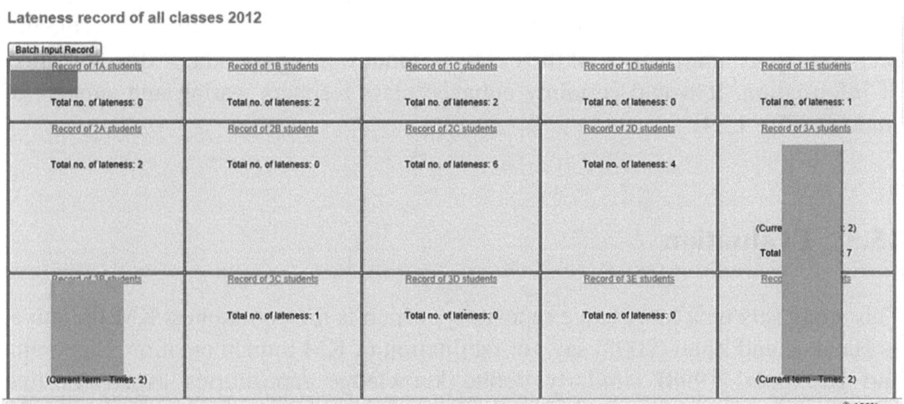

Fig. 15.2 The student lateness function of knowledge base

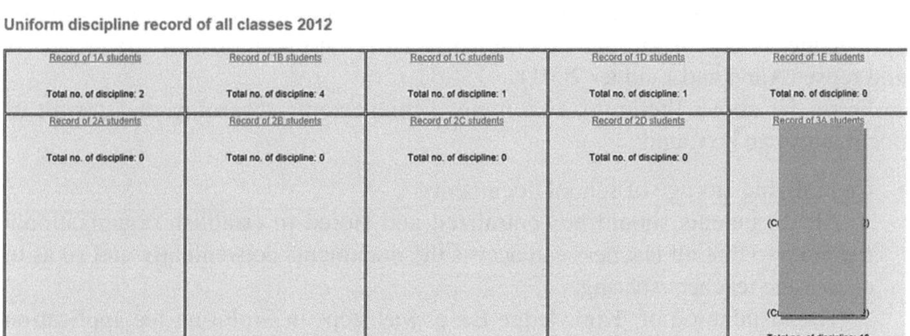

Fig. 15.3 The uniform irregularities record function of knowledge base

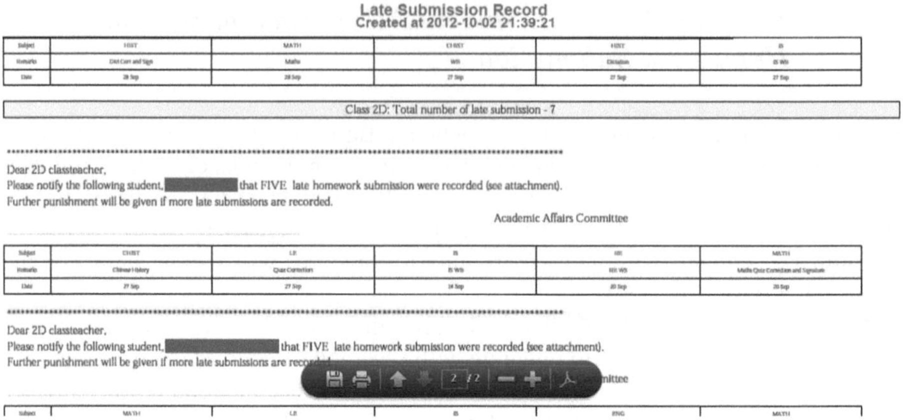

Fig. 15.4 The homework late submission record function of knowledge base

The PDF report with compiled information could be saved in less storage space and easily opened in any computer. Class teachers could easily and more conveniently access students' information of their class without waiting for others' dissemination of information. It would certainly enhance class teachers' caring and support to students (Fig. 15.4).

15.5 Evaluation

This study sets up a knowledge repository, which is the commonest KM initiative, as Handzic and Zhou (2005) say, for facilitation of KM implementation. Liebowitz and Beckman (1998) similarly define knowledge repositories as an 'on-line computer-based storehouse of expertise, knowledge, experiences, and documentation about a domain of expertise. In creating a knowledge repository, knowledge is collected, summarized, and integrated across sources.' The objective of building knowledge repositories as a central storage was to capture and keep organizational knowledge as organizational experience or corporate memories for later access and reuse (Alavi and Leidner 2001).

From the above literature, two major achievements regarding the storing of documents can be found:

- Centralizing storage of school documents

  All documents should be centralized and stored to establish organizational memory so that all teachers can access the documents conveniently and so as to encourage teachers sharing.

  The installation of 'Knowledge Base' was steps in exploring the application of the conceptualization of a knowledge repository in the school. Knowledge Base was designed to integrate different kinds of information, such as student photos, students' behavioural records, students' academic records and analysis so that teachers could access the information conveniently thereby facilitating knowledge use. Because the information in the Knowledge Base was uploaded by the school, teachers were not required to upload their information.

The researcher collected data from both observation and interview and found that teachers usually stored their documents in their desktop and notebook computers, but only Department Heads and Committee Heads were aware of the needs to keep their documents in the repository. It might be related to their customs and awareness to the school's needs. Department Heads and Committee Heads were more aware of the school's needs, so they were used to store knowledge simultaneously at the school repository.

- Enhancing usage of the stored documents by teachers
  Fayyad and Uthurusamy (2002) pointed out that the organizational ability of knowledge retention has exceeded that of knowledge utilization so that such organizational memories might easily become 'tombs'. Documents, information and even knowledge stored in the repository might be seldom used after uploading the documents in the repository. The storage of documents alone in the repository does not facilitate knowledge sharing and the process of KM. Thus, one of the most challenging research questions with regard to building effective knowledge repositories for organizations was to find technologies (tools and methods) that make stored knowledge more effective to be used rather than to be stored.

  Knowledge Base stored abundant students' information extracted from the school's Web-Based School Administration System (WEBSAMS) with analysis. The content of the stored information was found to be critical for teachers' motivation to access. The information was reorganized and analysed to identify whether there were patterns for monitoring students' academic performance. Such information was used to be restricted in some middle managers and administrators in schools. However, class teachers, with the aid of the KM system, could easily access the information to check whether their students have improvement or not. Subject Department Heads were able to retrieve the academic performance of the students easily and to organize appropriate action to help our students. For example, Subject Department Heads might organize remedial lessons to the students who got the performance under standard score.

  The researcher conducted some informal interviews with teachers and asked them about the usability of Knowledge Base. Teachers expressed their appreciation for the design of the Knowledge Base because they regarded the information stored in the repository was very useful. Teachers have also given some suggestions, e.g. compiling students' behavioural information in a class to produce a PDF page for class teachers' convenience, so that teachers can easily monitor the behavioural performance of the students and take corresponding action to them. The suggestion was adopted and the system was upgraded correspondingly.

On the other hand, the researcher used a school-based teacher questionnaire to collect teachers' views related to KM implementation for evaluating KM efforts.

Table 15.1 Results of school-based teacher questionnaire 2010–2011

School year 2010–2011	5	4	3	2	1	Average
Q1. I think that our school has tried to develop, store and share resources for teaching resources of NSS curriculum	1	24	12	5	0	3.50
Q2. I think that the colleagues would like to share their teaching experience and skills with others, which gradually inculcate sharing culture	0	24	13	5	0	3.45
Q3. I think that the colleagues are trying to accumulate and categorize teaching resources for retrieval in the future	0	25	15	1	1	3.52

Remarks: 5, strongly agree; 4, agree; 3, neutral; 2, disagree; 1, strongly disagree

The school administrators administered a survey using a school-based teacher questionnaire soliciting teachers' views on the school's major concerns in the school year 2010–2011. The questionnaires were distributed to all teachers to solicit their feedback on their opinions. Forty-two out of sixty teachers (70 %) finished the questionnaire and returned it to school office. All questionnaires were filled anonymously to protect personal privacy. Table 15.1 shows the result of the school-based questionnaire of the school regarding KM implementation in 2010–2011. From the result of the survey, most teachers (Q1 average = 3.50) agreed that the school has tried to develop, store and share resources for teaching resources of New Senior Secondary (NSS) curriculum. They have observed that the resources have been built up for facilitating sharing resources among teachers. Moreover, most teachers (Q2 average = 3.45) agreed that the colleagues would like to share their teaching experience and skills with others, which gradually inculcate sharing culture. They seemed to have experience that colleagues shared their teaching experience and skills with others. Finally, most teachers (Q3 average = 3.52) agreed that the colleagues are trying to accumulate and categorize teaching resources for retrieval in the future. Teachers did notice that colleagues have been starting to save and file teaching resources for convenient retrieval in the future.

A similar questionnaire was also administered in school year 2011–2012.

The school administrators administered a survey using a school-based teacher questionnaire soliciting teachers' view on the school major concerns in the school year in the school year 2011–2012. The questionnaire was different from that of 2011–2012; there was an additional part asking teachers' opinion on the necessity of the major concerns to be continued in the coming 3 years 2012–2015. The questionnaires were distributed to all teachers to solicit their feedback on their opinions. Sixty-five out of sixty-seven teachers (97 %) finished the questionnaire and returned

Table 15.2 Results of school-based teacher questionnaire 2011–2012

School year 2011–2012	5	4	3	2	1	Average
Q1. I am satisfied with setting up KM core team in 2011–2012	1	14	49	1	0	3.18
Q2. I am satisfied with building a knowledge sharing platform on intranet in 2011–2012	4	28	31	2	1	3.48
Q3. I am satisfied with promoting knowledge sharing in our school in 2011–2012	4	29	30	2	1	3.50
Q4. I am satisfied with developing, storing and sharing teaching resources in 2011–2012	5	37	21	2	1	3.65
Q5. I think that building up a knowledge sharing platform on intranet should be continually implemented in 2012–2015	6	36	22	1	0	3.67
Q6. I think that promoting knowledge sharing in our school should be continually implemented in 2012–2015	7	40	16	2	0	3.74
Q7. I think that developing, storing and sharing teaching resources should be continually implemented in 2012–2015	12	42	11	0	0	3.95
Q8. I think that forming communities of practice (CoPs) should be continually implemented in 2012–2015	3	27	31	4	0	3.39

Remarks: 5, strongly agree; 4, agree; 3, neutral; 2, disagree; 1, strongly disagree

it to school office. All questionnaires were filled anonymously to protect personal privacy. Table 15.2 shows the result of the school-based questionnaire of the school B regarding KM implementation in 2011–2012.

From the result of the survey, most questions received a positive response. From the evaluation of performance in 2011–2012, the highest score (3.65) could be found for Q.4, which teachers agreed that resources were developed, stored and shared in the school. This initiative should be continued in 2012–2015 (Q.7, average = 3.95). Most teachers agreed that the school performance in 'building up a knowledge sharing platform on intranet' (Q.2 average = 3.48) and 'promoting knowledge sharing in our school' (Q.3 average = 3.50) was satisfactory in 2011–2012. Teachers also agreed that the two abovementioned initiatives 'building up a knowledge sharing platform on intranet' (Q.5 average = 3.67) and 'promoting knowledge sharing in our school' (Q.6 average = 3.74) should be continued in 2012–2015, and also there are increasing trends in sustaining the initiatives in 2012–2015. Nevertheless, teachers seemed have reservations about the school performance of setting up KM core team (Q1. average = 3.18). On the other hand, forming communities of practice (CoP) (Q.8. average = 3.39)) should be sustained in 2012–2015.

Conclusion

The school has recognized knowledge as their strategic intangible asset and key resource. The experience that the school has retained the knowledge for sharing among members can make a contribution to KM theories and practice, because few studies have been conducted in a school setting; this study, which was conducted in a school, could serve as a model case.

This study sets up a knowledge repository not only to compile information in centralized storage but also to foster teachers to access such information for further analysis and following-up action to those students in need, so that teachers can take care to their students. Before building up such repository, most data and information has only been retained within the school administrators and middle managers. Frontline teachers could not easily access such valuable information. After such information has been shared, the school administrators and middle managers can share not only the information with teachers but also share know-how to take care of students with most teachers. Knowledge sharing in the school can be enhanced by providing necessary information to be accessed by teachers. Then, the whole school can have collaboration to take acute and immediate response to students who may have problems identified from students' information. The school can help students perform better with both teachers' assistance and administrative support with collegiality and synergy.

On the other hand, the school has already stepped further to develop knowledge by further enhancement in knowledge sharing in the other approach – people/interaction-based approach. However, owing to the limitation of space, the author cannot present the progress of the people/interaction-based approach.

References

Alavi, M., & Leidner, D. (2001). Knowledge management and knowledge management systems: Conceptual foundations and research issues. *MIS Quarterly, 25*(1), 107–136.

Chu, K. W., Wang, M. H., Zhou, S. H., Yuen, H. K. A. (2009). Teacher perception of knowledge management: A case study in a secondary school. In *Proceedings of the 2009 4th international conference on e-learning, Toronto, Canada,* 16–17 July 2009.

Chu, K. W., Wang, M. H., & Yuen, H. K. A. (2011). Implementing knowledge management in school environment: Teacher perception. *Knowledge Management & E-Learning: An International Journal, 3*(2), 139–152.

Dalkir, K. (2011). *Knowledge management in theory and practice*. Cambridge: MIT.

Davison, R., Martinsons, M., & Kock, N. (2004). Principles of canonical action research. *Information System Journal, 14*, 65–86.

Fayyad, U., & Uthurusamy, R. (2002). Evolving into data mining solutions for insight. *Communications of the ACM, 45*(8), 28–31.

Handzic, M., & Zhou, A. Z. (2005). *Knowledge management: An integrative approach*. Oxford: Chandos Publishing.

Liebowitz, J., & Beckman, T. J. (1998). *Knowledge organizations: What every manager should know*. Boca Raton: CRC Press.
McNiff, J., & Whitehead, J. (2006). *All you need to know about action research*. London: Sage.
Nonaka, I., & Takeuchi, H. (1995). *The knowledge-creating company: How Japanese companies create the dynamics of innovation*. New York: Oxford University Press.
Organisation for Economic Co-operation and Development. (2004). *Raising the quality of educational performance at school*. Paris: OECD.
Petrides, L. A., & Nodine, T. R. (2003). *Knowledge management in education: Defining the landscape* (Report). Half Moon Bay: Institute for the Study of Knowledge Management in Education.
Sallis, E., & Jones, G. (2002). *Knowledge management in education: Enhancing learning & education*. New York: Psychology Press.
Thambi, M., & O'Toole, P. (2012). Applying a knowledge management taxonomy to secondary schools. *School Leadership & Management, 32*(1), 91–102.

Chapter 16
Smartphone Usage, Social Relations and Life Satisfaction of Hong Kong College Students

Raymond Chi Fai Chui

Abstract Does smartphone usage relate to individual well-being? This study examined the relationship between smartphone usage, social relations and life satisfaction of Hong Kong college students. A cross-sectional survey study was administered to 244 male and 399 female college students aged 18–27 years from nine universities in Hong Kong. Results indicated that smartphone usage had a negative association with peer relations and family relations, while it had a positive relationship with life satisfaction. Moreover, peer and family relations were positively associated with life satisfaction. These results suggested that smartphone usage had a positive direct relationship with life satisfaction and a negative indirect relationship with it. Finally, peer and family relations were found to suppress the positive association between smartphone usage and life satisfaction.

Keywords Smartphone usage • Life satisfaction • Social relations • College students

16.1 Introduction

The usage of smartphones has become an indispensable part of one's personal life. Apart from using smartphone to communicate with others, it can be used to browse the Internet, search for information, play online and offline games, access to social networking services, and utilize various software applications for working purposes. The multiple functions of smartphone attract a large number of people to adopt and use it. The smartphone penetration rate in Hong Kong is 62.8 %, while the mobile Internet usage rate is the highest in the Asia Pacific region with 95.6 % going online everyday (Our Mobile Planet 2013). Moreover, 71.2 % Hong Kong users used smartphone for social networking. Yet, the use of social networking mobile applications is associated with smartphone addiction which is likely to cause psychosocial problems (Salehan and Negahban 2013). Therefore, the public has

R.C.F. Chui (✉)
Department of Social Work and Community Research Centre,
Hong Kong Shue Yan University, Hong Kong, China
e-mail: cfchui@hksyu.edu

© Springer Science+Business Media Singapore 2015

W.W.K. Ma et al. (eds.), *New Media, Knowledge Practices and Multiliteracies*,
DOI 10.1007/978-981-287-209-8_16

raised concerns over the maladaptive and addictive use of smartphone. Meanwhile, comparing to other user groups, college students had a more rapid adoption of smartphone usage (Lepp et al. 2014). Given the high smartphone adoption rate and usage for social networking, it is worthwhile to explore the level of smartphone usage of college students in Hong Kong.

16.2 Smartphone Usage and Life Satisfaction

Related to the psychological well-being of college students, the influence of smartphone addiction is similar to that of the Internet addiction (Beranuy et al. 2009). There are different constructs of psychological well-being, including: stress, depression, anxiety, loneliness, and life satisfaction. Overdependence on smartphone led to the compulsive usage and could become a stressor (Lee et al. 2014). Kraut et al. (1998) suggested that Internet addiction created a sense of isolation and loneliness because it reduced the user's interaction with the real world. Studies have also revealed that mobile phone addiction was associated with anxiety (Hong et al. 2012), stress (Lee et al. 2014; Thomee et al. 2011), depression (Lu et al. 2011), and life satisfaction (Lepp et al. 2014). The motivations for smartphone usage were also indirectly related to loneliness, self-esteem, and depression (Namsu Park and Lee 2012). Addictive mobile phone usage created anxiety due to the overwhelming obligation of individuals to remain constantly connected to various social networks through the mobile phone (Merlo 2008). Mobile phone users were expected to be reachable at all times (Thomee et al. 2011). Therefore, intensive mobile phone usage can disturb the sleeping quality.

Although the above studies indicated the negative association between smartphone use and individual well-being, they had some limitations. Lee et al. (2014) focused only on the relationship of smartphone usage with stress. Namsu Park and Lee (2012) explored the association of individual well-being with the motivations of smartphone usage rather than the level of smartphone usage. Lepp et al. (2014) was the only study focused on the smartphone usage and life satisfaction of college students, but the sample was limited to one university in the United States.

Life satisfaction is the perception of an individual on one's life. As it is one of the major constructs that reflect the quality of life and positive states of individuals (Diener et al. 1999), this paper uses life satisfaction as an indicator of individual subjective well-being. In order to supplement existing research, this study examines the association between smartphone usage and life satisfaction of college students. This study tests whether the result is similar in Hong Kong to that in previous studies, with an anticipation that:

H1: Smartphone usage is negatively related with life satisfaction.

16.3 Smartphone Usage and Social Relations

Smartphone is an important communication tool which college students like to use to maintain close social ties. The motivations for smartphone usage of college students was positive related to bonding relations (Namkee Park et al. 2013). Mobile phones allow users to connect with other people without any space and time limitations, and can be used to provide information about the location and time of social activities. A study on adolescents found that mobile phones provided a direct communication channel for adolescent users to connect with their peer groups and parents that enhanced their social interactions and relations (Kalogeraki and Papadaki 2010). Mobile phones created a sense of independence and autonomy from family and made the adolescent closely connected to their peer groups, while they serve as coordinating devices that increased the interactions among family members. A study on college students had a similar result that mobile phones provided direct contact with family members (Chen and Katz 2009). College students used mobile phones to share experience, obtain support from their family members, and help to fulfill family caring roles. Hence, using a mobile phone can generate trust and enhance parent-child relations. The above studies suggested that a smartphone is a social communication tool which can facilitate family and peer relations. This study wants to find out whether the usage of smartphones is positively related to social relations as suggested by previous studies. It is proposed that:

H2: Smartphone usage is positively related with peer relations and family relations.

16.4 Family Relations, Peer Relations, and Life Satisfaction

The quality of social relations was significantly associated with life satisfaction (Diener et al. 1999). Family relations and peer relations were positively associated with adolescents' life satisfaction across different cultures (Schwarz et al. 2012). Family relations are important to the happiness in life in Chinese societies which emphasize family values (Chang 2007). Parent-child relations are important to Chinese adolescents because the feeling of acceptance and approval from parents are emphasized under the tradition of filial piety in this collectivist society (Leung and Zhang 2000). Hence, life satisfaction was positively associated with parent-child relations among Hong Kong Chinese adolescents. Moreover, more positive family functioning was a predictor of better adolescent life satisfaction (Shek 1998).

Friendships are especially important during adolescence which is in the stage of identity formation and developing independence (Bukowski et al. 2009). Friendships help adolescents to fulfill developmental needs. The importance of friendship continues from adolescence to the young adult. If the young adult cannot have stable and long-lasting relations with others, they may feel being isolated and their personal development and well-being will worsen (Crain 2011). The effects of peer relations on life satisfaction could extend into the middle adulthood (Marion et al. 2013). Peer rejection led to poor self-esteem, adjustment difficulties, and loneliness. Therefore, the following hypothesis is derived:

H3: Peer relations and family relations mediate the relationship between a smartphone and life satisfaction.

16.5 Data Collection and Measurements

16.5.1 Procedure and Participants

A cross-sectional quantitative survey was conducted in this study. Data were collected between January and February 2014. College students in nine universities in Hong Kong were invited to participate. A self-administered questionnaire was distributed to the college students in these universities through student research helpers. A total number of 643 questionnaires were returned. Thirty-eight percent of the respondents were male and 62 % were female. Respondents' age ranged from 18 to 27 years ($M = 20.93$, $SD = 1.32$).

16.5.2 Measures

The four variables were assessed via self-report measures. Smartphone usage was assessed by the smartphone addiction scale (SAS) (Kwon et al. 2013). It is a 33-item index scored on a 6-point Likert scale. The higher score represents more serious smartphone addiction. Life satisfaction was assessed via the Satisfaction with Life Scale (SWLS) that reflects the positive side of an individuals' experience (Pavot and Diener 2009). This 5-item instrument scored on a 7-point Likert scale. The higher score represents higher levels of life satisfaction. Peer relations were assessed by the Index of Peer Relations (IPR). It is a 25-item instrument scored on a 5-point Likert scale (Hudson 1990). The higher score represents fewer peer relation problems. The Index of Family Relations (IFR) was used to measure family relations of respondents. It is a 25-item scale scored on a 7-point Likert scale (Hudson 1997). The higher score indicates lower severity of problems that participants have in their relations with family members. All these scales were highly reliable, with a Cronbach's alpha between 0.891 and 0.956.

16.6 Results

16.6.1 Bivariate Analyses

Table 16.1 indicates the bivariate correlations among the study variables. As predicted, peer relations and family relations were positively related to life satisfaction. Participants who had better peer relations and better family relations reported greater life satisfaction. However, in contrast to the hypothesis, smartphone usage was inversely related to peer relations and family relations. Participants who had higher level of usage reported poor peer relations and family relations. Moreover, smartphone usage was not related to life satisfaction.

16.6.2 Multivariate Analyses

Hierarchical regression analysis was applied in the study to examine the relationships among smartphone usage, peer relations, family relations, and life satisfaction. Listwise deletion was used to handle missing data in the regression. Table 16.2

Table 16.1 Correlation matrix of dependent (life satisfaction) and independent variables

	Variable			
Variable	1	2	3	4
1 Life satisfaction	–			
2 Peer relations	.337***	–		
3 Family relations	.387***	.395***	–	
4 Smartphone usage	.032	–.204***	–.116**	–

Note. * $p<.05$; ** $p<.01$; *** $p<.001$

Table 16.2 Multiple regression analyses: smartphone usage, peer relations, family relations, and life satisfaction

	Life satisfaction		
Variables	*B* (Coefficients)	*β* (Standardized beta)	*t*
Smartphone usage	0.007	.028	.677
R^2	.001		
Smartphone usage	0.031	.111	2.987**
Peer relations	0.120	.237	5.804***
Family relations	0.080	.307	7.723***
R^2	.202		
R^2 change	.201***		

Note. * $p<.05$; ** $p<.01$; *** $p<.001$

indicates the results of the hierarchical regression analyses. Smartphone usage was entered in the first block. Peer relations and family relations were entered in the second block. The results showed that smartphone usage was not related to life satisfaction in the first block. However, when peers relations and family relations were added to the model in the second block, smartphone usage was significantly positive in association with life satisfaction. Peer relations and family relations also had a significantly positive relationship with life satisfaction. These three variables explained 20.4 % of the variance in life satisfaction. Those with higher levels of peer relations and family relations had higher levels of life satisfaction. In contrast to the hypothesis, those with higher levels of smartphone usage had higher levels of life satisfaction.

A Sobel test (Sobel 1982) was employed to test the mediating effect of peer relations and family relations on the association between smartphone usage and life satisfaction. Results of the Sobel test indicated that the mediating effect was significant. The relationships between smartphone usage and life satisfaction were partially mediated through peer relations ($Z = -3.90, p < .001$) and family relations ($Z = -2.81$, $p = .005$). As shown in Table 16.2, smartphone usage has a negative indirect association and a positive direct association with life satisfaction. Smartphone usage has a negative and modest relationship with peer relations ($\beta = -.204, p < .001$) and family relations ($\beta = -.116$, $p = .003$); whereas peer relations have a positive and modest relationship with life satisfaction ($\beta = .237$, $p < .001$), and family relations have a positive and moderate relationship with life satisfaction ($\beta = -307$, $p < .001$). However, smartphone usage has a positive and direct modest relationship with life satisfaction ($\beta = .111, p = .003$).

16.7 Discussions

Smartphone usage had a positive direct relationship with life satisfaction and a negative indirect association with it through peer and family relations. The relationship between smartphone usage and life satisfaction was not significant in the bivariate analysis, but the relationship was significant in multiple analyses after controlling peer relations and family relations. Peer relations and family relations were found suppressing the positive relationship between smartphone usage and life satisfaction. Smartphone usage had a significant negative relationship with peer relations and family relations. At the same time, these two variables had a significant positive relationship with life satisfaction. These results created a suppression effect on the relationship between smartphone usage and life satisfaction.

Inconsistent with previous studies, smartphone usage was found to be positively related to life satisfaction. One of the possible explanations is that life satisfaction reflects the positive experience of individuals. Satisfaction can be obtained when positive experience gained from the smartphone usage in various entertaining purposes. For example, high level of physiological and aesthetic leisure satisfaction from online games was associated with high level of life satisfaction (Wang et al. 2008). However, the positive influence of smartphone usage needs to be clarified in further study by using other well-being measures.

This study is meaningful that it indicates the inverse association between smartphone usage and social relations. This finding is consistent with previous studies on the Internet that excessive and problematic usage was associated with poor quality of interpersonal relations (Liu and Kuo 2007; Milani et al. 2009). Excessive Internet users tend to spend less time to talk to peers and family members and participate in social activities (Suhail and Bargees 2006). All these supported that the overuse of smartphone in inappropriate ways may worsen social relations. Therefore, appropriate usages of smartphone should be promoted among college students.

There are a few limitations in this study. This is a cross-sectional study that fails to test the causal influences between variables. Therefore, a longitudinal study is necessary to test the predictive effects of the variables. Moreover, convenient sampling lacks a good sampling frame for a dispersed population and lacks evidence for representativeness so that the findings may not be generalized to all college students. In order to improve the generalizability of this study, probability and random sampling approach should be employed in the future studies.

References

Beranuy, M., Oberst, U., Carbonell, X., & Chamarro, A. (2009). Problematic Internet and mobile phone use and clinical symptoms in college students: The role of emotional intelligence. *Computers in Human Behavior, 25*(5), 1182–1187. doi:http://dx.doi.org/10.1016/j.chb.2009.03.001.

Bukowski, W. M., Motzoi, C., & Meyer, F. (2009). Friendship as process, function, and outcome. In K. H. Rubin, W. M. Bukowski, & B. Laursen (Eds.), *Handbook of peer interactions, relationships, and groups, social, emotional, and personality development in context* (pp. 217–231). New York: Cambridge University Press.

Chang, H. (2007). Depressive symptom manifestation and help-seeking among Chinese college students in Taiwan. *International Journal of Psychology, 42*(3), 200–206. doi:10.1080/00207590600878665.

Chen, Y.-F., & Katz, J. E. (2009). Extending family to school life: College students' use of the mobile phone. *International Journal of Human-Computer Studies, 67*(2), 179–191. doi:http://dx.doi.org/10.1016/j.ijhcs.2008.09.002.

Crain, W. (2011). *Theories of development: Concepts and applications*. Pearson: Upper Saddle River.

Diener, E., Suh, E. M., Lucas, R. E., & Smith, H. L. (1999). Subjective well-being: Three decades of progress. *Psychological Bulletin, 125*(2), 276–302.

Hong, F.-Y., Chiu, S.-I., & Huang, D.-H. (2012). A model of the relationship between psychological characteristics, mobile phone addiction and use of mobile phones by Taiwanese university female students. *Computers in Human Behavior, 28*(6), 2152–2159. doi:http://dx.doi.org/10.1016/j.chb.2c012.06.020.

Hudson, W. (1990). A short-form scale to measure peer relations dysfunction. *Journal of Social Service Research, 13*(4), 57–69. doi:10.1300/J079v13n04_04.

Hudson, W. (1997). *The WALMYR assessment scales scoring manual*. Tallahassee: WALMYR Publishing Company.

Kalogeraki, S., & Papadaki, M. (2010). The impact of mobile use on teenagers' socialization. *International Journal of Interdisciplinary Social Sciences, 5*(4), 121–134.

Kraut, R., Patterson, M., Lundmark, V., Kiesler, S., Mukopadhyaay, T., & Scherlis, W. (1998). Internet paradox: A social technology that reduces social involvement and psychological well-being? *American Psychologist, 53*(9), 1017–1031.

Kwon, M., Lee, J.-Y., Won, W.-Y., Park, J.-W., Min, J.-A., Hahn, C., Gu, X., Choi, J. H., & Kim, D.-J. (2013). Development and validation of a Smartphone Addiction Scale (SAS). *PLoS ONE, 8*(2), 1–7. doi:10.1371/journal.pone.0056936.

Lee, Y.-K., Chang, C.-T., Lin, Y., & Cheng, Z.-H. (2014). The dark side of smartphone usage: Psychological traits, compulsive behavior and technostress. *Computers in Human Behavior, 31*, 373–383. doi:http://dx.doi.org/10.1016/j.chb.2013.10.047.

Lepp, A., Barkley, J. E., & Karpinski, A. C. (2014). The relationship between cell phone use, academic performance, anxiety, and satisfaction with life in college students. *Computers in Human Behavior, 31*, 343–350. doi:http://dx.doi.org/10.1016/j.chb.2013.10.049.

Leung, J.-P., & Zhang, L.-W. (2000). Modelling life satisfaction of Chinese adolescents in Hong Kong. *International Journal of Behavioral Development, 24*(1), 99–104. doi:10.1080/016502500383520.

Liu, C.-Y., & Kuo, F.-Y. (2007). A study of Internet addiction through the lens of the interpersonal theory. *Cyberpsychology & Behavior: The Impact of the Internet, Multimedia and Virtual Reality on Behavior and Society, 10*(6), 799–804.

Lu, X., Watanabe, J., Liu, Q., Uji, M., Shono, M., & Kitamura, T. (2011). Internet and mobile phone text-messaging dependency: Factor structure and correlation with dysphoric mood among Japanese adults. *Computers in Human Behavior, 27*(5), 1702–1709.

Marion, D., Laursen, B., Zettergren, P., & Bergman, L. (2013). Predicting life satisfaction during middle adulthood from peer relationships during mid-adolescence. *Journal of Youth and Adolescence, 42*(8), 1299–1307. doi:10.1007/s10964-013-9969-6.

Merlo, L. (2008). Increased cell phone use may heighten symptoms of anxiety. *Primary Psychiatry, 15*(5), 27–28.

Milani, L., Osualdella, D., & Di Blasio, P. (2009). Quality of interpersonal relationships and problematic Internet use in adolescence. *CyberPsychology & Behavior, 12*(6), 681–684. doi:10.1089/cpb.2009.0071.

Our Mobile Planet. (2013). *Smartphone penetration*. Retrieved May 14, 2014, from http://think.withgoogle.com/mobileplanet/en/graph/?country=hk&category=DETAILS&topic=Q00&stat=Q00_1&wave=2013&age=all&gender=all&chart_type=&active=country

Park, N., & Lee, H. (2012). Social implications of smartphone use: Korean college students' smartphone use and psychological well-being. *CyberPsychology, Behavior & Social Networking, 15*(9), 491–497. doi:10.1089/cyber.2011.0580.

Park, N., Kim, Y.-C., Shon, H. Y., & Shim, H. (2013). Factors influencing smartphone use and dependency in South Korea. *Computers in Human Behavior, 29*(4), 1763–1770. doi:http://dx.doi.org/10.1016/j.chb.2013.02.008.

Pavot, W., & Diener, E. (2009). Review of the satisfaction with life scale. In E. Diener (Ed.), *Assessing well-being: The collected works of Ed Diener* (pp. 101–117). Dordrecht: Springer.

Salehan, M., & Negahban, A. (2013). Social networking on smartphones: When mobile phones become addictive. *Computers in Human Behavior, 29*(6), 2632–2639. doi:http://dx.doi.org/10.1016/j.chb.2013.07.003.

Schwarz, B., Mayer, B., Gisela, T., Ben-Arieh, A., Friedlmeier, M., Lubiewska, K., Mishra, R. & Peltzer, K. (2012). Does the importance of parent and peer relationships for adolescents' life satisfaction vary across cultures? *The Journal of Early Adolescence, 32*(1), 55–80. doi:10.1177/0272431611419508.

Shek, D. T. L. (1998). Longitudinal study of the relationship between family functioning and adolescent psychological well-being. *Journal of Youth Studies, 1*(2), 195–209.

Sobel, M. E. (1982). Asymptotic intervals for indirect effects in structural equations models. In S. Leinhart (Ed.), *Sociological methodology* (pp. 290–312). San Francisco: Jossey-Bass.

Suhail, K., & Bargees, Z. (2006). Effects of excessive internet use on undergraduate students in Pakistan. *CyberPsychology & Behavior, 9*(3), 297–307. doi:10.1089/cpb.2006.9.297.

Thomee, S., Harenstam, A., & Hagberg, M. (2011). Mobile phone use and stress, sleep disturbances, and symptoms of depression among young adults – A prospective cohort study. *BMC Public Health, 11*(1), 66–76.

Wang, E. S.-T., Chen, L. S.-L., Lin, J. Y.-C., & Wang, M. C.-H. (2008). The relationship between leisure satisfaction and life satisfaction of adolescents concerning online games. *Adolescence, 43*(169), 177–184.

Chapter 17
Concept of Cultural Differences Between Chinese and Western University Culture Based on the Idea of Isomerism

Chengen Li, Tieshan Hou, and Liang Chang

Abstract Chinese higher education has entered the stage of connotative development, and the important status of university culture as the main position of university soft power construction is unceasingly highlighting. Chinese modern university, as an exotic adopted from western university system, is always the most violent domain of east-west cultural exchange and confrontation. For a long time, in the development of Chinese university culture, influence from western university system has always been an unavoidable confusion. Through analysis and comparison, the Chinese and western university cultures can be regarded as isomers, which is a concept based on chemistry, the differences and conflicts between which are the results of isomerism. Through the analysis of isomerism between the Chinese and western university cultures, this paper proposed and constructed the university culture "isomers model," which provides a new research paradigm for the construction and development of Chinese characteristic university culture.

Keywords Chinese culture • Western culture • University cultures • Isomer • Cultural differences • Paradigm

---

Project supported by the National Social Science Fund of China (Grant No. 10BSH029) and Socialist theory and the union development research subject of Dalian University of Technology.

C. Li
Faculty of Humanities and Social Science, Dalian University of Technology,
Dalian, Liaoning China
e-mail: licn@dlut.edu.cn

T. Hou
Faculty of Management and Economics, Dalian University of Technology,
Dalian, Liaoning China
e-mail: htieshan@263.com

L. Chang (✉)
School of Physics and optoelectronic Technology, Dalian University of Technology,
Dalian, Liaoning China
e-mail: changl@dlut.edu.cn

© Springer Science+Business Media Singapore 2015

W.W.K. Ma et al. (eds.), *New Media, Knowledge Practices and Multiliteracies*,
DOI 10.1007/978-981-287-209-8_17

17.1 Introduction

Culture is the nation's blood, and it is also the spiritual home of the people. Since the 18th CPC National Congress, China's higher education cause has entered the connotative development stage, with a focus on quality improvement. The third plenary session of the 18th CPC national congress has approved "The decision to deepen reforms on several major issues comprehensively," which formally kicked off the reform program. Under the new circumstances, the CCP, the governments of all levels, and the higher educational world have realized that without first-class culture, there is no first-class university. And Chinese characteristic university culture will become a powerful drive for connotative development of Chinese higher education. Therefore, research on university culture and its construction is a very basic, strategic, and prospective program (Yun 2002).

In recent years, university culture as a hot topic in higher education research has been paid more and more attention. But in current research, there are two problems that should not be ignored. One problem is that because modern Chinese university is "exotic," with a history of only about a 100 years. Hence, in the research on university culture, many researchers will naturally pay more attention to the birthplace of modern university—universities in Europe and the United States, which gradually formed the research tendency that European and American university cultures are supreme. The other problem is that most studies are macroscopic instead of microscopic, with a low feasibility. At the same time, the basic structure of university culture, the relationship among university culture constitutes, and the priority issues are neglected, and the research methods have a lot of limitations. Analysis shows that the main reason for the two tendencies lies in the limitations of the research scope and research method (Wu 2013). Therefore, the author attempts to take the "university of science and technology" as the perspective of study, analyze the constitutes of university culture, and screen the key factors in the structure, in a bid to come up with a new approach to establish and promote Chinese characteristic university culture system.

17.1.1 "The Western Confusion" in the Process of Developing Chinese University Culture

Chinese university culture has undergone three historical stages. The first stage extended from pre-Qin period to the end of the Qing Dynasty, with Jixia Academy, ancient college, Imperial College, and academies appeared in succession. They undertook the function of higher education institutions and constituted the "classical" type of university in China. Of course, strictly speaking, these institutions cannot be called universities in the real sense, but their main features and functions are very similar. For Chinese universities at this stage, the biggest feature is that they were closely integrated with Confucianism, which almost remained unchanged over 2,000 years of feudal society. So this stage is called classical Chinese university culture. The second stage began in the Westernization Movement in the late Qing Dynasty and lasted till the new China was established. This stage is an important period for the establishment and development of real sense modern Chinese university, which echoed the transformation of Chinese modern society. Peiyang University and Peking University were the earliest modern Chinese transplantations of western university system. Over the past 100 years, modern Chinese university first transplanted Japanese university and then followed the example of European style and finally converted to American mode. At this stage, the dominant western culture caused severe impact on the Chinese traditional culture, with university becoming the most intense field for the confrontation. In general, Chinese university culture in this stage was more influenced by western culture than that of the east, which produced far-reaching effect on the development of modern Chinese society. The third stage began from the establishment of the PRC and has gone through continuous development and prosperity. Thus, Chinese university entered a new era. In the past 60 years, Chinese university experienced twists and turns, but the importance of university culture has gradually been acknowledged and gained concern from all sectors of society. Especially since the reform and opening up, various cultural thoughts became one of the most notable features for this stage of university culture. For a time, the construction of university culture has become the hot topic of research in higher education, with all thoughts and practices surging in.

In recent years, in theoretical study and in the practice of establishing Chinese university culture, there occurred disagreement and debates on how to treat the culture differences between the Chinese and western university cultures. Some researchers think that after 800 years of development, the western modern university is very heavy in culture and has formed a mature university culture development pattern. While with only 100-year-old history, it is natural for Chinese university to learn from the west and model on it, and this practice is also widely adopted by domestic colleges and universities. Of course, there are also some universities and researchers who believe that China has accumulated a rich cultural heritage, and the renaissance of traditional Chinese culture has become a trend. Besides, there are great differences in culture heritage, values, ideology and social development level, and social systems. So, in the collision and interaction, the drive for culture identity and the objection to western culture have both been aroused in the culture choice of Chinese university. Even today, researchers still obsess over the choice between Chinese and western inclination. Therefore, how to look at the east-west cultural differences scientifically, rationally, and objectively and how to make the Chinese and western university cultures reconcile and borrow from each other, i.e., "the western confusion," have become unavoidable problems that we have to resolve.

17.2 The Phenomenon of a Preliminary Study of University Cultural Isomerism

17.2.1 Isomers and Isomerism

To follow up the research on the topic of east-west university culture differences, conflicts, and fusion, the concepts of "isomer" and "isomerism" are introduced here in this paper. Isomers are chemical concepts, referring to organic compounds with the same molecular formula, but different atomic arrangements (see Fig. 17.1.). Isomerism refers to the phenomenon of isomers having the same molecular formula, but with different spatial structures. Moreover, isomers have different physical and chemical properties, and isomerism exists widely in organic compounds. Isomerism is mainly caused by heterogeneous carbon chain, heterogeneous functional group position, and heterogeneous functional group category. A small change in atomic arrangement or functional group coupling position will lead to varieties in physical and chemical properties.

17.2.2 Criterion for Chinese and Western University Culture Isomerism

This paper claims that Chinese and western university cultures are a pair of isomers. First of all, this judgment is based on the Chinese and western civilizations' consensus on the constitutes of university culture that both Chinese and western university cultures are made up of spiritual culture, material culture, behavior culture, and system culture. This consensus confirms that both cultures have the same molecular structure. Secondly, Chinese and foreign researchers generally believe that university culture is divine, ideal, inclusive, invasive, scholarly, critical, historical, national, and unique, which means that they have the same or similar functions. The fundamental reason for university culture differences is that the functional groups, i.e., the expressive bearers of university culture, are heterogeneous in arrangement and category, giving rise to isomerism between university cultures.

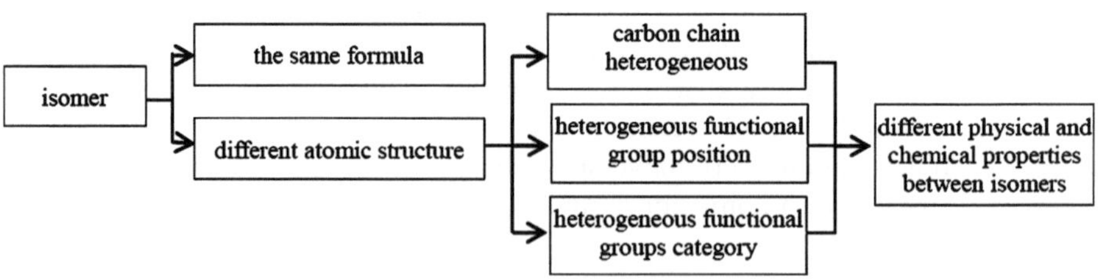

Fig. 17.1 Isomers concept diagram

17.2.3 The Meaning and Value of the Chinese and Western University Culture Isomerism

Research and insights into isomerism between Chinese and western university cultures help scientifically illustrate the conflicts and differences between them; help explore ways to compare, to refer to, and to integrate; and help cultivate the common ground, discard differences, and draw on experiences from the west in the process of establishing Chinese characteristic university culture, making it possible to employ what is good in the western university culture and to compensate our own culture creation. Thus, isomerism is the dialectical unity of Chinese and western university cultures and the kernel consistency between them.

17.3 Manifestations of University Cultural Isomerism

17.3.1 Overview of Isomerism Phenomenon Between Chinese and Western University Cultures

First, the historical origins of Chinese and western cultures are similar. Being an important part of the social culture, both were derived from the local culture and were closely related with social production and lifestyle, social structure, political system, ideology, and ways of thinking of different historical periods (Liao 2012). University culture of any country and any time has the common way of existence and cultural traits (Liu 2006). Civilization is the inherent value of culture; culture is the external form of civilization. The world's first-class universities, such as Harvard, Yale, Oxford, Cambridge, etc., without exception, almost all have distinct humanity traditions, a kind of spirit, and a kind of thinking throughout its entire history (Xian 2006). Therefore, higher education institutions, who shoulder the mission of culture inheritance, have become the common choice for the development of ancient civilizations both in the east and in the west. In the Chinese and foreign history of higher education, from the ancient colleges in West Zhou Dynasty to the academies in Song and Ming Dynasties, from the "Athens Lyceum" of ancient Greek, till the medieval and modern university, the aim of their establishment may differ greatly, but their function in culture inheritance is consistent.

Second, early Chinese and western university cultures both had some religious overtones. Modern university originated in Europe, and European University developed from grammar schools and convents of the church, so the cultural origin of modern university system is the medieval Christian culture (Wu 2013).

Religious cultural heritage of western university culture, such as the opening ceremony, degree and awarding ceremony, etc., is still partially preserved, in the teaching and research aspects of modern university. With more than 2,000 years under the rule of feudal monarchy, Chinese classical university culture was featured with Confucianism, and Buddhism, Taoism, and the traditional Confucian "Rites" had a history tab of Chinese classical university culture.

Third, both university culture in the east and west has the same educational function. Among all the functions of university culture, educational function is the primary one (Sun 2008). University culture, as the social identified norm and ideology, has education as its ontological function, with "literacy education" being the kernel content and "civilizing" being the basic method (Han 2009). This is because the relationship between culture and human is twofold. On the one hand, it is the relation between the subject and the object; culture is the objectification of human intrinsic power (Li 2006). It is man who created culture. On the other hand, culture, once formed, will become the growth environment, with ontological meaning for human existence. As Marx said: "people created the environment, and also, will be created by the environment" (Marx and Engels 2003). The subject of university culture is "people" in the university, but the object of university culture is also "university people." While creating university culture, university people also found themselves first unconsciously and then consciously shaped by the university culture (Han 2009). Chinese and western university cultures have their own cultural characteristics and unique forms of manifestation, but the pursuit of truth and the essence of talent cultivation are the same (Zhou 2008). Talent cultivation here is not confined to imparting knowledge and skills, but is based on Sue Home Linsky's (B.A. Cyxomjnhcknn) assertion of "cultivating the all-round development of people," which is in line with the traditional Chinese educational idea of "cultivating virtuous people." The educational function of university culture is reflected in how it guides, constraints, motivates, restrains, infiltrates, shapes, and influences university people and how the education helps in the formation of ideology and value consensus gradually, like the rain moistening things silently. Therefore, educational function is the common core of Chinese and western university cultures.

17.3.2 Overview of Isomerism Between Chinese and Western University Cultures

Although Chinese and western university cultures share the come core content, their evolution was restrained by different local civilization, history, geography, nationality, and basic national conditions. They became so different that there occurred violent conflicts in the process of interaction, exchange, and confrontation, which exactly reflected the existence of the typical "heterogeneous" phenomenon between Chinese and western university cultures.

Samuel Huntington (Huntington Samuel P), the renowned American political scientist, believes that university culture roots in the national culture, because the university knowledge production and transmission are closely associated with the symbols and values of social culture, making it possible for college culture to communicate with social culture fundamentally (Wu 2013). Therefore, originating from the European Renaissance period, western modern university culture bears the distinct characteristics of capitalist culture, the most distinctive feature of which is the support for the freedom, autonomy, and independence, the pursuit of them, and the encouragement for them. The inside and outside manifestations of western university culture are closely related with the European tradition of Christian culture, the long city-state system and civil society, and are a result of the combined effects of these factors (Liao 2012). In contrast, the ancient institutions of Chinese higher education and their goal never deviated from proclaiming "feudal loyalty." What the education advocated was "wherever you are, you are the king's servant." As ancient Chinese, higher education was always tightly attached to the feudal monarchy, cultivating national consciousness, meeting the real-life demand, and stressing cultural tradition, and cultural setting became the main characteristics classical Chinese university culture. On the one hand, it boosted and succeeded the glorious and resplendent ancient Chinese civilization. On the other hand, it also helped achieve the longest feudal society in the world. These features of classical Chinese university culture are obviously quite different from that of the western university, with the latter in pursuit of independence, freedom, and innovation. Even today, there are still traces of history in modern Chinese university culture.

Although Chinese modern university is the product of copying western university system, it has also inherited some characteristics of Chinese classical university culture. For example, Chinese university in history stressed the importance of school motto and the culture condensed from the motto and stressed the importance of cultivating students' spiritual state. After the founding of new China, as a result of copying the Russian model comprehensively, although to some extent, there occurred the regression of university culture, universities in China turned out to be stereotyped in culture and there was a lack of variety. Since the reform and opening up, China universities have achieved rapid development, with university culture connotation constantly enriched. Cultural inheritance and innovation has become the fourth social function of universities in the new era. At present, there is a spurt in the number of universities. But in terms of quality, their university cultures seem to be a bit premature, which, in time, will result in the "calcium deficiency" phenomenon. Therefore, the central government has made the timely strategic decision of "promoting connotation development of higher education." The construction of university culture with Chinese characteristics has become the first and foremost task, and its priority should be ensured.

In short, the "isomerism" in Chinese and western university cultures, especially in modern university cultures, is collectively shown in the fact that the renowned universities in Europe and America all have such a long history that they have formed their own characteristics in their tradition of humanism, science and technology, and industrialization and in the confronting development between civil society and the state. Chinese university culture, on the other hand, stresses national consciousness and highlights the social norm and individuals' self-discipline. University culture in Europe and the United States stresses technological rationality and individual freedom and highlights behavior norm and strength in nature (Zhou 2008).

17.4 Research Paradigm on University Culture Based on Isomerism Phenomenon

University culture is the foundation of university and the soul of university. To establish Chinese characteristic university culture, the premise is to accurately identify university culture and on the basis of which, to explore a practical model for cultural construction (Li and Peng 2008). Based on the preliminary judgment of isomers, and for the convenience of intensive study and thinking, this paper takes "Geert Hofstede's Cultural Onion model" and "Edward Fulton Denison's Organizational Culture model" as references and is attempting to establish a Model of Isomers (as is shown in Fig. 17.2).

Model of isomer between Chinese and western university cultures is made up of A, B, and C, three functional zones. Wherein, A represents the common "molecular skeleton" shared by Chinese and western university cultures. The skeleton is a kind of similar to the benzene ring structure of the conjugated system, with educational function at the core of university culture. Function Zone B represents the functional groups connected to the "molecular skeleton," and this area is the main functional area which gives rise to "heterogeneous" phenomenon/isomerism of Chinese and western university cultures. Note that the functional groups displayed in the model are only a part of the whole function, with more functional groups to be identified and screened in future studies. Function Zone C is the social cultural area, showing that

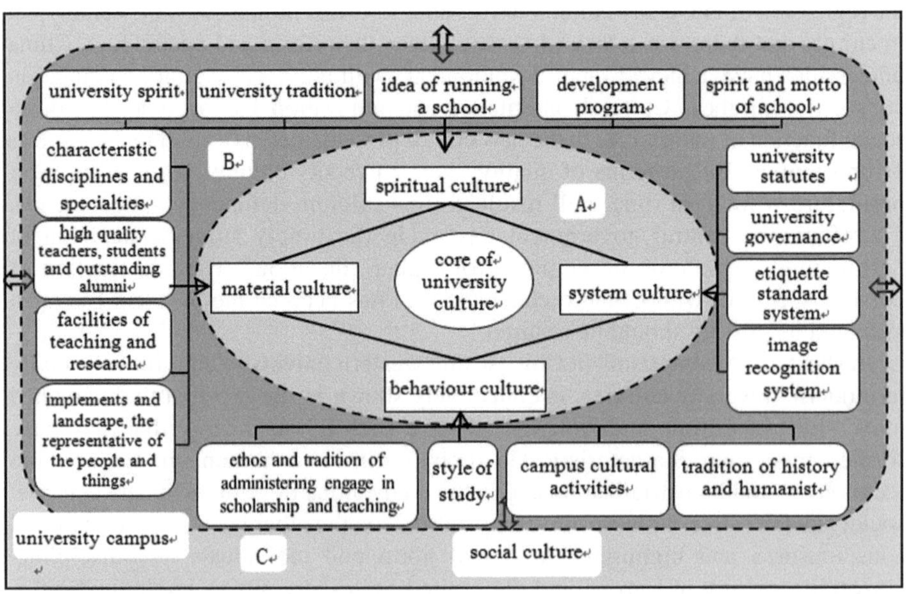

Fig. 17.2 Model of isomer between Chinese and western university culture

university culture is a subculture of social culture. Zone A and Zone B together form different university cultures, with campus being the boundary between them, which illustrates the interdependent relationship between university and university culture. At the same time, university culture and society culture remain relatively independent of each other, but there also exist mutual influence and interaction.

From the model of isomer between Chinese and western university cultures, we can see that differences and conflicts mainly come from "functional group position isomerism" or "functional group category isomerism" phenomenon in Function Zone B. The main reason for the isomerism is the influence of functional Zone C on the structure and categories of functional groups in Zone B. In the process of building Chinese characteristic university culture, researches and explorations should take Chinese characteristic (Zone C) and university culture (Zone A) as the two basic themes. Meanwhile, according to the model of isomer, by taking grip of the inherent laws of university culture development (Zone A), we should explore and screen all good traits in both Chinese and western university cultures (focusing on Zone B) and do some in-depth studies about the structures and categories of the functional groups behind these traits. In addition to this, we should note the internal and external conditions that facilitate the functional groups, and under the guidance of Chinese characteristic socialist culture (Zone C), we should try to transform functional groups (Zone B), so as to adapt to the construction and development of Chinese characteristic university culture. University culture constitutes an important part of advanced socialist culture. University culture and social cultures echo each other and exert influence on each other (Wang 2005). Chinese characteristic university culture will radiate towards the whole social culture and hence realize the support and guidance of advanced socialist culture.

References

Han, Y. M. (2009). Strengthen the university culture education function. *Educational Research, 351*(4), 89–93.

Li, P. (2006). University culture kernel and innovation personnel training. *Higher Education in China, 4*, 19–21.

Li, L., & Peng, S. W. (2008). Cultural model and the construction of university culture. *Social Science of Human Normal University, 2*, 117–120.

Liao, K. B. (2012). Chinese university of China's cultural transformation: History, current situation and path. *Zhejiang Social Sciences, 2*, 12–23.

Liu, H. (2006). Concerning the characteristics of the university culture, evolution and function. *Higher Education Exploration, 3*, 29–32.

Marx, K., & Engels, F. (2003). *The German ideology*. Beijing: People's Publishing House.

Sun, L. (2008). Theory of education function and realization way of university culture. *Higher Education in China, 22*, 30–32.

Wang, J. S. (2005). The scientific connotation of university culture. *Journal of Higher Education, 10*, 5–10.

Wu, L. B. (2013). Chinese university cultural dilemma and cultural innovation. *China Higher Education Research, 6*, 43–47.

Xian, Y. (2006). *The story of the university*. Beijing: Petroleum Industry Press.
Yun, G. R. (2002). To strengthen the university cultural study and promote the construction of university culture. *China University Teaching, 10*, 4–5.
Zhou, H. H. (2008). University cultural studies. *Higher Education in China, 7*, 23–24.

Chapter 18
Exploring the Effectiveness of Blended Learning in Cost and Management Accounting: An Empirical Study

Suet Ching Chak and Heidi Fung

Abstract This paper focuses on the effectiveness of the online quizzes provided by the textbook companion website for accounting students. The main objective of this study is to investigate the relationship between student academic performance and the quantity of online quizzes they had completed. Additionally, it attempts to understand students' motives of taking the quizzes. The subjects of this study were 129 second-year accounting students enrolled in an undergraduate course of Cost and Management Accounting in a private university in fall of 2013. Results indicate that online quizzes make a positive impact on final exam score and the end-of-semester grade under the assumption of the students taking adequate amount of online quizzes throughout the semester. The student initiatives in taking online quiz without bonus marks may come from perceived usefulness, instructor encouragement, self-motivation, and peer pressure.

Keywords Blended learning • Online quiz • Textbook companion website • Cost accounting • Student initiative • Academic performance

18.1 Introduction

Information and communication technology (ICT) has affected every aspect of our society during the new millennium. There is no exception for established businesses such as textbook publishing. Although the majority of textbooks are still printed in traditional paper format, most of the companies have provided online supplemental textbook companion website (TCW) to give a convenient platform for both

S.C. Chak ACMA (✉)
Hong Kong Shue Yan University, Hong Kong, HKSAR, China

PhD Candidate in Finance, Shanghai University of Finanace and Economics, China
e-mail: scchak@hksyu.edu

H. Fung
Hong Kong Shue Yan University, Hong Kong, HKSAR, China
e-mail: heidi@hksyu.edu

© Springer Science+Business Media Singapore 2015

W.W.K. Ma et al. (eds.), *New Media, Knowledge Practices and Multiliteracies*,
DOI 10.1007/978-981-287-209-8_18

instructors and students. The content of the TCW usually comprises of PowerPoint slides, quizzes, extra readings, and journal articles. As most users assume TCW is an effective learning tool, not many researches have been conducted on this new way of learning. Before Fung and Ma's (2013) study, there was no concrete data which showed the effects of TCW to accounting education. This study extends Fung and Ma's examination to the courses of Cost and Management Accounting.

Our study examines the effectiveness of TCW online quizzes and its contribution to academic success. Our methodology is to compare the student academic performance (both final exam and end-of-semester grades in the course of Cost and Management Accounting) with the number of online quizzes they had completed. This study also aims to understand student initiative in taking the online quizzes on a voluntary basis without bonus mark. The aforementioned then raised two research questions:

RQ1. How does the number of quiz completed make a noticeable impact on student academic performance?

RQ2. What are the factors affecting student initiative in taking online quizzes voluntarily without bonus marks?

18.2 Literature Review

18.2.1 Online Quiz

Along with the accessibility of computer network, online quizzes have been integrated in many face-to-face (F2F) courses in higher education. It is generally believed that supplementary online materials improve student performance (Potacco et al. 2008; Smolira 2008). As a learning and assessment tool, online quizzes were designed to improve the quality of the student learning experience (Ramsaran-Fowdar et al. 2011). Some instructors use online quizzes to reinforce their students' understanding of the course content. Studies also agreed that online quizzes enhance student learning experience and teaching effectiveness in F2F courses (Johnson and Kiviniemi 2009; Peng 2011).

18.2.2 Benefits of TCW

Once the textbook is adopted, TCW provides course-related materials conveniently to students and instructors through the Internet as they can easily access the supplementary materials from anywhere at anytime. Because some publishers make TCW resources available to the public, especially the area designed for the students, the benefits of these online supplements are being shared by many users who have not paid for the textbooks. Moreover, the content variety and its flexibility accommodate the diverse needs of the students. On the other hand, instructors have also benefited from using the readily available resources to release some of their time from preparing the teaching materials and/or marking exercise and have more time for other required duties or professional development.

Online quizzes are the key component of the TCW. Students use online quizzes to summarize, revise, and test how much progress they have made during the learning process (Hadsell 2009; Johnson and Kiviniemi 2009; Jonas and Norman 2011; Potacco et al. 2008). Although acquiring new knowledge is not the intended purpose of online quizzes, computer-generated quiz results have the advantage of catching the errors immediately after the student has submitted the answers, and it makes them more aware of their own weaknesses. For the instructors, besides the convenient and automatic marking feature, TCW also provides the overall grade distribution and other concrete data of the student performance in different areas. This helps instructors in readjusting their teaching focus for better learning outcome.

18.2.3 Previous Studies on Textbook at Higher Education

In the existing literature, there are very few researches conducted on the use of textbooks and their TCW supplements at tertiary level (Jonas and Norman 2011; Sellnow et al. 2005; Vandsburger and Duncan-Daston 2011). Jonas and Norman (2011) examined the relationship between student characteristics and the voluntary participation in TCW at the entry-level accounting courses. The result suggested factors such as students' perceptions of usefulness, their ability to explain the benefits of usage, and peer usage of the TCW could positively affect students' usage behavior. Sellnow et al. (2005) investigated student perceptions on the usage of technological supplements that accompanied a textbook of public speaking. The result indicated that students found the supplements less useful than they expected except when the online materials were assigned by the instructors. Disappointedly, no major investigation has been conducted on the relationship between the effectiveness of the resources and learning outcome before 2013.

Noticing this research gap, Fung and Ma (2013) conducted a study on how TCW online quizzes affect student performance in the course of Accounting Information Systems. Besides reviewing students' opinions of TCW supplements, more important, their study examined how online quizzes impacted student academic performance. Their analysis indicated that students who took the online quizzes generally received higher scores in both midterm test and final exam. But it did not take the student performance before the online quizzes into consideration. Additionally, only two variables (not taken online quiz versus taken online quiz) and 10 respondents were examined in their study.

18.3 Methodology

This study was conducted in the context of Cost and Management Accounting, a second-year course offered by the Department of Accounting in a private university in Hong Kong. The accounting undergraduate degree is a 4-year full-time program of which most of the students enrolled at the age of 18 or 19.

18.3.1 Background of the Study

18.3.1.1 Cost and Management Accounting (Costing) Course

Cost and Management Accounting (Costing) is an operational-level course under the field of management accounting. The objectives of the course include (1) to provide students the quantitative skills on job costing, budgeting, and cost analysis and (2) to develop students' generic and quantitative skills and apply what they learned in making business decisions and evaluating performance. The textbook adopted in fall of 2013 was *Introduction to Managerial Accounting*, which includes 13 chapters. The course was planned to cover eight chapters of the textbook within the 15-week semester. The grading criteria included class participations (10 %), textbook exercises (10 %), a midterm (20 %), and a final exam (60 %). Both midterm and final are closed-book exams. The 2-h midterm consisted of multiple-choice (MC) questions (60 %) and short questions (40 %). As all of the midterm questions were quantitative oriented, students who had higher mathematical skills were likely to perform better. On the contrary, the 3-h long final exam included four to five questions which equally comprised of both mathematical and essay-type questions, so a good command of English writing and costing skills are both essential to succeed.

18.3.1.2 Costing Textbook Companion Website (TCW)

Online Learning Center, the student edition of the TCW of the adopted textbook, is a free website which categorizes its learning tools into different sections such as practice quiz, alternative problems, practice exam, as well as PowerPoint presentations with narrative descriptions. Each of the 13 chapters includes 10 MC questions except Chapter 8 which comes with 12. There is no time limit to complete the quizzes. These quizzes are marked simultaneously by the computer system. When a student finishes and clicks "submit answers," he/she will get the scores and the correct answer of each question immediately (see Fig. 18.1). The alternative problems and practice exam sections consist of long questions with answer provided at the end of each question. Since the website is not password protected, anyone can visit and download the materials.

It was optional for the students to email the quiz results to the instructor. The quiz result showed the number and percentage of the correct/incorrect answers the student made, and the questions completed by the student were also included. From the collected data, the instructor sorted out the areas which seemed to be more difficult for most students. This information is very helpful for refining future pedagogic strategy.

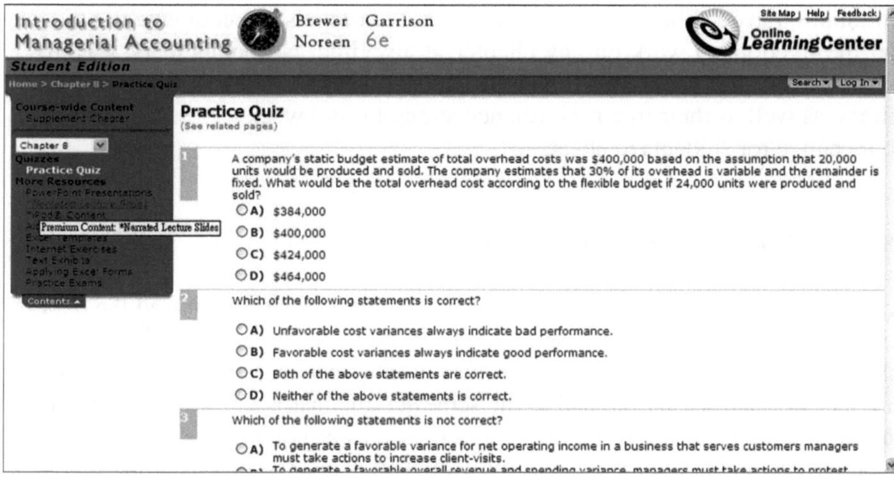

Fig. 18.1 An example of online quiz

18.3.2 Research Design

18.3.2.1 Subjects

The 129 participants in this research were the second-year accounting students who were required to take the course to meet their graduation requirements. There were five sections in the course and four of them taught by the same instructor and participated in the study. Each section consisted of around 31–33 students. Identical learning materials were distributed to the participants through ILN (Interactive Learning Network) which is a learning management system provided by the university. These learning materials included the important theories and exercises from the textbook but no MC question.

18.3.2.2 Lecturer's Influences

At the beginning of the semester, the instructor introduced the free textbook online learning platform in class. The instructor recommended that the students take the online quiz after studying each chapter and email the quiz results to him or her afterwards. Throughout the semester, the instructor kept reminding students to take the quizzes and then posted a submission list on ILN every 1 or 2 weeks. For privacy reason, the list only showed the student ID numbers but didn't show the test scores.

No submission deadline was set since it was not a compulsory requirement. Students had the freedom to work on any chapter at any time. No bonus mark was given because the instructor wanted to get the honest reflection of the students' voluntary efforts, as well as their true performance strengths and weaknesses. Hence there is no incentive for students to cheat.

18.3.2.3 Data Collection Procedures

After receiving the test scores through emails, the instructor organized the data by course sections. Information such as the dates of email delivery, dates quizzes were taken, test scores, and the question numbers of incorrect answers was all categorized in Excel worksheets. By the end of the semester, the instructor also added midterm and final exam scores, as well as the end-of-semester grade, onto the worksheets. In order to examine the progress of individual students, the grades of the first-year course, Introductory Accounting, was also added to the worksheet for comparison.

To acquire a general understanding of students' attitudes towards TCW and their initiatives in taking the online quiz, all the 129 participants were invited to take a voluntary and anonymous survey during class time by the end of the semester. The questionnaire included 36 questions which attempts to identify the student experience with TCW (see Appendix). Likert scale of seven was used for the questionnaire, and all the collected data was analyzed by SPSS.

18.4 Findings

During the semester, the instructor received a total of 563 emails reporting quiz results, and 335 of those were received before the midterm. As the midterm and online quizzes both were comprised of MC questions primarily, it is easy to explain why the student participations in taking the online quizzes from Chapters 1–4 were high. However, the instructor still received 228 emails (40 % of total) even after the midterm. The reporting emails also indicate the online quizzes were taken during the convenient time of the students, especially on the few days before the midterm and final exams were scheduled. Surprisingly, the instructor still received 14 reporting emails even after the final exam. Some students probably wish they could receive bonus mark when they performed poorly in the exam.

18.4.1 Descriptive Statistics of Variables

All participants were divided into nine subgroups based on the number (or frequency) of the chapters they completed. Group 0 represents the students who did not complete any quiz, while Group 8 represents the students who completed all eight chapters taught during the semester. The distribution of participation is shown in Fig. 18.2.

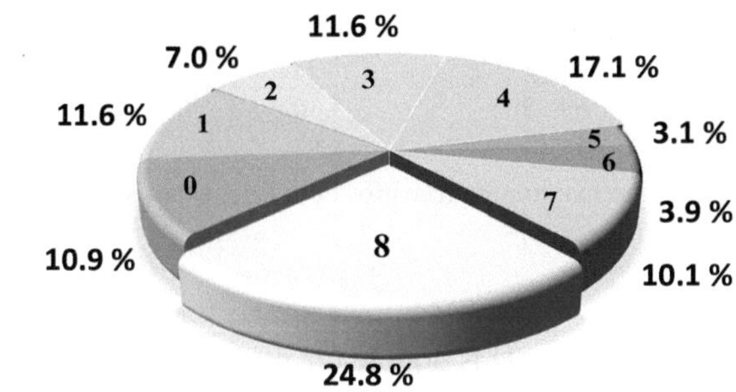

Sub group	N
0	14
1	15
2	9
3	15
4	22
5	4
6	5
7	13
8	32
Total	**129**

Fig. 18.2 Distribution of subgroups

Table 18.1 Description of the three main groups

Group	Category	Frequency*	*N*	%
L	Low motivated	0–2	38	29.4
M	Middle motivated	3–6	46	35.7
H	High motivated	7–8	45	34.9
		8	**129**	**100**

*Frequency is the number of chapter attempted by participants

There were 24.8 % (N=32) of participants who took all eight chapters, which is the highest number among all the subgroups. On the other hand, there were 10.9 % (N=14) of participants who did not take any online quiz.

In order to divide the total number of participants into three larger groups for more effective comparison, the nine subgroups were re-categorized into three main groups as follows: Group L (low motivated) with frequency 0–2, Group M (middle motivated) with frequency 3–6, and Group H (high motivated) with frequency 7–8. Afterwards, each of the three main groups consisted of approximately 1/3 of the participants (refer to Table 18.1).

18.4.2 Comparisons of Academic Results Between Groups

The scores of the online quizzes and final exam of each group are shown in Table 18.2. (Eighty-two is the maximum score for the online quizzes as each of the 82 MC questions weighs a point; the highest score for the final exam is 100 as usual.)

Group H, consisted of the highly motivated students who participated most frequently in the TCW, received the highest final exam score as expected. On the other hand, Group L, the least motivated group, also scored the lowest in the final.

Table 18.2 Summary of online quiz, final exam, and end-of-semester scores

Group	Online quiz	(1) Final exam	(2) End-of-semester	(2) minus (1) points uplifted by continuous assessment
L	7.08	62.28	64.21	1.93
M	32.57	65.85	69.35	3.50
H	64.60	70.87	75.44	4.57

The maximum score for online quiz is 82; the maximum scores for both final exam and end-of-semester grade are also 100

The number of online quizzes taken by Group H is double the number of Group M, and its average final exam score was also 5.02 points higher. The number of online quizzes taken by Group M was 4.6 times higher than the number of Group L, and its average final exam score was also 3.57 points higher. The statistical results reflected that the benefit from taking online quizzes became more substantial when students attempted seven or more chapters.

The final end-of-semester score was the sum of continuous assessment (40 %) and final exam (60 %). Continuous assessments included attendance, class participation, home exercises, and a midterm. As shown on Table 18.2, the end-of-semester scores of all groups were higher than the final exam scores (Group L: 1.93, Group M: 3.5, and Group H: 4.57). As students from Group H put the greatest efforts throughout the semester, therefore their continuous assessment scores were also the highest among the groups, and it is high enough to uplift their average score of the semester (see the right column "(2) minus (1)" on Table 18.2 for further details).

18.4.3 Comparisons to Previous Year's Academic Results

For this study, we compared the student performance in Costing with a first-year financial accounting course, Introductory Accounting. Although Cost Accounting was intended to raise students' analytical skills while Financial Accounting emphasized on financial reporting, both courses helped in establishing quantitative skills which is the strength of most accounting students. Therefore, it is likely that they would have similar performances in both courses. Since all the participants in this research took Cost Accounting with the same instructor, the instruction and evaluation methods were consistent between sections. Although the two instructors who taught Cost Accounting and Introductory Accounting might have different teaching and evaluation methods, the comparison of students' performance between these two courses still reflects the relative changes between the 2 years.

As shown in Table 18.3, we found that all the three groups had increased their scores in the second-year course. Group H, the highly motivated group, achieved the highest score gain as expected. However, the score gain of Group M was lower than the gain of Group L, even though students from Group M took more online quizzes. This situation is worthy of further investigation.

Table 18.3 Summary of score gain

Group	Score gain*	S.D.
L	7.11	12.23
M	3.91	9.30
H	11.33	9.74

*The score gains are calculated by using the end of semester score of the second-year course minus that of the first-year course

Table 18.4 Means of questions related to instructor encouragement

Q*	Description	*M*
13	I would not do the online quiz if my lecturer had not mentioned it	4.52
30	I would do the online quiz if the lecturer says it is useful	5.25

*The question number follows that printed on the questionnaire

To examine if there were significant differences among the groups, a one-way ANOVA with Tukey HSD post hoc was conducted. It was found that there were significant differences between the groups ($F=5.831$, $p=0.04<0.01$). The Tukey HSD post hoc multiple comparisons showed that (1) there were no significant differences either between Group L and Group M ($p=0.343$) or between Group L and Group H ($p=0.159$), but (2) Group H (mean = 11.33) was significantly higher than Group M (mean = 3.91) in the score gain ($p=0.003<0.01$) where at confidence level of 95 %, the mean difference was from 2.2544 to 12.5861.

18.4.4 Post Hoc Analysis

A total of 123 questionnaires were collected from 129 participants. The response rate was 95.34 %. The mean score of the 36 questions fell between 3.26 and 5.63 (min 1, max 7). It suggested students felt positive in general about the online quizzes.

There were 99.1 % of respondents who responded that they knew the website from their instructor and 84.4 % who had visited the website. Among them, more than 90 % took the online quizzes and reported the results. The instructor successfully convinced most students to take the quizzes by telling them its benefits (see Table 18.4).

It seemed perceived usefulness is the key motive for the students to take the online quizzes. According to Table 18.5, all the means are higher than 5, and Q12 got the highest score among all questions. The students would do more exercises for academic advancement. The means of questions related to the final exam (Q26 and Q27) is slightly lower than that of midterm (Q23 and Q24) as there were many qualitative essay questions in the final exam but most online quizzes are quantitative oriented.

Table 18.5 Means of questions related to perceived usefulness by students

Q	Description	*M*
12	I find the online quiz useful for my learning	5.63
22	Doing the online quiz increases my understanding of the course	5.24
23	Doing the online quiz helps me in preparing for the midterm	5.61
24	Doing the online quiz improves my midterm result	5.45
27	Doing the online quiz helps me in preparing for the final exam	5.19
26	Doing the online quiz improves my final exam result	5.02

Table 18.6 Means of questions related to self-motivation

Q	Description	*M*
18	I enjoy doing the online quiz	4.81
21	Doing the online quiz enhances my confidence in the course	4.89

Table 18.7 Means of questions related to peer pressure

Q	Description	*M*
29	I would do the online quiz if I know other schoolmates did it	4.67
35	I would recommend my schoolmates to do the online quiz in the future	4.72

When a student thought that his/her midterm result was improved by taking the online quizzes, this would enhance his/her confidence (Table 18.6, Q21). The enjoyment of getting instant feedback when completing a chapter of online quiz motivates them to take more. This could be a reason why many students completed two to three chapters in a row.

Table 18.7 suggests that peer pressure could influence learning behavior, but its impact is not significant in the course.

In addition, the statistics indicated that students found the quizzes moderately difficulty (Mean 4.29) and perceived the time spent on each chapter reasonable. These might also contribute to students' positive attitude towards this learning tool. To conclude, the respondents felt neutral in making these online quizzes as a mandatory requirement of the course.

18.4.5 Sum-Up of Findings

After analyzing all the collected data, three findings emerged from our study:

1. In general, taking TCW online quizzes helps in improving student performance in Cost Accounting; more frequent attempts will lead to greater gains in their academic performance.

2. Students must take a substantial number of exercises (seven chapters in this study) to obtain noticeable improvement. It means only the students who maintain continuous efforts will result in a beneficial outcome.
3. Student initiatives of taking online quizzes can be determined by many factors, including perceived usefulness, instructor encouragement, self-motivation, and peer influences.

18.5 Discussion

This study reveals the factors which contribute to student attitudes towards TCW online quiz. These factors are: (1) perceived usefulness, (2) instructor encouragement, (3) self-motivation or a sense of success from obtaining high scores in the quiz, and (4) peer influences and pressure.

18.5.1 Instructor's Influences and Social Pressure

With the instructor encouragement, approximately 90 % of the participants attempted at least one chapter of quizzes even though no bonus mark was given. The instructor's strategy of releasing the submission list online effectively motivated the students. An extremely high number of students decided to email the quiz results to the instructor within 1 or 2 days after the submission list was posted on ILN. Besides avoiding lagged behind, some students also felt pressure and ashamed when their ID numbers were not listed.

18.5.2 Bundle-Style Studying Pattern

The email delivery dates showed that students neither took the quizzes immediately after the class lecture nor finished up the exercises one by one as the class schedule. The record also showed the students took the online quizzes at their time of convenience; they worked on the quizzes when their workload was lighter and attempted multiple chapters at once. Many quiz results were emailed to the instructor right before the midterm and final exams; some results were sent even a few days after the final exam. This phenomenon can be explained in many ways. Firstly, many students liked to cram their ongoing workloads into the last few days before the exam approaching. Additionally, taking the online quizzes was an effective method for them to review their coursework. Another possible reason of taking a bundle of quizzes at once was the sense of success as most accounting students enjoyed working with numbers especially calculation. When they answered a chapter of quizzes correctly, the sense of success encouraged them to continue. Accordingly, the motivation of taking online quiz changed from passive to proactive.

18.5.3 The Effects of Taking Online Quiz on Academic Performance

This study concluded that online quizzes will create positive impacts on undergraduate accounting students but on the condition that students must continue working until they completed an adequate amount of chapters. Although there was no MC question in the final exam, and not many theoretical questions were included in the online quizzes, students still took the quizzes before the final exam, which implies they perceived TCW as a valuable tool of learning. This is a possible reason to explain why students who participated in online quiz received higher scores in the final exam.

Figure 18.3 shows the student motivation portfolio on taking online quizzes, in which "Motivation" represents the three main groups of participants and "Rewards" refers to the exam scores. As seen on Table 18.3 in Sect. 4.3, when comparing student academic performance in costing from the accounting course taken in the previous year, Group H, represented by the highly motivated students, had achieved an exceptional gain of 11.33 points; this increase is large enough to uplift a student grade from the low into the middle tier (indicated in Fig. 18.3, from Box 7 to Box 8) or from the middle to the high tier (Box 8–9). However, Group M, the average-motivated students, only made a score gain of 3.91; this increase is insufficient to uplift an academic score into a higher tier. Our analysis also found that Group L, the least motivated group, also made a score gain of 7.11 with a relative high standard deviation of 12.23, but it was uncertain whether the gain was high enough to change the tiers from low to middle or from middle to high (compare Box 1 and 2 and Box 2 and 3 respectively in Fig. 18.3). It is quite possible that many students were unmotivated and did not participate in the online quizzes but still smart enough to make a high score in the final exam, but this would require further investigation.

In addition, the learning gain could possibly be diminished at a later stage of the study as the growth of the learning process could never be kept at an infinite rate. Students might also stop taking the online quizzes after they had completed many chapters or move their focus from Cost Accounting to other areas after they already invested extended time in the course.

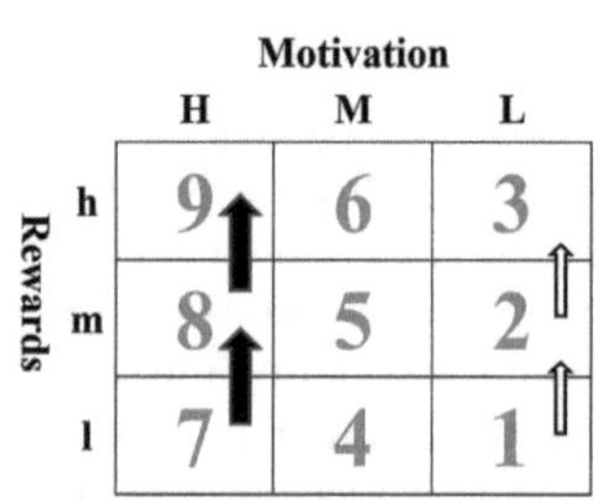

Fig. 18.3 Students' motivation portfolio on taking online quiz (Motivation refers to the number of chapters attempted by students. The three levels are high (*H*), middle (*M*), low (*L*). Rewards refer to academic results. The three levels are high (*h*), middle (*m*), low (*l*))

18.5.4 Limitations and Future Studies

Since the final exam of Cost Accounting comprised of essay questions, English writing skills became an underlying factor to determine student performance. Therefore, the exam scores we used in our calculation also took qualitative and comprehensive skills into account, which had been less emphasized from the online quizzes. As mentioned previously, taking online quizzes helped the students to define the scope of the final exam, improved their reading skills, and expanded their professional vocabulary, but it would not affect their writing skills. In order to find out more objective impacts on student performance brought about by online quizzes to the students, future study should focus solely on the effect of online quizzes to the quantitative areas of the final exam, and essay questions should be excluded from the calculation.

To determine whether the academic improvement (score gain) was a direct result from the online quiz, we compared the student performance in Cost Accounting with a first-year course, Financial Accounting. These two courses undoubtedly had different emphases, but they both required similar business knowledge, quantitative skills, and the ability of working with numbers. For future study, we suggest requiring students to take the same MC questions from the course content at the beginning and at the end of the semester to see the clear score gain.

Future study can also investigate whether the online quizzes were taken before, immediately after, or long after the class lectures and how these time differences affect score gain.

Conclusion

Our study found that online quizzes could be an effective learning tool for accounting students. It provides an excellent opportunity for the students to review what they have learned in class, refines their quantitative skills through the MC questions, and helps them to identify the scope of the final exam. To fully utilize this learning tool, completing a substantial number of online quizzes will bring noticeable academic improvement. We also realized the students who invested continuous efforts and took a series of exercises throughout the semester had shown the greatest increase in their exam scores. On the other hand, students also perceive the online quizzes on the textbook companion website (TCW) useful. Additionally, many other factors also affect the students' willingness of taking the online quizzes, such as the usefulness of the exercises, instructor encouragement, peer pressure, self-motivation, and intrinsic reward.

Appendix: Thirty-Six Questionnaire Items

Q1	The existence of the textbook companion website of the course ACCT210 was: _____ (1) Informed by my lecturer (2) Informed by my schoolmate (3) Discovered by myself (4) Others ________________________________		
Q2	I know the existence of textbook companion website of other course(s)	Y	N
Q3	I know this kind of companion website before studying ACCT210	Y	N
Q4	I have heard my schoolmate talking about the textbook companion website of ACCT210	Y	N
Q5	I have visited the textbook companion website of other course(s)	Y	N
Q6	I have visited the ACCT210 textbook companion website ***(If your answer is N, please go to question Q25)***	Y	N
Q7	I have tried the online quiz (multiple-choice (MC) questions) of the ACCT210 textbook companion website ***(If your answer is N, please go to question Q25)***	Y	N
Q8	I have sent my online quiz results to my lecturer	Y	N
Q9	I have recommended my schoolmates to do the online quiz	Y	N
Q10	I did the online quiz because my schoolmates suggested me to do so	Y	N
Q11–Q36	*Strongly* ***Disagree*** ***Neutral*** *Strongly* ***Agree*** **1** ←← **4** →→ **7**		
Q11	I find the ACCT210 textbook companion website easy to use		
Q12	I find the online quiz useful for my learning of ACCT210		
Q13	I would not do the online quiz if my lecturer had not mentioned about it		
Q14	I did the online quiz for I know my schoolmates have or would have done it		
Q15	I repeated the same quiz until I have all the questions answered correctly		
Q16	I sent my online quiz results to my lecturer because of bonus marks		
Q17	I find it convenient to access the online quiz		
Q18	I enjoy doing the online quiz		
Q19	I find the questions of the online quiz easy to answer		
Q20	The number of questions in each chapter of the online quiz is too many		
Q21	Doing the online quiz enhances my confidence in studying ACCT210		
Q22	Doing the online quiz increases my understanding of ACCT210		
Q23	Doing the online quiz helps me in preparing for the midterm test of ACCT210		
Q24	Doing the online quiz improves my ACCT210 midterm test result		
Q25	I believe the textbook companion website is useful for learning		
Q26	Doing the online quiz would improve my ACCT210 final exam result		
Q27	Doing the online quiz would help me in preparing for the final exam of ACCT210		
Q28	Doing the online quiz is time consuming		

(continued)

Q29	I would do the online quiz if I know my other schoolmates did it
Q30	I would do the online quiz if the lecturer says it is useful for my study
Q31	I would do the online quiz if my lecturer gives me bonus marks
Q32	I would do the online quiz even if the midterm test contains only essay questions
Q33	I would do the online quiz if the final exam has MC questions
Q34	I would use the textbook companion website of other course(s) in the future
Q35	I would recommend my schoolmates to do the online quiz in the future
Q36	The lecturer should make the online quiz a compulsory task of the course

References

Fung, H., & Ma, W. W. K. (2013). Exploring the effectiveness of hybrid learning in accounting information systems – An empirical study. In S. K. S. Cheung et al. (Eds.), *ICHL 2013, LNCS 8038, hybrid learning and continuing education* (pp. 178–189). Berlin/Heidelberg: Springer.

Hadsell, L. (2009). The effect of quiz timing on exam performance. *Journal of Education for Business, 84*(3), 135–141.

Johnson, B. C., & Kiviniemi, M. T. (2009). The effect of online chapter quizzes on exam performance in an undergraduate social psychology course. *Teaching Psychology, 36*(1), 33–37.

Jonas, G. A., & Norman, C. S. (2011). Textbook websites: User technology acceptance behaviour. *Behaviour & Information Technology, 30*(2), 147–159.

Peng, Z. (2011). The Web-enhanced instruction mode: Evidence from undergraduate finance graduates with embedded online assessments. *Business Education Innovation Journal, 3*(2), 82–91.

Potacco, D. R., Ramirez-Levine, R., Chisholm, D. R., & De Young, S. (2008). Online supplemental resources in developmental mathematics. *Research & Teaching in Developmental Education, 25*(1), 45–53.

Ramsaran-Fowdar, R. R., Baguant, P., & Fowdar, S. (2011). A critical analysis of e-Assessment with particular emphasis on the use of different types of online quizzes. *International Journal of Learning, 18*(1), 191–202.

Sellnow, D. D., Child, J. T., & Ahlfeldt, S. L. (2005). Textbook technology supplements: What are they good for? *Communication Education, 54*(3), 243–253.

Smolira, J. C. (2008). Student perceptions of online homework in introductory finance courses. *Journal of Education for Business, 84*(2), 90–95.

Vandsburger, E., & Duncan-Daston, R. (2011). Evaluating the study guide as a tool for increasing students' accountability for reading the textbook. *Journal of College Reading and Learning, 42*(1), 6–23.

Part IV
Multiliteracies

Chapter 19
Variable-Centered and Person-Centered Approaches to Studying the VARK Learning Style Inventory

Wilfred W.F. Lau, Allan H.K. Yuen, and Albert Chan

Abstract With the increased integration of technology in education process, teachers are challenged to personalize and create interactive learning environments to fulfill students' needs. An understanding of how an individual's preferred learning style interacts with the instructional medium presented is needed. This study examined the VARK (visual, aural, read/write, and kinesthetic) learning style inventory using the variable-centered and person-centered approaches. Based on a sample of 807 Secondary 1 (Grade 7) students in Hong Kong, confirmatory factor analysis (CFA) using the correlated trait–correlated uniqueness (CTCU) model affirmed that the model fits the responses from the inventory well. Latent class analysis (LCA) identified five meaningful subgroups of students (all rounded (6.2 %), mediocre (16.2 %), kinesthetic oriented (21.9 %), read/write oriented (50.4 %), and uninvolved (5.3 %)).

Keywords Variable-centered approach • Person-centered approach • Learning style • VARK • Multimodality

19.1 Introduction

Research on learning style can be traced back to the mid-1940s when several such models emerged. The major studies of style stemmed from the work of differential psychology, which examines measurable differences between individuals, and that of cognitive psychology, which investigates the processes and abilities in cognition (Riding and Rayner 1998). Among the pioneering work in the area, Witkin and Goodenough's (1981) theory of field dependence/independence is one of the most

W.W.F. Lau (✉) • A. Chan
Faculty of Education, The University of Hong Kong, Hong Kong, China
e-mail: wwflau@hku.hk; albert.chan.mr@live.com

A.H.K. Yuen
The University of Hong Kong, Hong Kong, China
e-mail: hkyuen@hku.hk

© Springer Science+Business Media Singapore 2015
W.W.K. Ma et al. (eds.), *New Media, Knowledge Practices and Multiliteracies*,
DOI 10.1007/978-981-287-209-8_19

well known in the literature. Field-independent people tend to perceive figures separated from the environment, while field-dependent people simply perceive the environment as a whole. The Embedded Figures Test (EFT) and Group Embedded Figures Test (GEFT) are used to assess field dependence/independence by asking each participant to locate a simple figure from a large complex figure.

Pask and Scott (1972) identified two types of learners: (1) serial learners who favor bottom-up strategy for information processing and (2) holist learners who favor top-down strategy for information processing. The Pask Smugglers Test was developed to measure participants' tendency to learn information in a local and/or global manner. Marton and Säljö (1976) categorized students' strategies for learning as deep or surface approach. Deep approach learners seek underlying meaning of concepts and structures that links different concepts together. Surface approach learners simply memorize materials and do not look for structures. The deep and surface approaches to learning form the basis of Biggs' Study Process Questionnaire (Biggs 1987), which attempts to identify motives and strategies in individual learners.

19.2 Conceptualization of Learning Style

Over the past several decades, a proliferation of learning style models has been reported in the literature. Apart from the problems of reliability and validity of many instruments, some instruments appear to be similar to others, and therefore a conceptualization of the underlying models seems necessary. Curry (1983) made an early effort to achieve this goal. She proposed an onion model that reconceptualizes learning style into three layers: instructional preference, information processing, and cognitive personality. The outermost layer, instructional preference, refers to individuals' preferred learning environment. As it has direct interaction with the external influences, it is considered to be the least stable. The Learning Preference Inventory (Rezler and Rezmovic 1981) is one of the instruments in this layer. The second layer, information processing, deals with the intellectual ability of individuals to process information. It is relatively more stable than instructional preference and yet can be modified by learning strategies. Kolb's Learning Style Inventory (1976) provides one such example. Finally, the innermost layer, cognitive personality, represents "an underlying and relatively permanent personality dimension" (pp. 8–9). The EFT/GEFT (Witkin 1962) and Myers–Briggs Type Indicator (MBTI) (Myers 1962) are instruments in this layer.

Having reviewed over 30 instruments labeled as cognitive/learning styles in detail, Riding and Cheema (1991) suggested two fundamental dimensions to categorize styles, namely, wholist–analytic and verbalizer–imager. The wholist–analytic dimension describes individual preferences for processing information as a whole (wholist) or as separate components (analytic). Witkin's field dependence–independence model (Witkin 1962) and Pask's holist–serialist model (Pask and Scott 1972) are styles in this dimension. The other dimension, verbalizer–imager, represents individual preferences in delineating information either as words (verbalizer) or as images (imager). The verbalizer–imager style (Riding and Taylor 1976) and the verbalizer–visualizer style (Richardson 1977) are two examples of styles in this dimension.

Drawing on the style research of Grigerenko and Sternberg (1995), Rayner and Riding (1997) discussed a learning style framework incorporating three approaches: personality-centered, cognitive-centered, and learning-centered. Personality-centered approaches were not explored further owing to this approach's limited influence on style-based theory and the fact that it has been included only in MBTI model. Cognitive-centered approaches encompass styles that reflect individual differences in cognitive and perceptual functioning. The two fundamental dimensions of styles by Riding and Cheema (1991), wholist–analytic and verbalizer–imager, provide the basis for categorizing models using these approaches. The integration of the two dimensions results in a new model called Cognitive Styles Analysis (CSA) (Riding 1991). Learning-centered approaches distinguish themselves by the following features: a great concern for individual differences in pedagogy, the emergence of new learning constructs and concepts, and the development of new assessment instruments in response to emerging constructs and concepts. These approaches subsequently focus on the discussion of process-based models, preference-based models, and cognitive skills-based models. Process-based models represent those that are characterized by information perception and processing. Kolb's Experiential Learning Model (Kolb 1976, 1984) is one such example. Preference-based models emphasize elements of an individual's favorable learning environment such as temperature, motivation, independent/group study, and time of study, with Dunn and Dunn's Model (Dunn et al. 1989) as one example. Cognitive skills-based models are identified in terms of the number of cognitive skills like field dependency, perceptual modality, and memory.

19.3 The VARK Questionnaire

A bewildering array of learning style models has brought confusion and chaos to researchers in the field. Mitchell (1994) reported that there are over 100 such models found in the literature, although quite a number of these are not worthy of consideration. Coffield et al. (2004) reviewed 13 major learning style models and found only one possessed desirable psychometric properties in terms of internal consistency, reliability, and validity. Despite the controversy over whether learning style can be utilized as an instructionally useful concept when planning and delivering instruction, Evans and Cools (2011) concluded that "overall, we are positive about the conceptual, methodological, and practical evolutions that have recently taken place in the learning styles field" (p. 253). For example, Lau and Yuen (2009, 2010, 2011) found that learning style, as measured by the Gregorc Style Delineator (GSD), was a significant predictor of programming performance.

This study investigated the psychometric properties of a learning style inventory called VARK (visual, aural, read/write, and kinesthetic) in a Chinese sample. According to Fleming (2001), who designed the inventory, individuals have four perceptual preferences for perceiving and processing information. Visual learners tend to learn and think through visual images including charts, graphs, and diagrams. Aural learners learn best through speeches and group discussions. Learners who prefer read/write would choose to perceive and process information through printed medium. Kinesthetic learners are those who prefer to gain hands-on experiences through physical experimentation to approach problems.

While intuitively appealing as a measure of learning style, the inventory has also been critiqued for its inadequate reliability and validity. To our knowledge, only one study by Leite et al. (2010) showed preliminary support for the validity of the VARK scores. The authors found that the correlated trait–correlated uniqueness (CTCU) model provided the best fit to the data compared with the correlated trait–correlated method (CTCM) and the correlated trait–correlated method minus 1 (CT-C(M-1)) models: $\chi^2(1,100) = 18,779.444$, $p < 0.01$, CFI = 0.845, TLI = 0.905, RMSEA = 0.034, and SRMR = 0.049. The reliability estimates for the subscales visual, aural, read/write, and kinesthetic of the inventory were 0.85, 0.82, 0.84, and 0.77, which were considered adequate.

In view of this, this study examined the VARK inventory using the variable-centered and person-centered approaches. With regard to the former approach, we examined the inventory's psychometric properties with confirmatory factor analysis (CFA). For the latter approach, we performed latent class analysis (LCA) to determine whether there exist unobserved meaningful classes of individuals based on their responses to the items in the inventory.

19.4 Variable-Centered and Person-Centered Approaches to Data Analysis

Poncheri and Ward (2008) noted that there are different focuses and assumptions underlying the variable-centered and person-centered approaches to data analysis. The variable-centered approach intends to analyze the relationships between variables with the assumption that such relationships are generalizable to a homogenous population. This approach is broadly adopted in statistical analyses such as correlations, regressions, and structural equation models. The person-centered approach takes the view that there are individual differences to the variables under consideration. It assumes that unobserved subgroups of population exist (heterogeneous population) and that findings can only be generalized to a certain class or cluster in a population. Cluster analysis and LCA are examples of statistical procedures using the approach. Ainley and Buckley (2010) concluded that these two analytic approaches are complementary and "the insights they yield provide a more complete picture of both person and process as they underpin student learning" (p. 13).

19.5 Method

19.5.1 Sample

A convenient sample consisting of six secondary schools was collected in the study. In order to provide a sample that reflects the high, middle, and low academic profile of students, two schools were invited for each profile. A whole class was used as a clustered sample. Four to five intact classes of Secondary 1 (Grade 7) students from each of the sample schools participated in the study. A briefing session was conducted for each class of students to explain the detailed procedure of the data collection. Students responded to a self-reported paper-based survey in order to understand their learning styles. They were asked to spend about 10 min to complete the survey. The sample size was 807, of which there were 46.7 % male students and 46.3 % female students. 6.9 % of the students did not report their gender in the survey.

19.5.2 Measure

The VARK inventory comprised four subscales, namely, visual, aural, read/write, and kinesthetic. It contains 16 questions with four options. Each option represents a learning style preference. The total number of item-level measurement is thus 64, with each response being dichotomous. The VARK questionnaire version 7.1 was used (Fleming 2011).

19.5.3 Analysis Strategy

All analyses were carried out with Mplus 7 (Muthén and Muthén 1998–2012). To assess construct validity for the VARK inventory in our sample, multitrait–multimethod CFA was conducted (Leite et al. 2010). In particular, Leite et al. (2010) recommended using the CTCU model. As such, we chose this model for CFA (see Fig. 19.1). As the responses of the VARK items are dichotomous, Leite et al. (2010) suggested using the mean- and variance-adjusted weighted least square estimator (WLSMV) for analyzing categorical indicators, and thus this estimation method was used in this study.

Independent LCAs were performed to determine the optimal number of latent classes. Fit indices were evaluated for unconditional models (without covariates) with one to six classes. The following three criteria for selecting the optimal number of latent classes were recommended by Muthén and Muthén (2000): (a) the Bayesian information criterion (BIC) and a sample-size-adjusted version of the BIC (Adj. BIC), with lower scores indicating better model fits; (b) entropy, with higher values showing that individuals are classified into their most likely classes; and (c) the theoretical

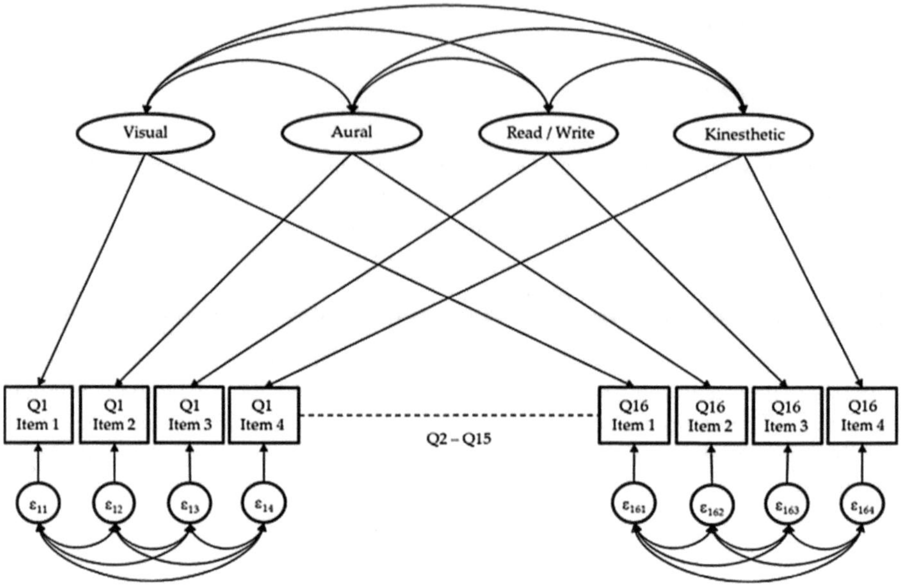

Fig. 19.1 The CTCU model

significance and practical usefulness of the latent classes. Later, Nylund et al. (2007) found that the Adj. BIC and the bootstrapped likelihood ratio test (BLRT), which statistically compares of the goodness of fit of a given model with a model of one fewer class, were consistently the best indicators for determining the number of classes in various mixture models.

19.6 Results

The majority of the students (79.3 %) showed single modal preference and read/write modality preference shared the highest proportion among the single modality category. Bimodal (13 %), trimodal (1.9 %), and multimodal (0.6 %) preferences were relatively fewer in number.

Using the CTCU model, all the standardized factor loadings were significant. This means that they were explained less by error than by the hypothesized constructs (Hair et al. 2006). Fit indices indicated that the model provided an acceptable fit to the data: $\chi^2(1{,}888)=2{,}470.972$, $p<0.001$, CFI = 0.921, TLI = 0.916, RMSEA = 0.02, SRMR = 0.07 (Hu and Bentler 1999). The reliability estimates for subscales visual, aural, read/write, and kinesthetic of the VARK inventory in this study were 0.83, 0.80, 0.81, and 0.78, which were considered adequate (Nunnally 1978) and were similar to those reported by Leite et al. (2010).

From Table 19.1, following the recommendation of Muthén and Muthén (2000), it seems that the 6-class solution should be chosen based on the BIC and Adj. BIC conditions. The entropy criterion suggests that the 3-class solution fits the data best,

Table 19.1 Model fit indices for the 1-, 2-, 3-, 4-, 5-, and 6-class solutions

	1-class	2-class	3-class	4-class	5-class	6-class
AIC	16,074	15,040	14,712	14,557	14,512	14,470
BIC	16,112	15,101	14,796	14,665	14,643	14,625
Sample-size-adjusted BIC	16,086	15,059	14,739	14,592	14,554	14,520
Entropy	n/a	0.923	0.957	0.937	0.808	0.828
VLMRLRT	n/a	0.000	0.000	0.001	0.021	0.263
LMRALRT	n/a	0.000	0.000	0.002	0.024	0.274

Note: *AIC* Akaike Information Criterion, *BIC* Bayesian Information Criterion, *VLMRLRT* Vuong-Lo-Mendell-Rubin Likelihood Ratio Test, *LMRALRT* Lo-Mendell-Rubin Adjusted Likelihood Ratio Test

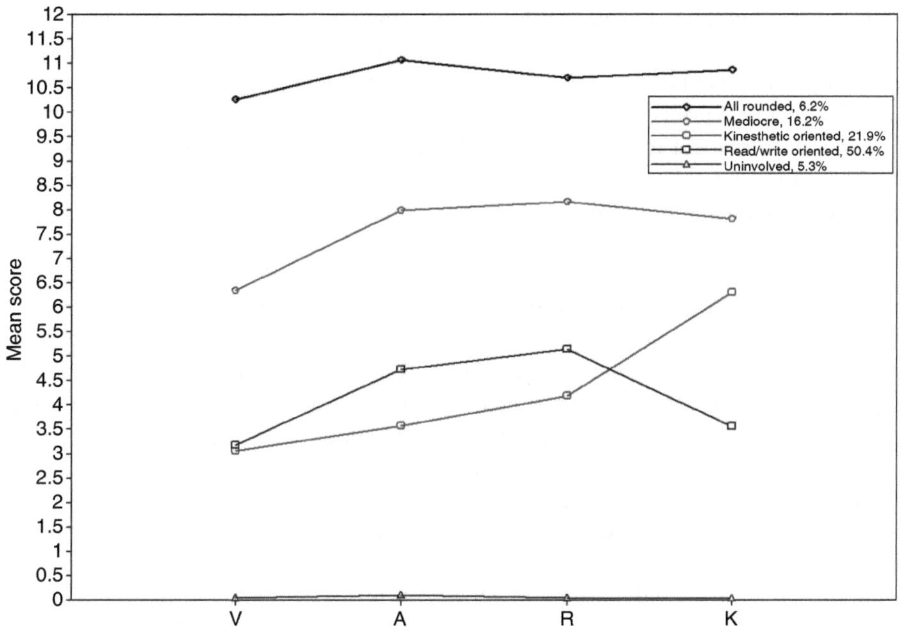

Fig. 19.2 Latent class solution with 5 classes

whereas the results from the two LRTs show that the 5-class solution provides a good fit to the data. As Nylund et al. (2007) demonstrated that BLRT gives reliable indicators for the optimal number of latent classes, we selected the 5-class solution. The average individual posterior probabilities for being assigned to a certain latent class were 0.791, 0.998, 0.874, 0.912, and 0.896, which indicate a clear classification. According to the mean score profiles shown in Fig. 19.2, we labeled the 5 classes as (1) all rounded (6.2 %), (2) mediocre (16.2 %), (3) kinesthetic oriented (21.9 %), (4) read/write oriented (50.4 %), and (5) uninvolved (5.3 %).

19.7 Discussion and Conclusion

This study set out to investigate the VARK learning style inventory using the variable-centered and person-centered approaches. Results from CFA using the CTCU model affirmed that the model fits the data in this study well, which is consistent with the analysis performed with sample collected in the United States (Leite et al. 2010). There is some preliminary evidence to support construct validity of the inventory in a Chinese context. Messick (1995) argued that there are six unified conceptions of construct validity, namely, content, substantive, structural, generalizability, external, and consequential validities. Specifically, this study demonstrates the inventory's structural validity, which assesses the consistency of the empirical relationships between targeted constructs and their indicators with the hypothesized structure and generalizability validity, which assesses whether the properties of a scale can be generalized to and across various population groups, settings, and tasks.

Another important contribution of this study is that it identified five meaningful subgroups of students using LCA based on their responses to the inventory. To our knowledge, our work is the first attempt to profile Chinese junior secondary school students with respect to the inventory. While only convenience sample was used in this study, the relatively large sample size from six secondary schools does provide some degree of representativeness of the student population in Hong Kong. All rounded and uninvolved learners accounted for a small percent in the sample (11.5 %). Over 70 % of the learners were either kinesthetic oriented or read/write oriented. It is not surprising to find that many students still prefer read/write as the dominant modality to perceive and process information through printed medium. Yet a substantial number of students (21.9 %) are more inclined to gain hands-on experiences through physical experimentation to approach problems. The implication of these findings for teachers today is that they should recognize the existence of groups of students with different perceptual preferences and endeavor to meet the diverse needs of these student groups.

As the use of hypermedia systems has been increasingly commonplace in interactive learning environments, there is a lack of empirical evidence to evaluate their influence on learners and learning in general. It is our belief that a student-centered pedagogy should begin with an informed understanding of how students utilize their multiple senses to make sense of the perceived information and this study represents a major step in this direction.

References

Ainley, M., & Buckley, S. (2010). Understanding educational achievement: Person, process and content. In S. Rodrigues (Ed.), *Using analytical frameworks for classroom research: Collecting data and analysing narrative* (pp. 1–18). London/New York: Routledge.

Biggs, J. B. (1987). *Student approaches to learning and studying*. Hawthorn: Australian Council for Educational Research.

Coffield, F., Moseley, D., Hall, E., & Ecclestone, K. (2004). *Should we be using learning styles? What research has to say to practitioners*. Retrieved September 25, 2013, from http://itslifejimbutnotasweknowit.org.uk/files/LSRC_LearningStyles.pdf

Curry, L. (1983). *An organization of learning styles theory and constructs*. Paper presented at the Annual Meeting of the American Educational Research Association, Montreal, Quebec, Canada.

Dunn, R., Dunn, K., & Price, G. E. (1989). *Learning styles inventory*. Lawrence: Price Systems.

Evans, C., & Cools, E. (2011). Applying styles research to educational practice. *Learning and Individual Differences, 21*(3), 249–254.

Fleming, N. D. (2001). *Teaching and learning styles: VARK strategies*. Christchurch: Author.

Fleming, N. D. (2011). *The VARK questionnaire*. Retrieved October 3, 2013, from http://www.vark-learn.com/english/page.asp?p=questionnaire

Grigerenko, E. L., & Sternberg, R. J. (1995). Thinking styles. In D. H. Saklofske & M. Zeidner (Eds.), *International handbook of personality and intelligence* (pp. 205–230). New York: Plenum Press.

Hair, J. F., Black, B., Babin, B., Anderson, R. E., & Tatham, R. L. (2006). *Multivariate data analysis* (6th ed.). Upper Saddle River: Prentice Hall.

Hu, L.-T., & Bentler, P. M. (1999). Cutoff criteria for fit indexes in covariance structure analysis: Conventional criteria versus new alternatives. *Structural Equation Modeling, 6*(1), 1–55.

Kolb, D. A. (1976). *The learning styles inventory: Technical manual*. Boston: McBer & Company.

Kolb, D. A. (1984). *Experiential learning: Experience as the source of learning and development*. Englewood Cliffs: Prentice-Hall.

Lau, W. W. F., & Yuen, A. H. K. (2009). Exploring the effects of gender and learning styles on computer programming performance: Implications for programming pedagogy. *British Journal of Educational Technology, 40*(4), 696–712.

Lau, W. W. F., & Yuen, A. H. K. (2010). Promoting conceptual change of learning sorting algorithm through the diagnosis of mental models: The effects of gender and learning styles. *Computers & Education, 54*(1), 275–288.

Lau, W. W. F., & Yuen, A. H. K. (2011). Modelling programming performance: Beyond the influence of learner characteristics. *Computers & Education, 57*(1), 1202–1213.

Leite, W. L., Svinicki, M., & Shi, Y. (2010). Attempted validation of the scores of the VARK: Learning styles inventory with multitrait-multimethod confirmatory factor analysis models. *Educational and Psychological Measurement, 70*(2), 323–339.

Marton, F., & Säljö, R. (1976). On qualitative differences in learning, I: Outcome and process. *British Journal of Educational Psychology, 46*, 4–11.

Messick, S. (1995). Validity of psychological assessment: Validation of inferences from persons' responses and performances as scientific inquiry into score meaning. *American Psychologist, 50*, 741–749.

Mitchell, D. P. (1994). Learning style: A critical analysis of the concept and its assessment. In R. Hoey (Ed.), *Design for learning: Aspects of educational technology* (pp. 5–10). London: Kogan Page.

Muthén, L. K., & Muthén, B. O. (1998–2012). *Mplus user's guide* (7th ed.). Los Angeles: Muthén & Muthén.

Muthén, B., & Muthén, L. K. (2000). Integrating person-centered and variable-centered analysis: Growth mixture modeling with latent trajectory classes. *Alcoholism: Clinical and Experimental Research, 24*(6), 882–891.

Myers, I. B. (1962). *The Myers-Briggs type indicator manual*. Princeton: The Educational Testing Service.

Nunnally, J. C. (1978). *Psychometric theory*. New York: McGraw-Hill.

Nylund, K., Asparouhov, T., & Muthén, B. (2007). Deciding on the number of classes in latent class analysis and growth mixture modeling: A Monte Carlo simulation study. *Structural Equation Modeling, 14*, 535–569.

Pask, G., & Scott, B. C. E. (1972). Learning strategies and individual competence. *International Journal of Man-Machine Studies, 4*, 217–253.

Poncheri, R. M., & Ward, S. J. (2008). *Personality remix: Integrating variable-centered and person-centered approaches to personality.* Paper presented at the 23rd annual meeting of the Society for Industrial and Organizational Psychology, San Francisco, CA.
Rayner, S., & Riding, R. (1997). Towards a categorisation of cognitive styles and learning styles. *Educational Psychology, 17*(1/2), 5–28.
Rezler, A. G., & Rezmovic, V. (1981). The learning preference inventory. *Journal of Applied Health, 10*, 28–34.
Richardson, A. (1977). Verbaliser-visualiser: A cognitive style dimension. *Journal of Mental Imagery, 1*, 109–126.
Riding, R. (1991). *Cognitive styles analysis.* Birmingham: Learning and Training Technology.
Riding, R., & Cheema, I. (1991). Cognitive styles-an overview and integration. *Educational Psychology, 11*(3/4), 193–215.
Riding, R., & Rayner, S. (1998). *Cognitive styles and learning strategies: Understanding style differences in learning and behaviour.* London: David Fulton Publishers.
Riding, R. J., & Taylor, E. M. (1976). Imagery performance and prose comprehension in 7 year old children. *Educational Studies, 2*, 21–27.
Witkin, H. A. (1962). *Psychological differentiation: Studies of development.* New York: Wiley.
Witkin, H. A., & Goodenough, D. R. (1981). *Cognitive styles: Essence and origins.* New York: International Universities Press.

Chapter 20
The Impact of ICT on Pedagogical Practices in an Interdisciplinary Approach

Kathryn Reed

Abstract Technological, pedagogical and content knowledge (TPACK) is a growing area of research that describes the knowledge base required by teachers to proficiently use educational technologies. However, few studies have focused on TPACK in an interdisciplinary approach. This paper reviews the literature related to interdisciplinary approaches in school contexts and outlines the differing views of TPACK. A conceptual framework using ICT-PCK based on Angeli and Valanides (2009) conceptualisation of ICT-TPCK as a distinct body of knowledge is proposed.

Keywords Interdisciplinary • ICT • Pedagogical practices • TPACK

20.1 Introduction

Empirical research into the underpinnings of technological, pedagogical and content knowledge (TPACK) is still in the early stages, and a review of the literature by Voogt et al. (2013a) found that it is a complex concept that can be understood in differing ways. In the literature, the acronyms TPACK and TPCK are used, and this paper takes a similar approach to Voogt et al. (2013a) by using the TPACK or TPCK acronyms according to the research article's terminology. Most TPACK literature considers it as stemming from Shulman's (1986) concept of pedagogical content knowledge (PCK) (e.g. Abbitt 2011; Graham 2011; Voogt et al. 2013a). Nonetheless, Voogt et al. (2013a) argue the literature points to three views: as an extension of PCK (Cox and Graham 2009; Niess 2005), as the interplay between pedagogy, content and technology and the intersections of these three domains (Mishra and Koehler 2006) or as a body of knowledge that is distinct (Angeli and Valanides 2009). Much of the research using the TPACK framework focuses on single disciplines such as science and mathematics, and there has been little research into how information and communication technology (ICT) is impacting on teacher pedagogical practices in an interdisciplinary approach. In recent years there has been an interest in

K. Reed (✉)
Faculty of Education, The University of Hong Kong, Hong Kong, China
e-mail: reedkj1@hku.hk

© Springer Science+Business Media Singapore 2015
W.W.K. Ma et al. (eds.), *New Media, Knowledge Practices and Multiliteracies*,
DOI 10.1007/978-981-287-209-8_20

interdisciplinary curriculum models by teachers and policymakers at secondary school level, as a way of preparing students to be flexible thinkers, who can approach new problems from multiple perspectives by connecting different fields of knowledge (Boix-Mansilla 2010; CDC-HKEAA 2014). This paper will firstly outline the research questions for the current study exploring the impact of ICT in an interdisciplinary approach, then review the key concepts of interdisciplinary and TPACK in the literature and finally outline the conceptual framework.

The focus of the study is the impact of ICT on teachers' pedagogical practices in an interdisciplinary unit of study, and accordingly, two broad research questions emerge:

- How do teachers approach teaching an interdisciplinary unit of study?
- In what ways are teachers using ICT in an interdisciplinary unit of study?

The first research question explores teachers' understanding of the term interdisciplinary, the pedagogical practices they intend to use and the reasons for choosing these pedagogical practices in an interdisciplinary unit of study. Secondary school teachers generally operate in a discrete disciplinary structure, and this question investigates teachers' understanding of interdisciplinary approaches along with their educational beliefs and experiences. The second research question centres on ICT in an interdisciplinary unit of study by exploring how and why ICT pedagogical practices are employed in the unit of study. This is because ICT pedagogical practices may be aligned to the requirements of particular disciplines. Therefore, teachers' ICT competence and confidence may not necessarily transmit to the pedagogical practices required using an interdisciplinary approach, and they may be required to develop their ICT pedagogical practices.

20.2 Literature Review

20.2.1 Why an Interdisciplinary Approach?

Secondary school curricula are often organised with a timetable of discrete disciplines. A discipline is not solely the content area or facts used to form the subject knowledge (Moss et al. 2008; Nissani 1995). Each discipline potentially has a different set of learning tools, as well as exploring different subject matter or phenomena (Beane 1995; Moss et al. 2008). Curricula with interdisciplinary elements include Liberal Studies in Hong Kong (CDC-HKEAA 2014) and the International Baccalaureate Middle Years Programme (MYP) (Boix-Mansilla 2010). However, interdisciplinary approaches have been explored by educationalists for many years, e.g. Hopkins (1937) (as cited in Beane 1997), Jacobs (1989) and Tchudi and Lafer (1996). An interdisciplinary approach integrates knowledge from across multiple disciplines (Hammond and McCallum 2009). Similarly, Nissani (1995) suggests a working definition of an interdisciplinary curriculum as bringing together two or more distinctive disciplines.

Although it is acknowledged that a single-subject curriculum can also offer opportunities to undertake authentic real-world problems (Brown 2008), interdisciplinary learning has been advocated as a way of making connections between disciplines (e.g. Boix-Mansilla 2010; Brown 2008). Empirical research from primary and secondary school contexts offers evidence that interdisciplinary approaches can contribute to helping students make connections across disciplines and real-life situations (Rennie et al. 2011; Venville et al. 2000; Zhbanova et al. 2010). Students can also engage in issues that are relevant and motivating (Beane 1997; Brown 2008) and more closely matches the way people approach problems outside of the classroom (Griffin et al. 2012). Consequently interdisciplinary approaches may offer opportunities for students to develop their ability to transfer knowledge and skills into other contexts in order to prepare students to develop the capabilities required by knowledge societies. Venville et al. (2000) argue that a key issue for interdisciplinary approaches is that teachers may feel less confident about advising students about the subject knowledge they are less familiar with and question their own ability to teach in this way.

20.2.2 Differing Views of TPCK

TPACK is a conceptual framework to describe the knowledge base that teachers require to proficiently use technology and involves an alignment of the pedagogy, content and technology knowledge (Voogt et al. 2013a). The number of peer-reviewed papers on the ERIC database that have TPACK or TPCK in either the title and/or abstract on the 10th November 2013 was 104. Many of these papers focused on approaches to teaching that included in-service and pre-service professional development, beliefs and attitudes. The disciplinary orientation of nearly a third of the studies was on mathematics and science, with a few examples of interdisciplinary approaches in mathematics, science and social sciences.

Mishra and Koehler's (2006) TPCK framework has been widely used to consider teachers' knowledge and use of educational technologies (Voogt et al. 2013b). The initial series of papers by Koehler and Mishra (2005) and Mishra and Koehler (2006) referred to TPCK rather than TPACK. In 2007 Thompson and Mishra (2007) published an editorial paper announcing the change from TPCK to TPACK as it both emphasises the three types of knowledge they believe to be essential to technology integration and also the integrated nature of these domains. Other similar terms used in the literature are ICT-TPCK as a strand of TPCK (Angeli and Valanides 2009) and technology-enhanced PCK or TPCK (Niess 2005).

Voogt et al. (2013a) found that all 55 papers in their data set agreed that TPACK originated from Shulman's (1986) concept of PCK. Stevens et al. (2005) explain that Shulman argued that "research on teaching had focused on the wrong target" (p. 113) by not focusing on how teachers think about the interaction of pedagogy and content knowledge. PCK is considered an important feature of teaching as it involves integrating domain knowledge with appropriate pedagogical approaches so that students can understand the subject matter (Voogt et al. 2013a). From reviewing TPACK literature, Voogt et al. (2013a) argue that there are three different understandings: (1) TPCK as an extension of PCK (Cox and Graham 2009; Niess 2005), (2) TPCK as a development of the understandings of the three domains of content, pedagogy and technology knowledge and the interplay between them (Mishra and Koehler 2006) and (3) ICT-TPCK as a distinct body of a knowledge (Angeli and Valanides 2009). Each of these perspectives will now be looked at in turn.

One view of TPCK is technology-enhanced PCK (Niess 2005). In her case study research with five pre-service science and mathematics teachers, Niess (2005) explains that TPCK requires a consideration of multiple domains of knowledge, and she suggests that courses to prepare student teachers need to consider how to guide pre-service teachers in expanding their understanding of the interactions between the knowledge of their subject area and their knowledge of technology (Niess 2005). Abbitt (2011) describes TPACK as a response to the growth in using educational technologies by integrating technology into Shulman's (1986) concept of pedagogical content knowledge (PCK). He remarks that both Niess (2005) and Mishra and Koehler (2006) emphasise the interplay between technology and PCK. However, Mishra and Koehler (2006) include technology knowledge as a third domain more explicitly along with pedagogical knowledge and content knowledge (Abbitt 2011). In their conceptual analysis, Cox and Graham (2009) claim that PCK has always included technologies and that, as digital technologies become ubiquitous, TPACK transforms into PCK. Cox and Graham (2009) argue that TPACK is extended as new technologies emerge.

TPCK as a development of understanding in all three domains is a second view of TPCK presented by Koehler and Mishra (2005) and Mishra and Koehler (2006). This necessitates that the teacher looks further than technical aspects and considers the importance of the interplay of technology knowledge, pedagogical knowledge and content knowledge (Mishra et al. 2009). Mishra and Koehler (2006) claim that: "Quality teaching requires developing nuanced understanding of the complex relationships between technology, content, and pedagogy, and using this understanding to develop appropriate context specific strategies and representations" (p. 1029). Voogt et al. (2013a) argue that Mishra and Koehler (2006) present TPCK as a development of understanding in the three domains and their intersections, whereas Niess (2005) views TPCK as an enhancement of PCK. However, these authors point out that researchers have found that the seven knowledge domains as conceptualised by Mishra and Koehler are problematic because it is difficult to agree of what are examples of each construct, e.g. Archambault and Barnett (2010) and Cox and Graham (2009).

Angeli and Valanides (2005, 2009) present a third view of TPCK, as ICT-related PCK (2005) and ICT-TPCK (2009), which they describe as a unique body of knowledge. Their research into pre-service teacher preparation found ICT preparation focused on technical understanding of various software applications rather than how to teach with ICT (Angeli and Valanides 2005). After mapping two ICT-enhanced design tasks, Angeli and Valanides (2009) found that pre-service primary teachers' ICT-TPCK competency improved over the course of a semester. Voogt et al. (2013a) support the view that TPACK should be seen as a distinct body of knowledge, and they are surprised that few studies in their review discussed the meaning of TPACK for specific subject areas. They see TPACK as distinct from technology integration and a knowledge base where content needs to be considered (Voogt et al. 2013a).

20.3 The Conceptual Framework for the Study

The present study proposes to view TPACK as a distinct body of knowledge within the context of teachers' overall pedagogical practices in an interdisciplinary unit of study, with these practices informed by the teachers' characteristics and ICT knowledge (Fig. 20.1). Beliefs about technology and pedagogy are closely intertwined (Voogt et al. 2013a). Therefore, the conceptual framework will look at teacher characteristics and ICT knowledge in terms of their educational values and beliefs, ICT skills and beliefs as well as previous interdisciplinary experience. The top section of the conceptual framework shows a two-way process

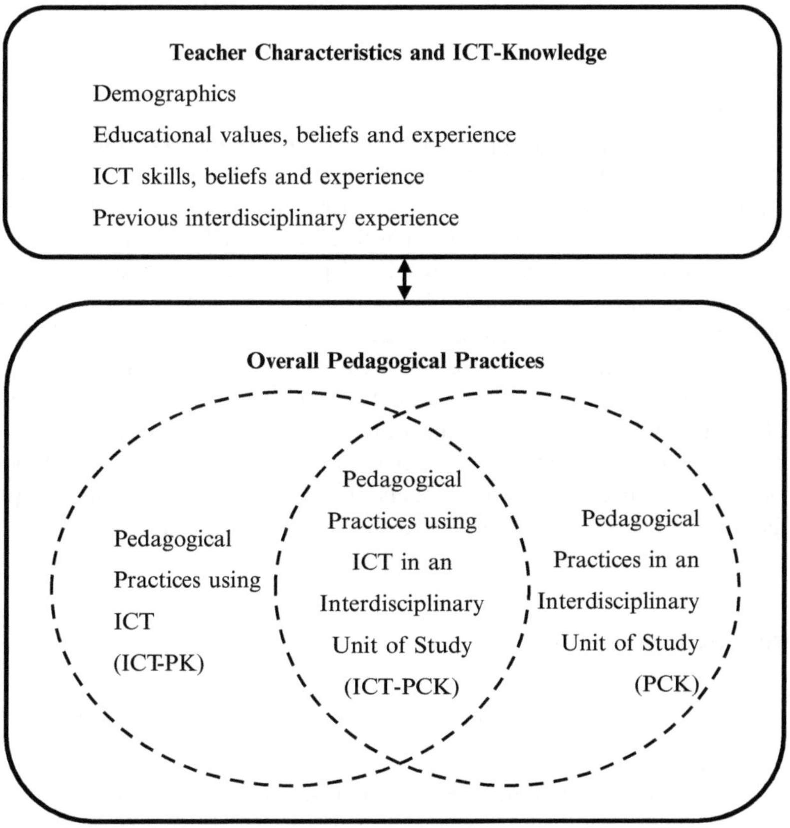

Fig. 20.1 Diagrammatic representation of the conceptual framework

between teachers' beliefs, values, experiences and ICT knowledge that will have helped shape their pedagogical practices.

The lower section of the conceptual framework covers teachers' overall pedagogical practices, which are informed by teacher characteristics and ICT knowledge. Overall pedagogical practices encompasses: the pedagogical practices used in an interdisciplinary unit (PCK), the pedagogical practices using ICT (PK-ICT) and the intersection of these, where ICT-PCK are the pedagogical practices using ICT in an interdisciplinary unit. PK-ICT are the skills and competencies teachers have developed for approaches using ICT in the disciplines they teach. PCK includes the approaches the teachers intend to use to cover content, skills and concepts to assist students make interdisciplinary links. ICT-PCK is conceptualised as a body knowledge within the context of teachers' overall pedagogical practices which has been constructed from PK-ICT and PCK when engaged in an interdisciplinary approach. The term ICT-PCK is used which is a variation of Angeli and Valanides (2009) conceptualization ICT-TPCK being a strand of TPCK, which is restricted to ICT. The research will focus on pedagogical practices and ICT, and so the construct will be referred to as ICT-PCK because this more accurately describes the focus of the study as it is investigating ICT as opposed to technology more generally.

Conclusion
Although interdisciplinary approaches have been advocated and investigated for a number of years, there is little research into the impact of ICT and interdisciplinary approaches in secondary schools. Frequently, TPACK research has been carried out looking at particular disciplines such as mathematics and science. The interaction between teachers' pedagogical practices and their characteristics and ICT knowledge is indicated on the conceptual framework for the present study. The conceptual framework uses the term ICT-PCK in an interdisciplinary approach, where ICT-PCK is viewed as a distinct body of knowledge within teachers' overall pedagogical practices constructed from PK-ICT and PCK. The research questions are intended to reveal how ICT is impacting on the pedagogical practices in an interdisciplinary approach both theoretically by investigating the concept of ICT-PCK and practically in terms of facilitating factors, as well as issues and concerns that may arise.

References

Abbitt, J. T. (2011). Measuring technological pedagogical content knowledge in preservice teacher education: A review of current methods and instruments. *Journal of Research on Technology in Education, 43*(4), 281–300.

Angeli, C., & Valanides, N. (2005). Preservice elementary teachers as information and communication technology designers: An instructional systems design model based on an expanded view of pedagogical content knowledge. *Journal of Computer Assisted Learning, 21*(4), 292–302.

Angeli, C., & Valanides, N. (2009). Epistemological and methodological issues for the conceptualization, development, and assessment of ICT–TPCK: Advances in technological pedagogical content knowledge (TPCK). *Computers & Education, 52*(1), 154–168.

Archambault, L. M., & Barnett, J. H. (2010). Revisiting technological pedagogical content knowledge: Exploring the TPACK framework. *Computers & Education, 55*(4), 1656–1662.

Beane, J. A. (1995). Curriculum integration and the disciplines of knowledge. *The Phi Delta Kappan, 76*(8), 616–622.

Beane, J. A. (1997). *Curriculum integration: Designing the core of democratic education.* Williston: Teachers College Press.

Boix-Mansilla, V. (2010). *MYP guide to interdisciplinary teaching and learning*. Retrieved May 22, 2012, from http://occ.ibo.org/ibis/documents/myp/m_g_mypxx_mon_1005_1_e.pdf

Brown, S. W. (2008). Assessment is not a dirty word. In D. M. Moss, A. Osborn, & D. Kaufman (Eds.), *Interdisciplinary education in the age of assessment*. New York: Routledge.

CDC-HKEAA. (2014). *Liberal studies curriculum and assessment guide* (Secondary 4–6, pp. 1–232). Retrieved May 7, 2014, from http://334.edb.hkedcity.net/doc/eng/curriculum/LS%20C&A%20Guide_updated_e.pdf

Cox, S., & Graham, C. R. (2009). Diagramming TPACK in practice: Using an elaborated model of the TPACK framework to analyze and depict teacher knowledge. *TechTrends: Linking Research & Practice to Improve Learning, 53*(5), 60–69.

Graham, C. R. (2011). Theoretical considerations for understanding technological pedagogical content knowledge (TPACK). *Computers & Education, 57*(3), 1953–1960.

Griffin, P., Care, E., & McGaw, B. (2012). The changing role of education and schools. In P. Griffin, B. McGaw, & E. Care (Eds.), *Assessment and teaching of 21st century skills* (pp. 1–15). Dordrecht: Springer.

Hammond, C., & McCallum, F. (2009). Interdisciplinary: Bridging the university and field of practice divide. *Australian Journal of Teacher Education, 34*(2), 50–63.

Jacobs, H. H. (1989). The growing need for interdisciplinary curriculum content. In H. H. Jacobs (Ed.), *Interdisciplinary curriculum: Design and implementation* (p. 97). Alexandria: Association for Supervision and Curriculum Development.

Koehler, M., & Mishra, P. (2005). What happens when teachers design educational technology? The development of technological pedagogical content knowledge. *Journal of Educational Computing Research, 32*(2), 131–152.

Mishra, P., & Koehler, M. (2006). Technological pedagogical content knowledge: A framework for teacher knowledge. *Teachers College Record, 108*(6), 1017–1054.

Mishra, P., Koehler, M., & Kereluik, K. (2009). The song remains the same: Looking back to the future of educational technology. *TechTrends: Linking Research & Practice to Improve Learning, 53*(5), 48–53.

Moss, D. M., Osborn, T. A., & Kaufman, D. (Eds.). (2008). *Interdisciplinary education in the age of assessment*. New York: Routledge.

Niess, M. (2005). Preparing teachers to teach science and mathematics with technology: Developing a technology pedagogical content knowledge. *Teaching and Teacher Education, 21*(5), 509–523.

Nissani, M. (1995). Fruits, salads, and smoothies: A working definition of interdisciplinary. *The Journal of Educational Thought, 29*(2), 121–128.

Rennie, L. J., Venville, G., & Wallace, J. (2011). Learning science in an integrated classroom: Finding balance through theoretical triangulation. *Journal of Curriculum Studies, 43*(2), 139–162.

Shulman, L. S. (1986). Those who understand: Knowledge growth in teaching. *Educational Researcher, 15*(2), 4–14.

Stevens, R., Wineburg, S., Herrenkohl, L. R., & Bell, P. (2005). Comparative understanding of school subjects: Past, present, and future. *Review of Educational Research, 75*(2), 125–157.

Tchudi, S., & Lafer, S. (1996). *The interdisciplinary teacher's handbook: Integrated teaching across the curriculum*. Portsmouth: Boynton/Cook Publishers.

Thompson, A., & Mishra, P. (2007). Breaking news: TPCK becomes TPACK! *Journal of Computing in Teacher Education, 24*(2), 38/64.
Venville, G., Wallace, J., Rennie, L., & Malone, J. (2000). Bridging the boundaries of compartmentalised knowledge: Student learning in an integrated environment. *Research in Science and Technological Education, 18*(1), 23–35.
Voogt, J., Fisser, P., Pareja Roblin, N., Tondeur, J., & van Braak, J. (2013a). Technological pedagogical content knowledge – A review of the literature. *Journal of Computer Assisted Learning, 29*(2), 109–121.
Voogt, J., Knezek, G., Cox, M., Knezek, D., & ten Brummelhuis, A. (2013b). Under which conditions does ICT have a positive effect on teaching and learning? A Call to Action. *Journal of Computer Assisted Learning, 29*(1), 4–14.
Zhbanova, K., Rule, A., Montgomery, S., & Nielsen, L. (2010). Defining the difference: Comparing integrated and traditional single-subject lessons. *Early Childhood Education Journal, 38*(4), 251–258.

Chapter 21
Students' Perception of Using ePortfolios for Learning in Higher Education

Danlin Yang, Alexandra Chiu-Yee Ngai, and Hing Keung Hung

Abstract ePortfolio is implemented in a higher education institute in Hong Kong with the objective of building the capacity of students in managing and monitoring their own learning in technology-enhanced environment, and at the same time, it is important for the institute to understand the students' perspectives in creating the ePortfolios for the ongoing development. As a student-centered learning tool, the study aims to find out whether the ePortfolios could help students learn to document their learning process, showcase their learning outcomes and perform self-reflection on their own learning. Moreover, the purpose of this study was to gain insights from students' perceptions of the usefulness of ePortfolios for further implementation. Semi-structured interviews were conducted on seven students selected from different programs to understand their perceptions of learning and how they perceive the benefits of ePortfolio creation to learning. It is found that not all students could perceive the objectives of ePortfolio creation which would help them to organize, manage, and reflect on learning and that it is still a long way for freshmen to perceive the benefits of student-centered learning by creating ePortfolios. It is crucial for the institute to consider how to develop the awareness of students to become active learners with the creation of ePortfolios and with the guidance of teachers.

Keywords ePortfolios • Students' perception • ePortfolio implementation • Higher education

21.1 Introduction

With the implementation of the new 3-3-4 academic structure in Hong Kong secondary school curriculum, the bachelor degree programs in education offered in Hong Kong were expanded from 4 to 5 years, and a new series of general education courses were designed to focus on the development of students' learning experience (Fisher et al. 2012). Portfolios, as a collection of individual artifacts for

D. Yang • A.C.-Y. Ngai • H.K. Hung (✉)
Centre for Learning, Teaching and Technology,
Hong Kong Institute of Education, Hong Kong, China
e-mail: dyang@ied.edu.hk; acyngai@ied.edu.hk; vhung@ied.edu.hk

© Springer Science+Business Media Singapore 2015

W.W.K. Ma et al. (eds.), *New Media, Knowledge Practices and Multiliteracies*,
DOI 10.1007/978-981-287-209-8_21

documentation and record of the personal growth, have been introduced to support student learning in global context (Parker et al. 2012; Bolliger and Shepherd 2010). Nowadays, with the development of information technology, institutions of higher education are utilizing ePortfolios to collect digital artifacts demonstrating students' learning in a technology-enhanced platform (Singh and Ritzhaupt 2006). It is believed that ePortfolio, integrated with emerging Web 2.0 technology, has potential to leverage the learning (Alexiou and Paraskeva 2010). Therefore, ePortfolios are implemented as a technologically supported tool for students to manage their learning process, consolidate their learning outcomes, and reflect upon their learning.

In light of the advantages of ePortfolios to support learning, the institute gradually regarded integrating ePortfolios into academic courses that have great potential to enhance students' learning. Since the learner is, of course, central to the learning process, it is necessary to take into consideration the perspectives of students using ePortfolios for learning. In this regard, this paper is aimed not only to evaluate the usefulness of ePortfolios from students' perspectives but also to illuminate the improvement of ePortfolio implementation for higher education.

The following sections of this paper begin with the literature review on ePortfolios, followed by the qualitative analysis of students discourse on their perception of the ePortfolio implementation in higher education. We conclude this paper with the future directions of ePortfolio implementation.

21.2 Literature Review

21.2.1 The Definition of ePortfolios

With the increasingly popularity of ePortfolios in tertiary education (Batson 2002), there are numerous definitions and interpretations of the term. As known, ePortfolio is short for electronic portfolio. It is acknowledged that ePortfolios are collections of electronic artifacts integrating multimedia elements and represent the accomplishments of learners (Lorenzo and Ittelson 2005). However, ePortfolios are not just used to store learners' artifacts digitally. They are meant to be exhibitions of learners' progress and accomplishments (Paulson et al. 1991), as well as a digital container for learners to collect and organize their multimedia artifacts (Abrami and Barrett 2005). To conclude, an ePortfolio is a collection of digital resources as learning evidence to show an individual's personal development and achievements (Beetham 2005).

21.2.2 The Purposes of ePortfolios

ePortfolios are implemented for a variety of purposes as indicated in literatures, such as recording students' learning process and outcomes for assessment (Gülbahar and Tinmaz 2006), continuous reflective practices for improvement over time

(Zubizarreta 2009), for enhancement of students' ability of self-regulated learning (Alexiou and Paraskeva 2010), and demonstrating one's achievements at any time such as job interview.

The aim of ePortfolio implementation in our context is to build students capacity to manage, organize, and reflect on their learning process and outcomes throughout the learning journey.

21.2.3 Students' Perceptions of ePortfolios

Since ePortfolios are for individuals to organize and manage their own learning, students should play a central role in their self-managed student-centered ePortfolio activities. Therefore, it is important to have a better understanding on students' perceptions of using ePortfolios for learning along with the institute's objectives on ePortfolio implementation.

Bolliger and Shepherd (2010) conducted a web-based questionnaire and collected the threaded of discussion from 40 students in regard to their perspectives of communication connectedness, their value, and their learning through ePortfolio integration. The research reported that ePortfolios can foster sustained learning communities for the students in online graduate programs.

Tosh et al. (2005) addresses four themes, which will help to enhance the engagement of students with their ePortfolios: buy-in, motivation, assessment, and ePortfolio technology. The research shows the needs to understand the viewpoints of students in the implementation of the ePortfolio to ensure students active engagement. By focusing on preservices teachers' attitudes and perceptions towards the process of electronic portfolio creation, 33 teacher candidates were selected and studied under qualitative research method. After 5 weeks of ePortfolio activities, semi-structured interviews were conducted on a one-on-one basis in order to determine their perspectives and attitudes towards the ePortfolio creation process. The results showed that electronic portfolio creation process was perceived as a desired teaching process; and the participants developed positive attitudes towards this process. The findings supported that ePortfolio should be a part of teacher education and be included in the policies of education institutes.

Another study conducted by Denton and Wicks (2013), implemented electronic portfolios through social media platforms and collected 33 graduate students' perceptions on using it. The results have shown that the participants perceived electronic portfolios as online diaries and also a convenient tool for organizing and showcasing artifacts, but they didn't identify the connection between social media and ePortfolios with their learning. And the study indicated the importance of training students to analyze and reflect in the ePortfolio implementation.

It is reviewed that ePortfolios can promote students' learning in higher education. However, little studies have focused on students' perception of creating ePortfolios for learning. If students do not perceive the use of ePortfolios as an integral part of managing their learning, then the goals of the implementing ePortfolios in the courses may not have achieved and strategies of the implementation may need to be reviewed.

Therefore, it led us to ask:

- What is the impact of the ePortfolio implementation on the students' learning?
- What is the students' perception of using ePortfolios for their learning?

21.3 Research Design

ePortfolio was introduced to students of an institute in Hong Kong to empower students in managing and critically reflecting upon their learning and to become lifelong learners. The implementation started from students' year-1 study that is aimed at facilitating students to be familiar with the ePortfolio concept, so that the students can start managing their own learning at the early stage of their undergraduate study by documenting their works and engaging in continuous reflection on their own learning. Three core courses were integrated for the implementation at year 1: the General Education (GE) Foundation course and two courses from the English Enhancement (EE) Program. The ePortfolio activities included writing reflective journals and uploading artifacts as evidences of learning in these courses.

The briefing sessions to introduce the concept of using ePortfolios for their learning and the training workshops are being conducted for students to have a basic understanding of ePortfolios and tailor their ePortfolios for self-managing their learning process. It is expected that the students would transfer what they have learned to other learning contexts for continuous reflection and development upon their learning throughout their undergraduate study at the institute.

To evaluate the impact of the full-scale implementation on year-1 students and to understand the students' perceptions of using ePortfolios in their studies, both qualitative and quantitative methods were employed with 688 surveys received and in-depth interview conducted with seven students. The focus in this paper is to have a deep understanding of students' perceptions of using ePortfolios for their learning. Semi-structured interviews were used as a qualitative instrument for the study. Interviews were favored because they are suitable for gaining insight into the experience and knowledge of others (Schostak 2005).

Using a theoretical criterion sampling strategy (Byrne 2001), we were looking for the respondents who have experience in using ePortfolios in their learning. A convenience sampling technique is used to identify the students for interview. A number of emails were sent out to invite students to participate in the interview. Seven year-1 students replied and agreed to participate. The interviews were conducted in January–March 2014. One of the main questions in the interview was, "What are the purposes of creating ePortfolios?," followed-up by questions asking about their perception of learning and whether they perceived any relationships with the use of ePortfolios. All interviews were audio recorded and transcribed for analysis.

Students participated in the semi-structural in-depth interviews on a voluntary basis, and the categories of responses may be weighted towards the more conscientious students or the students with a particular point to make.

The data analysis consisted of coding the interview transcripts. Two researchers were involved in the qualitative analysis, which consisted of three types of coding procedures: open, axial, and selective coding. The researchers coded responses line by line, formed categories and subcategories, and explored the interrelationship of the categories (Parker et al. 2012). Results from the analysis are discussed in the following sections.

21.4 Findings and Discussions

The study identified students' perceptions of learning with ePortfolios at a local higher education institution and discussed the factors which influence their dependency upon learning with ePortfolios. Student perceptions on learning and the possible justifications in the students' perceptions are discussed.

21.4.1 Students' Perception of Learning with ePortfolios

In general, the majority of respondents believed that the creation of the ePortfolios did help their learning. A participant indicated that the ePortfolio was a valuable or enjoyable experience. However, not all respondents enjoyed the ePortfolio development. In these instances, using ePortfolios became a burden instead of a useful tool for their learning. One participant mentioned having difficulty in understanding the relevance of the ePortfolio to support learning. The students' perception on the purposes of using ePortfolios is investigated below.

To understand students' perception of the purposes of ePortfolios, three categories of responses are identified from coding and pattern categorization. The first category, *assignments submission*, suggests that participants perceived ePortfolios as a platform to hand in assignments to teachers. Evidentiary comments for this included the following:

> I just uploaded files. I perceived it as a platform for handing in assignments.
>
> …the ePortfolios help me learn how to submit assignments on the Internet.

And two participants mentioned that they have difficulty in understanding the difference between ePortfolio platform and the learning management system (LMS), as they see that the ePortfolio platform serves the same purposes as the LMS, that is, for submitting assignments. It is also acknowledged that students who were confused between the purposes of the two platforms perceived little value in using ePortfolios in their courses and for their learning. From their responses, they regarded that using ePortfolios was externally from demands of course assessment instead of self-directed learning. Although they fulfilled all ePortfolio requirements in their ePortfolio pages, the students could not be identified as understanding the concept of using ePortfolios to manage their own learning with ePortfolios. They regarded ePortfolio as a platform for them to upload the assignments to accomplish the teachers' tasks. That is to say, they passively accepted to use ePortfolios for handing in assignments rather than using ePortfolios for reflection or knowledge building.

The second category, *organization and showcase*, suggests that participants affirmed ePortfolios as a useful tool for recording, organizing, and presenting their assignments and achievements. Supporting comments included:

> I want to put all the materials centrally together. I can organize them together using the platform which can be exported to another file in the future for showcasing.
>
> I think it focuses on showcasing, and it can let me have a place to put all my things together.

Additionally, three students mentioned that ePortfolios were beneficial for their job interviews in the future and that they can use it to demonstrate their skills and abilities. One participant stated:

> I think it is useful for one's future, such as when you go to work in the society, when you apply for jobs, or just for your own reference.

Students in this category perceived ePortfolio as an important platform for them to document their digital artifacts as evidence of learning, also see the usefulness of using ePortfolios for showcase to others in future, especially for job finding. However, although the students realized ePortfolio as a useful tool for them to organize their artifacts, they did not mention to use ePortfolios to achieve their learning goals or manage their learning. They have the awareness that ePortfolio is useful, but they have not integrated it for their learning.

The last category *reflective learning* suggests that participants realized ePortfolios as an area for students to reflect upon what they have learned. Two participants addressed that performing reflection can help their learning and personal development. The students, who valued the importance of ePortfolios for their learning, constructed their knowledge actively by keeping record of the evidences of learning and writing reflective journals on ePortfolios about what they have learned. What the students mentioned:

> Such as images, links, presentations, and other multimedia elements, the paper-based format doesn't have these functions, but ePortfolios can include all of them… I think it can help students reflect on what they learnt regularly.
>
> I enjoyed writing journals. The professor told us that we have the freedom to express on anything we wanted to. It helped me to recall what I have learnt from the GE class more quickly.

In summary, not all of the respondents perceived the concept of using ePortfolios as a tool to help them to organize their learning artifacts, to reflect upon their learning, and to manage their learning. Respondents who regarded ePortfolios as an online assignment submission platform were more concerned about how to submit and the frequency of submission. This paradox clearly warrants further exploration as learners are unlikely to benefit from the process if they misunderstood the main purposes of using ePortfolios. Therefore, it is necessary for teachers and administrators to have a clear shared understanding of how the implementation of ePortfolios links with the students' perception of learning.

As evidenced by the categories above, the students who perceived the values of using ePortfolios for learning believed that ePortfolios have benefits on their learning and were actively building their ePortfolios to reflect on their performance for improvement, while some students who just completed their ePortfolio pages fulfilling the basic requirements did not realize the connection between using ePortfolios and their personal development. As Hartnell-Young (2006) put it, learning is a process that requires learners to actively build knowledge. From the perspective of Jonassen (1991), knowledge is actively constructed by students. Therefore, it is essential to transform the students who lack the motivation to use ePortfolios for their learning to take responsibility of their learning and become self-regulated learners.

Since it is found that ePortfolios can promote deep learning by engaging students with reflection, it is significant for the institute to integrate ePortfolio implementation with student-centered approach to improve their motivation. That is to say, it is important for the institute to think about ePortfolio implementation from the perspectives of learners to motivate students' learning enthusiasm and engage students in active learning with ePortfolios. Also, it is important for the institute to consider strategies aiming at promoting the concept of learning with ePortfolios.

21.4.2 The Role of Teachers

One point of interest is that three participants mentioned the teachers as an important role for their learning with ePortfolios. In their perspective, the feedbacks given by teachers to their ePortfolios motivated them to reflect on what they have written and forced them to take more time to reflect further and polish the ePortfolios. For example, one participant indicated that the teacher who guided the ePortfolio development motivated her to keep on reflecting on what she has learned, while other students who did not receive teachers' feedbacks regularly mentioned that they just regarded ePortfolios as a platform to submit their assignments and did not update their ePortfolios regularly without the teachers' requirement.

Results from this study indicated that feedbacks from teachers played an important role in encouraging the enthusiasm of students for managing their ePortfolios and reflecting on learning. It is suggested that learning is mediated by discourse rather than merely received from teachers' instruction (Vygotsky 1978). That is to say, the important role of teachers is not as a dispenser of knowledge. As for students, teachers play the role of facilitators and guides. They help students grow, change, and learn. Therefore, it is suggested to address the attention of the communication between teachers and students throughout the process of the ePortfolio implementation.

With the teachers' feedbacks, students can reflect their ideas continuously towards deeper learning, which can lead students to begin to integrate ePortfolios into their learning landscape to support their continuous development.

Conclusion

This paper has analyzed students' responses to using ePortfolios based on their perception of learning in their year-1 study. It is acknowledged that the students' perceptions of the usefulness of ePortfolios are vital concern to whether the implementation can achieve the goal of enhancing students managing in learning with ePortfolios. According to the findings, most of the students are aware that ePortfolios can help them in their learning. However, not all of the students used ePortfolios for self-managing their own learning and monitoring their personal improvement. It is crucial for the institute to consider how to develop the awareness of students to become active learners with the support of ePortfolios. Besides, teachers' guidance and encouragement on the ePortfolio development are also important throughout the process. With their guidance, students have a better understanding of integrating ePortfolios with reflection for their learning. Referring to the students' perspective, this paper analyzed some problems of students' learning with ePortfolios to facilitate further implementation and ongoing improvement of ePortfolio initiatives. But there is one potential weakness of this study is that the data were collected by convenience sampling, therefore, selected participants were not generalized to represent all year-1 students. Further studies could explore students' perception of learning with ePortfolios in their final year of study to see the effectiveness of ePortfolios and any change on students' perception of learning. The perceptions of this study may also warrant further exploration.

References

Abrami, P., & Barrett, H. (2005). Directions for research and development on electronic portfolios. *La Revue Canadienne De l'apprentissage Et De La Technologie* [Canadian Journal of Learning and Technology], *31*(3), 1–15.

Alexiou, A., & Paraskeva, F. (2010). Enhancing self-regulated learning skills through the implementation of an e-portfolio tool. *Procedia-Social and Behavioral Sciences, 2*(2), 3048–3054.

Batson, T. (2002). *The electronic portfolio boom: What's it all about*. Retrieved April 10, 2014, from http://campustechnology.com/articles/2002/11/the-electronic-portfolio-boom-whats-it-all-about.aspx?sc_lang=en

Beetham, H. (2005). *E-portfolios in post-16 learning in the UK: Developments, issues and opportunities*. Retrieved April 10, 2014, from http://www.jisc.ac.uk/media/documents/themes/elearning/eportfolioped.pdf

Bolliger, D., & Shepherd, C. (2010). Student perceptions of ePortfolio integration in online courses. *Distance Education, 31*(3), 295–314.

Byrne, M. (2001). Sampling for qualitative research. *AORN Journal, 73*(2), 494–498.

Denton, D. W., & Wicks, D. (2013). Implementing electronic portfolios through social media platforms: Steps and student perceptions. *Journal of Asynchronous Learning Networks, 17*(1), 123–133.

Fisher, D., Cheung, H. L., Pickard, V., Chen, Y., Chan, Y. F., & Wong, M. C. (2012). ePortfolios for higher education: A Hong Kong perspective. In D. Cambridge (Ed.), *E-portfolios and global diffusion: Solutions for collaborative education* (p. 149). Hershey: IGI Global.

Gülbahar, Y., & Tinmaz, H. (2006). Implementing project-based learning and E-portfolio assessment in an undergraduate course. *Journal of Research on Technology in Education, 38*(3), 309–327.

Hartnell-Young, E. (2006). ePortfolios for knowledge and learning. In A. Jafari & C. Kaufman (Eds.), *Handbook of research on ePortfolios* (pp. 124–133). Hersey: IGI Global.

Jonassen, D. H. (1991). Objectivism versus constructivism: Do we need a new philosophical paradigm? *Educational Technology Research and Development, 39*(3), 5–14.

Lorenzo, G., & Ittelson, J. (2005). An overview of e-portfolios. *Educause Learning Initiative, 1*, 1–27.

Parker, M., Ndoye, A., & Ritzhaupt, A. D. (2012). Qualitative analysis of student perceptions of E-portfolios in a teacher education program. *Journal of Digital Learning in Teacher Education, 28*(3), 99–107.

Paulson, F. L., Paulson, P. R., & Meyer, C. A. (1991). What makes a portfolio a portfolio. *Educational Leadership, 48*(5), 60–63.

Schostak, J. (2005). *Interviewing and representation in qualitative research.* Maidenhead: McGraw-Hill International.

Singh, O., & Ritzhaupt, A. (2006). Student perspective of organizational uses of eportfolios in higher education. *World Conference on Educational Multimedia, Hypermedia and Telecommunications, 2006*(1), 1717–1722.

Tosh, D., Light, T. P., Fleming, K., & Haywood, J. (2005). Engagement with electronic portfolios: Challenges from the student perspective. *La Revue Canadienne De l'apprentissage Et De La Technologie* [Canadian Journal of Learning and Technology], *31*(3), 89–110.

Vygotsky, L. S. (1978). *Mind in society: The development of higher psychological processes.* Cambridge, MA: Harvard University Press.

Zubizarreta, J. (2009). *The learning portfolio: Reflective practice for improving student learning.* San Francisco: Wiley.

Chapter 22
Investigating the Relationship Between Students' Attitude Towards Video Production Project and Their Generic Skills Enhancement

Heidi Fung and Will W.K. Ma

Abstract Over the past decade there has been a growing concern for higher education to pay greater attention to the development of students' generic skills. The development of generic skills requires learning settings that focus on process and student-centered learning. According to the potential benefits of using role-playing and video production as learning activity, it is presumed that integrating the two into curriculum creates a good platform that helps in the development of various types of generic skills. As prior research demonstrated that students' attitude towards learning would have a direct influence on students' learning behavior and outcome, this research study aims to investigate the relationship between students' attitude towards role-playing video production project (RVP) and the improvement of students' generic skills. This study also examines if there is any association between students' perception of using smartphones in learning and their generic skills enhancement.

Keywords Generic skills • Student-produced video • Role-playing • Accounting information systems • Students' attitude • Smartphones

H. Fung (✉)
Hong Kong Shue Yan University, Hong Kong, HKSAR, China
e-mail: heidi@hksyu.edu

W.W.K. Ma
Online Communication Research Centre, Department of Journalism and Communication, Hong Kong Shue Yan University, Hong Kong, China
e-mail: wkma@hksyu.edu

© Springer Science+Business Media Singapore 2015

W.W.K. Ma et al. (eds.), *New Media, Knowledge Practices and Multiliteracies*, DOI 10.1007/978-981-287-209-8_22

22.1 Introduction

As generic skills were perceived as being important to graduates' future careers, increasingly, higher education institutions are being expected to aid the development of students' generic skills (Chapman and O'Neill 2010; Luca and Oliver 2002). Instructors of higher education need to redesign learning activities that aid producing graduates with discipline knowledge as well as generic skills. Previous research on the development of generic skills revealed the importance of learning settings that are student-centered and focus on process (Luca and Oliver 2002). The potential benefits of role-playing pedagogy (Billings 2012; Joyner and Young 2006; Lei-Da et al. 2003; Oreilly 2013; Shapiro and Leopold 2012; Stroessner et al. 2009) and the advantages of student-produced video assignment (Cox et al. 2010; Greene and Crespi 2012; Gromik 2012; Hung et al. 2004; Kearney and Schuck 2006) infer that a combination of the two would be an effective approach for enhancing generic skills.

However, research literature on investigating the effectiveness of student-produced role-playing video project in the enhancement of student's generic skills is limited. Moreover, in this information era, youth have got used to the stimulation of a multimedia world, especially when smartphones appear to be an "extended part" of the human body. Today's students are not satisfied with the traditional passive learning mode but are expecting a more active and engaging educational experience (Greene and Crespi 2012). Despite the accessibility of smartphones, there are only a few researches that have examined the affordances of audiovisual recording features of smartphones (Gromik 2012; Naismith et al. 2004).

It is generally agreed that the attitudes and perceptions people hold determine what they do. To extend the concept into the context of video production project with the use of smartphones, this study aims to investigate the relationship between students' attitude towards role-playing video production project (RVP) and students' generic skills improvement. It also attempts to examine if there is any association between students' perception of using smartphones in learning and their generic skills enhancement.

The aforementioned purposes then raise the research questions of this study:

RQ1. What are students' attitudes towards RVP?

RQ2. What are students' perceptions of using smartphones in learning?

RQ3. Is there any relationship between students' attitude towards RVP and students' generic skill improvement?

RQ4. Is there any relationship between students' perception of using smartphones in learning with students' generic skill improvement?

22.2 Literature Review

With the rapid development in information and communication technology (ICT), today's students have grown up in a multimedia world. They would expect more than the traditional one-way lecturing and PowerPoint slides in their learning experience (Greene and Crespi 2012). In addition, as employers have put more emphasis on generic skills, higher education pedagogy should be developed from the integration of education theory, current technology, an understanding of the abilities and interests of the learner as well as the expectation from the employers.

22.2.1 Role-Playing Pedagogy

In regard to student engagement, role-playing is a commonly used activity in teaching and learning process. There has been extensive literature about using role-playing for teaching and learning. Previous studies indicated potential benefits of role-playing to learning outcome. Role-playing encourages student engagement, promotes active learning, and supports higher-order thinking skills (Billings 2012; Joyner and Young 2006; Lei-Da et al. 2003; Oreilly 2013; Shapiro and Leopold 2012; Stroessner et al. 2009).

Role-playing facilitates deeper and more critical understanding of course material (Shapiro and Leopold 2012). Students were able to practice and develop skills during role-playing (McKeachie 1986, cited in Joyner and Young 2006). Stroessner et al. (2009) indicated that role-playing produces beneficial psychological consequences and improvement in academic skills. Besides enhancing cognitive skills (Lei-Da et al. 2003; Stroessner et al. 2009), role-playing also increases student's motivation and confidence (Lei-Da et al. 2003; Shapiro and Leopold 2012). Despite the benefits that have been assumed to arise from role-playing, Stroessner et al. (2009) argued that the empirical foundation of these claims is limited. Moreover, only a few research studies in the existing literature spotlighted the effectiveness of role-playing for enhancing students' generic skills.

22.2.2 Student Video Production Activity

Digital video is frequently employed by the teachers for increasing student engagement. In addition to using documentary video or educator-produced video, student-generated digital video projects are becoming more common. In general, student feedback and evaluation in relation to student-created video approach is positive (Greene and Crespi 2012; Hung et al. 2004). Students perceived it a useful activity for their learning (Gromik 2012). Having students to produce video not only yields a richer understanding of the subject matter but also promotes active learning and student engagement (Cox et al. 2010; Greene and Crespi 2012; Kearney and Schuck 2006; Sadik 2008). As video production activity offers a high level of student autonomy, it encourages student motivation and enthusiasm (Cox et al. 2010; Hung et al. 2004; Kearney and Schuck 2006). Previous studies indicated that student-generated video activities promote higher-order thinking and enhance confidence and communication skills (Cox et al. 2010; Kearney and

Schuck 2006). However, most of these studies were conducted at primary or secondary schools. Research literature on student-produced videos as an active learning assignment at tertiary education is limited (Greene and Crespi 2012).

22.2.3 Smartphones

As smartphones become more accessible to younger consumers, it is not difficult to find college students carrying smartphones with them everywhere. According to the survey "Smartphone Using and Consumption Habit of Hong Kong Students" conducted by the Hong Kong Computer Society (HKCS) Youth Club in 2013, 90 % of the 529 student respondents were using smartphones. Among the smartphone users, 83 % spent more than 1 h on smartphone per day and nearly half of them spent over 3 h on smartphones per day. Naismith et al. (2004) identified potential teaching practice for constructive learning by integrating smartphones into the curriculum.

Previous studies show that students appreciated smartphones' photo and video recording features for reporting and sharing content over the Internet (Gromik 2012). As a valuable and accessible device to the youth, smartphones might be a convenient and effective instrument to enhance learning. According to Taleb and Sohrabi (2012), the most educational uses of mobiles by university students are calculator usage, text messaging, and English dictionary. In the student focus group interviews conducted by Gikas and Grant (2013), the participants have described many advantages of mobile devices, such as smartphones, for their learning. For example, with the mobile devices, students can access information quickly and communicate with their fellow classmates and the instructor in a convenient way. The video and voice recording feature of the devices enable students interact with course content in a variety of ways and facilitate class discussion and collaborative learning. Mobile devices also support situated learning of which learning takes place in the same context in which it is applied. Despite the popularity of smartphones in the young generation, integrating smartphones into curriculum is still at the infant stage. Research about how smartphones are being used to support teaching and learning is limited (Gikas and Grant 2013).

22.2.4 Generic Skills

Generic skills, also known as soft skills, key skills, common skills, essential skills, employability skills, basic skills, necessary skills, competencies skills, and transferable skills (Yassin et al. 2008), refer to "skills that are common to more than one work site, more than one occupation or more than one field of knowledge" (NBEET 1996, cited in Luca and Oliver 2002, p. 1). Kember and Leung (2009) has come up with a list of generic competencies that the graduates should possess. The list of generic competencies includes critical thinking, creative thinking, self-managed learning, adaptability, problem-solving, communication skills, interpersonal skills and teamwork competencies, and computer literacy. All these generic competencies have proved acceptable across different disciplines.

Over the past decade there has been a growing concern for higher education to pay greater attention to the development of students' generic skills. While technical knowledge is vital to the success of an employee's work, more and more employers are stressing the importance of nontechnical skills (Freudenberg et al. 2011; Low et al. 2013). Since 1980s, many employers and professional bodies have called for more "work-ready" graduates who are adaptable, independent, and self-directed learner (Chapman and O'Neill 2010; Luca and Oliver 2002). Kember and Leung (2009) argued that "..., there is a general agreement that a university education should result in graduates developing a range of generic capabilities, which equip them for life-long learning" (p. 17).

22.2.5 Attitude-Behavior Relationship

There is a general agreement that attitude is one of the factors that influence behavior. Attitude simply refers an index of the degree to which a person likes or dislikes about the object. According to the theory of reasoned action, a person's positive or negative evaluation of performing the behavior, which termed as attitude towards the behavior, determines a person's intention to act (Ajzen and Fishbein 1980). Prior research suggested that student's attitude towards learning would have a direct influence on student's learning. Regarding the context of textbook online support, Fung and Ma (2013) revealed that students' attitude towards the online support positively associated with their usage behavior and students who have used the online support outperformed those who have not used. Moreover, integrating information technology into curriculum would be an effective way to support learning. Users with negative attitudes about the technology might lead to negative repercussions and weaken the benefits of the system (Brown et al. 2002). Students' attitude towards blended learning is an important factor influencing their usage behavior of educational technology (Fung and Yuen 2012). Similarly, students' behavior is influenced by their perception of what will work for them (Vandsburger and Duncan-Daston 2011).

Based on the attitude-behavior relationship demonstrated in previous research, it is presumed that students' attitude towards the RVP and their perception of using smartphones in their learning influence their learning behavior that would have an effect on learning outcome. Accordingly, we posited that:

H1: There would be a significant relationship between students' attitude towards video production project and their generic skill improvement.

H2: There would be a significant relationship between students' perception of using smartphones in learning and their generic skill improvement.

22.3 Methodology

The goals of this study are to investigate the relationship between students' attitude towards RVP and students' generic skills improvement and examine if there is any association between students' perception of using smartphones in learning and their generic skills enhancement. In order to answer the research questions of this study, quantitative approach was used to understand students' attitude and perception and to analyze the associations of the constructs. A survey was conducted to collect the required data.

22.3.1 Background of the Study

This study was located in the ground of an undergraduate third year Accounting Information Systems (AIS) course in a private university in Hong Kong. AIS is a compulsory third year semester course of a 4-year undergraduate Accounting program. The objective of the course is to help students acquire the necessary knowledge and understanding of contemporary information systems from an accountant's perspective. The duration of the course is 15 weeks and students were taught in one 3-h class per week. In order to encourage student engagement and active learning, together with the integration of ICT in learning, the instructor has chosen the video production project (RVP) as part of the continuous assessment.

In this group project, students needed to use smartphones to film and edit a 15-min video of an assigned topic using the genre of role-playing. In order to enhance team building skill, each group (group of 5) of students was formed in random. The assigned topics were related to the business cycles of an organization, and each group of students was responsible for some activities of the cycle. Students were expected to present in the video the procedures of the activities, the possible threats of the activities, and the internal controls measures to protect the organization.

The students were required to submit the finished video 4 weeks after the instructor had notified them the assigned topics. After reading relevant materials, students needed to design the scenarios and different characters for the video. All students were required to act in the video. In addition to producing the video, students were required to submit weekly reflection journals reporting their progress of the project and the problems they have encountered. They also needed to indicate the contributions of each member. The student-produced videos would then be broadcasted in class as teaching material and for peer evaluation. The evaluation was based on the content and the quality of the video. Although this was a group project, individual member's contribution to the project was counted in instructor evaluation.

22.3.2 Participants

The data of this study was collected in the fall semester 2013. The participants in this study were 151 undergraduate year three accounting students enrolled in AIS. These students were allocated into five sections. Since all the five sections were taught by the same instructor, all the participants have gained the same information of the course.

22.3.3 Data Collection Instrument and Data Analysis

In order to understand the students' attitude towards the RVP and their perceptions of using smartphones in learning, all the 151 students were invited to do a questionnaire after the completion of the project. The questionnaire also included questions for collecting students' perceptions of the improvement on generic skills. Although the survey was conducted in class, students have a free will to participate and the purpose of the survey was clearly stated on the questionnaire.

The questionnaire includes three constructs which are Attitude towards RVP (ATT), seven items; Perception of using smartphones in learning (PHO), four items; and Generic skill improvement (GEN), nine items (see Appendix). The items of the ATT and PHO were adopted from Cox et al. (2010) and Greene and Crespi (2012). Since the RVP was not carried out in class, students' behavior during the process was not accessible. In order to collect data on whether students have improvement in generic skills through this project, it is necessary to rely on the student's self-report on their perceptions of generic skill improvement. The GEN items of the questionnaire were adopted from Kember and Leung (2009). Likert scale of 7 was used for the questionnaire.

SPSS statistical package was used to analyze these quantitative data. The data was validated by reliability (Cronbach's alpha) and validity (factor analysis) and further analysis using regression to test the hypotheses.

22.4 Findings

22.4.1 Students' Feedback

In general, students hold a positive attitude towards the video production project (see Appendix). There were 62.7 % of the respondents who agreed that doing the project was a positive learning experience. The result of the survey also reveals that 61.6 % and 59.6 % of the students agreed that the RVP was an innovative assignment and an interesting experience, respectively. There were 55.6 % of the respondents who agreed that it was an enjoyable experience to do the project and 53 % were glad that they have been involved in the project.

Regarding the improvement in generic skills, over 62 % of the students agreed that their generic skills (except the self-management learning capability) have improved via this project. Moreover, the survey shows that 82 % of respondents perceived smartphones a valuable tool in their university learning and over 56 % have responded that using smartphones to do learning task is interesting, innovative, and motivating.

22.4.2 Instrument Validation

Internal consistency was tested by reliability; Cronbach's α-value where values greater than 0.7 is considered reliable (Nunnally and Bernstein 1994). The α values for ATT, PHO, and GEN were 0.923, 0.903, and 0.918, respectively.

It showed that all the constructs were reliable and internal consistent. All the items were then examined using factor analysis. It was found that the constructs were all distinct without any significant cross-loadings, exhibited discriminant validity. The factor loading for each item is greater than 0.5 which is considered significant and exhibited convergent validity (Hair et al. 2010). Therefore, the instrument is both reliable and valid (see Table 22.1).

Table 22.1 Factor analysis

		Component			
		1	2	3	α
ATT	ATT1	.119	**.815**	.194	0.923
	ATT2	.253	**.754**	.306	
	ATT3	.245	**.651**	.145	
	ATT4	.379	**.796**	.161	
	ATT5	.226	**.830**	.254	
	ATT6	.336	**.747**	.040	
	ATT7	.358	**.708**	.269	
PHO	PHO1	.284	.063	**.740**	0.903
	PHO2	.175	.268	**.854**	
	PHO3	.214	.337	**.823**	
	PHO4	.126	.238	**.878**	
GEN	GEN1	**.615**	.367	.066	0.918
	GEN2	**.730**	.304	.122	
	GEN3	**.733**	.263	.135	
	GEN4	**.699**	.353	.236	
	GEN5	**.722**	.330	.201	
	GEN6	**.762**	.146	.162	
	GEN7	**.812**	.209	.156	
	GEN8	**.710**	.176	.134	
	GEN9	**.713**	.117	.196	
	Eigen values	9.772	2.134	1.757	
	% of variance	48.862	10.672	8.784	

Table 22.2 Model summary

Model summary					ANOVA	
Model	*R*	R^2	Adjusted R^2	Std. error of the estimate	F	Sig.
1	.659[a]	.435	.427	.5791	55.774	.000

[a]Predictors: (Constant), Smart Phone, Attitude

Table 22.3 Hypotheses testing results

Model		Unstandardized coefficients		Standardized coefficients		
		B	Std. Error	Beta	*t*	Sig.
1	(Constant)	2.054	.273		7.526	.000
	Attitude	.437	.060	.537	7.285	.000
	Smartphone	.147	.057	.192	2.602	.010

22.4.3 Hypotheses Testing Results

The summed mean score for each construct is calculated. Then, regression analysis was used to test the hypotheses. The overall testing model was significant ($p<0.001$) and the R-square was 0.435. That means the overall model explained 43.5 % of the variance of the dependent variable (GEN) (see Table 22.2).

H1 was supported. It was found that the path was significant and the standardized coefficient was 0.537 (unstandardized coefficients 0.437, std. error 0.060, $p<0.001$). That is, for every standardized unit of ATT increased, there would be 0.537 standardized unit of GEN increased. The higher the ATT, the higher the GEN. H2 was supported. It was found that the path was significant and the standardized coefficient was 0.192 (unstandardized coefficients 0.147, std. error 0.057, $p<0.01$). That is, for every standardized unit of PHO increased, there would be 0.192 standardized unit of GEN increased. The higher the PHO, the higher the GEN (see Table 22.3 and Fig. 22.1).

22.5 Discussion

Despite the encouraging results of this study that in general students hold a positive attitude towards the RVP, it can be observed that students have different extents of acceptance towards different attributes of the project. Instructors are suggested to put effort in understanding the rationale behind students' response, especially for those unfavorable items, so as to modify the project design for lifting students' positive attitude towards the project.

The result of this study shows consistency with the findings of previous research on role-playing pedagogy (Billings 2012; Joyner and Young 2006; Lei-Da et al. 2003; Shapiro and Leopold 2012; Stroessner et al. 2009) and video production activity (Cox et al. 2010; Greene and Crespi 2012; Gromik 2012; Hung et al. 2004; Kearney and Schuck 2006), and the RVP takes the advantages of both role-playing

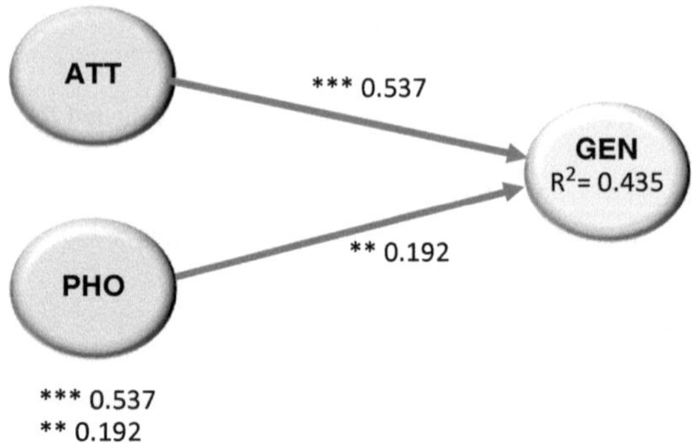

Fig. 22.1 Summary of the testing model

and video production. In general, students reflected that RVP is motivating and useful. Besides promoting active learning and student engagement, the RVP also facilitates a richer understanding of the subject matter and helps the development of different types of skills. Similar to the situation of students' attitude towards the RVP discussed in the previous paragraph, the impact of the RVP to different generic skills varies. It would be valuable to find out how the project aids the improvement of different generic skills with the purpose of adjusting the project for better enhancement of generic skills.

Although RVP is not the only approach for generic skills development, as the potential benefits of RVP have been demonstrated, instructors are encouraged to consider using a similar approach when designing the curriculum in order to support student learning of discipline knowledge as well as the generic skills. Though an alternate term for generic skills is transferable skills, different industries would have their preference on graduate's generic skills. To meet the needs of employers, instructors are suggested to design learning activities that give more emphasis to the development of the industry-required generic skills.

This study demonstrates the association between students' attitude towards the RVP and the self-report generic skills enhancement. In general, the more positive the students' attitudes towards the RVP, the further improvement in generic skills they have perceived. In order to foster positive attitude towards a learning activity, the focus should be on expounding the benefits of RVP to student learning (Brown et al. 2002). Instructors are suggested to clearly inform students the purposes and benefits of using RVP in the course. When students gain a better understanding of the rationale behind the adoption of RVP, they would have a more positive feeling towards RVP. With a positive attitude, students are expected to be more involved in the project, which probably would result in a greater improvement in their knowledge and skills.

The association between students' perception of using smartphones in learning and the improvement in generic skills was also established in this study. Herrington and Parker (2013) confirmed that emerging technologies can be used in every stage of the learning cycle. Their study demonstrated that emerging technologies were "the delivery mechanism, the means for communication and articulation, the tool for collaboration, the platform for the publication of final products, and importantly, the cognitive tools for thinking and creating valuable technology-based products" (p. 614). As the mobile devices such as smartphones and tablet computers become students' necessities, instructors are suggested to examine the potential benefits of these emerging technologies and consider integrating these accessible devices into the curriculum.

22.5.1 Limitations and Future Studies

This study investigated the relationship between students' attitude towards RVP and generic skills improvement. Although the results demonstrated the potential benefits of RVP to student learning, it is essential to understand how generic skills enhancement occurs in the process. Further research is needed to explore in-depth how the improvement of different types of generic skills occurs throughout the project.

Because of the limited scale of this study, the findings may not generalize to other course context. Previous study indicated that students' perception of the suitability of ICT integration differs depending on the type of course in which they are participating (Frey et al. 2003). The course context of this study, AIS, is a subject related to information technology. Students might be more willing to accept the project and using smartphones because they might perceive it relevant to the course nature. Similar research could be conducted in other courses and at other disciplines.

This study uses students' self-report perception as a measurement of the generic skills improvement. Since the RVP required the students to do the project on their own, their behaviors were not directly accessible to an observer. Though students' self-report data provide a certain degree of accuracy on student learning, future research needs to consider other methods to measure the student learning. For instance, aptitude test with the use of scenarios could be used to measure students' generic skills before and after the RVP. Analyzing students' reflection journals would be an alternative way to understand the process of the project and the development of generic skills.

Though *H2* (there would be a significant relationship between students' perception of using smartphones in learning and their generic skill improvement) of this study was supported by a weak correlation, it is expected to arouse the interest of educators and researchers about the potential association of the variables. Further work is clearly needed to ensure the relationship.

Conclusion

In conclusion, this study reveals the correlation between students' attitude towards the RVP and the generic skills enhancement, along with the relationship between students' perception of using smartphones in learning and the improvement in generic skills. It provides valuable evidence for the possible educational value of the RVP to student generic skill improvement. As a practical issue, the result of this study provides empirical evidence for instructors of different disciplines to consider taking advantage of RVP for effective learning. As smartphones being accessible devices to today's students, instructors are suggested to consider how to utilize these advanced technology in supporting teaching and learning.

Appendix: Survey Instrument Items

	Constructs: items	*M*	SD	[a]Cumulative percent
Student's attitude towards the video production project (ATT)				
(Adopted from Cox et al. 2010; Greene and Crespi 2012)				
ATT1	It was an *innovative assignment*	4.71	1.164	61.6
ATT2	It was an *enjoyable experience*	4.66	1.206	55.6
ATT3	It was a *fair assessment task*	4.43	1.105	46.6
ATT4	I am *glad* that I have involved in the project	4.65	1.097	53
ATT5	It was an *interesting experience*	4.74	1.187	59.6
ATT6	It was a *useful experience*	4.49	1.142	49.7
ATT7	It was a *positive learning experience*	4.84	0.990	62.7
Student's perception of using smartphone in learning (PHO)				
(Adopted from Greene and Crespi 2012)				
PHO1	In general, smartphone is a *valuable* tool in my university study	5.36	1.012	82.0
PHO2	Using smartphone to do learning task is *interesting*	4.82	1.118	62.7
PHO3	Using smartphone to do learning task is *innovative*	4.74	1.155	56.7
PHO4	Using smartphone to do learning task is *motivating*	4.65	1.238	50.3
Student's perceived improvement in generic skill (GEN)				
(Adopted from Kember and Leung 2009)				
GEN1	(Critical thinking) I have become *more willing to consider different points of view*	4.75	0.969	63.3
GEN2	(Self-management learning) I have become *more confident of my ability* to pursue further learning	4.55	1.033	48.7
GEN3	(Adaptability) I have learnt how to be *more adaptable*	4.79	0.945	62.0
GEN4	(Adaptability) I have become *more willing to change my views and accept new ideas*	4.85	1.052	65.3
GEN5	(Problem-solving) I have *improved my ability to use knowledge to solve problems* in my study	4.78	0.929	64.5
GEN6	(Communication skills) I have *developed my ability to communicate effectively* with others	4.94	0.964	68.0
GEN7	(Communication skills) I have *improved my ability to express ideas*	4.83	0.979	64.7
GEN8	(Interpersonal skills and group work) I have learnt to *become an effective team member*	4.91	0.929	71.3
GEN9	(Interpersonal skills and group work) I feel *confident in dealing with a wide range of people*	4.77	1.071	65.3

[a]*Note:* cumulative percent of respondents who have chosen 5, 6, or 7 (i.e., agree to strongly agree)

References

Ajzen, I., & Fishbein, M. (1980). *Understanding attitudes and predicting social behavior.* New York: Prentice-Hall.

Billings, D. M. (2012). Role-Play revisited. *The Journal of Continuing Education in Nursing, 43*(5), 201–202. Retrieved April 8, 2013, from http://dx.doi.org/10.3928/00220124-20120424-04

Brown, S. A., Massey, A. P., Montoya-Weiss, M. M., & Burkman, J. R. (2002). Do I really have to? User acceptance of mandated technology. *European Journal of Information Systems, 11*(4), 283–295.

Chapman, E., & O'Neill, M. (2010). Defining and assessing generic competencies in Australian universities: Ongoing challenges. *Education Research and Perspectives, 37*(1), 105–125.

Cox, A. M., Vasconcelos, A. C., & Holdridge, P. (2010). Diversifying assessment through multimedia creation in a non-technical module: Reflections on the MAIK project. *Assessment & Evaluation in Higher Education, 35*(7), 831–846.

Freudenberg, B., Brimble, M., & Cameron, C. (2011). WIL and generic skill development: The development of business students' generic skills through work-integrated learning. *Asia-Pacific Journal of Cooperative Education, 12*(2), 79–93.

Frey, A., Faul, A., & Yankelov, P. (2003). Student perceptions of web-assisted teaching strategies. *Journal of Social Work Education, 39*(3), 443–457.

Fung, H., & Ma, W. W. K. (2013). Exploring the effectiveness of hybrid learning in accounting information systems – An empirical study. In S. K. S. Cheung et al. (Eds.), *Hybrid learning and continuing education* (LNCS 8038, pp. 178–189). Berlin/Heidelberg: Springer.

Fung, H., & Yuen, A. (2012). Factors affecting students' and teachers' use of LMS – Towards a holistic framework. In S. K. S. Cheung et al. (Eds.), *Hybrid learning* (LNCS 7411, pp. 306–316). Berlin/Heidelberg: Springer.

Gikas, J., & Grant, M. M. (2013). Mobile computing devices in higher education: Student perspectives on learning with cellphones, smartphones & social media. *Internet & Higher Education, 19*, 18–26.

Greene, H., & Crespi, C. (2012). The value of student created videos in the college classroom – An exploratory study in marketing and accounting. *International Journal of Arts and Sciences, 5*(1), 273–283.

Gromik, N. A. (2012). Cell phone video recording feature as a language learning tool: A case study. *Computers & Education, 58*(1), 223–230.

Hair, J. F., Black, W. C., Babin, B. J., & Anderson, R. E. (2010). *Multivariate data analysis: A global perspective* (7th ed.). Upper Saddle River: Pearson.

Herrington, J., & Parker, J. (2013). Emerging technologies as cognitive tools for authentic learning. *British Journal of Educational Technology, 44*(4), 607–615.

Hong Kong Computer Society (HKCS) Youth Club. (2013). *Survey report on smartphone using and consumption habit of Hong Kong Students*. Retrieved March 20, 2014, from https://www.hkcs.org.hk/en_hk/misc/press_release/20131104_1_eng.pdf

Hung, V. H. K., Keppell, M., & Jong, M. S. Y. (2004). Learner as producers: Using project based learning to enhance meaningful learning through digital video production. In R. Atkinson, C. McBeath, D. Jonas-Dwyer, & R. Phillips (Eds.), *Beyond the comfort zone: Proceedings of the 21svt ASCILITE Conference* (Vol. 1, pp. 428–436). Perth: ASCILITE.

Joyner, B., & Young, L. (2006). Teaching medical students using role play: Twelve tips for successful role plays. *Medical Teacher, 28*(3), 225–229.

Kearney, M., & Schuck, S. (2006). Spotlight on authentic learning: Student developed digital video projects. *Australasian Journal of Educational Technology, 22*(2), 189–208.

Kember, D., & Leung, D. Y. P. (2009). Development of a questionnaire for assessing students' perceptions of the teaching and learning environment and its use in quality assurance. *Learning Environments Research, 12*(1), 15–29.

Lei-Da, C., Achita, M., & Frolick, M. N. (2003). Investigating the use of role play training to improve the communication skills of IS professionals: Some empirical evidence. *The Journal of Computer Information Systems, 43*(3), 67–74.
Low, M., Samkin, G., & Liu, C. (2013). Accounting education and the provision of soft skills: Implications of the recent NZICA CA academic requirement changes. *E-Journal of Business Education & Scholarship of Teaching, 7*(1), 1–33.
Luca, J., & Oliver, R. (2002). Developing an instructional design strategy to support generic skills development. In *Australasian Society for Computers in Learning in Tertiary Education (ASCILITE). Conference* (19th: 2002). Auckland: UNITEC Institute of Technology.
Naismith, L., Lonsdale, P., Vavoula, G., & Sharples, M. (2004). *Literature review in mobile technologies and learning*. Harbourside/Bristol: Futurelab.
Nunnally, J. C., & Bernstein, I. H. (1994). *Psychometric theory*. New York: McGraw-Hill.
Oreilly, P. (2013). Implementing and assessing student performance skills and learning: A policy role-playing exercise. *International Journal of Education, 5*(1), 103–119.
Sadik, A. (2008). Digital storytelling: A meaningful technology-integrated approach for engaged student learning. *Educational Technology Research and Development, 56*(4), 487–506.
Shapiro, S., & Leopold, L. (2012). A critical role for role-playing pedagogy. *TESL Canada Journal, 29*(2), 120–130.
Stroessner, S. J., Beckerman, L. S., & Whittaker, A. (2009). All the world's a stage? Consequences of a role-playing pedagogy on psychological factors and writing and rhetorical skill in college undergraduates. *Journal of Educational Psychology, 101*(3), 605–620.
Taleb, Z., & Sohrabi, A. (2012). Learning on the move: The use of mobile technology to support learning for university students. *Procedia – Social and Behavioral Sciences, 69*, 1102–1109.
Vandsburger, E., & Duncan-Daston, R. (2011). Evaluating the study guide as a tool for increasing students' accountability for reading the textbook. *Journal of College Reading and Learning, 42*(1), 6–23.
Yassin, S., Hasan, F. A., Amin, W., & Amiruddin, N. (2008). Implementation of Generic Skills in the Curriculum. In *EDU-COM international conference* (2008: 4th). Khon Kaen.

Chapter 23
Enhancing Primary School Students' Story Writing by Mobile-Assisted Collaborative Learning: A Case Study

Wenting Zou and Xiaolei Li

Abstract Writing is generally perceived as a daunting task in language learning for primary school children. To improve engagement and activate the writing process, the present study implemented and evaluated the effectiveness of an innovative writing instruction strategy that combines two commonly used collaborative learning practices—collaborative writing and peer assessment—on a mobile learning platform, also described as Mobile-Assisted Collaborative Learning Pedagogy (MACLP). In this quasi-experimental study, two classes of 3rd graders ($N=73$) received sessions about Chinese story writing varied in two kinds of instructional designs: MACLP vs. traditional individual and paper-based writing graded by teacher. We compared students' learning gains after different interventions and probed students' perceptions towards MACLP in their writing process, with a special focus on whether students with high, average, and low prior Chinese language abilities benefit equally from MACLP.

Keywords Mobile-assisted language learning (MALL) • Collaborative writing • Peer assessment • Individual difference

23.1 Introduction

23.1.1 Problem Statement

Writing is perceived to be one of the most stressful and challenging tasks in Chinese language learning for elementary school students. They constantly express anxiety and demonstrate incompetency while dealing with writing tasks (Sun 2008).

W. Zou
CCC Heep Woh Primary School, Kowloon, Hong Kong
e-mail: ellenzou2012@gmail.com

X. Li (✉)
The University of Hong Kong, Hong Kong, China
e-mail: xiaolei1990@hotmail.com

© Springer Science+Business Media Singapore 2015

W.W.K. Ma et al. (eds.), *New Media, Knowledge Practices and Multiliteracies*,
DOI 10.1007/978-981-287-209-8_23

Lacking involvement, limited and incorrect use of vocabulary, and badly structured paragraphs are the common defects in primary school students' compositions (Huang 2008; Wong et al. 2011). To address these problems, effective and quality instructions are developed to support the writing process (Graham and Perin 2007). Traditional writing instructions are constantly criticized for multiple aspects: (1) teacher centered, (2) exam-oriented, and (3) fail to involve students' life experiences (Shen and Nie 2013). Under the pressure of public examinations, many instructors are negligent of the true purpose of writing, thus fail to guide students to explore and express the passion and natural emotion stimulated by real life. Students have nothing to write about but fabricate stories or plagiarize model essays to finish the tasks. Resulted from inappropriate scaffolding, certain number of primary children remains low writing capabilities all the way through middle schools.

Over the past decade, substantial amount of literature has tapped into the reform of traditional writing instruction in search for innovative pedagogical designs to teach Chinese writing. For instance, Zheng (2008) proposed that group discussions, role-playing, and peer assessment might be recipes for activating students' interests and increasing engagement in writing attempts. Based on empirical practices, the present study aims at examining whether collaborative writing combined with peer assessment can successfully improve students' writing performances, with a particular focus on whether students with different levels of prior language achievement benefit equally from MACLP.

23.1.2 Research Questions

Due to the limited literature on examining the effectiveness of mobile-assisted collaborative learning in Chinese writing instruction in primary schools, this study aims to fill the blank and address the following research questions:

Q1. Does MACLP impose significant effects on students' learning gains in the writing task?

Q2. Did students with different levels of Chinese language abilities benefit equally from MACLP?

Q3. What are students' perceptions towards MACLP in the writing task?

23.2 Literature Review

23.2.1 Collaborative Writing

According to Social Constructivist Theory (Vygotsky 1978) and Social View of Writing Process Theory (Faigley 1986; Tompkins 2008), writing is no longer seen as a solitary endeavor. Instead, writing is considered as a social activity in which co-participation and guided instruction are essential (De Smedt and Van Keer 2014). Rice and Huguley (1994) highlight the major activities of collaborative writing: it is performed collectively by more than one person to produce a single text, and writing is any activity that leads to a completed document, including idea generating, researching, planning and organizing, drafting, revising, and editing. The potentials and effectiveness of collaborative writing were noted by ample studies. For instance, Fernández Dobao and Blum (2012) study indicates that groups wrote more accurate texts than individual learners. Besides positive impact on writing performance, collaborative writing also has notable effects on noncognitive aspects such as motivation (Schultz 1997), enjoyment (Paquette 2009), learning attitudes, and lowering writing anxiety (De Bernardi and Antolini 2007). Despite of many perceived benefits, collaborative writing is not always successful under certain conditions, especially in primary schools. For example, dissensions over the task assignment (Lin and Maarof 2013), unwillingness to offer opinions, and failure to finish the writing task in the allocated time (Storch 2005). However, previous literature mainly focuses on the collaborative writing in English classrooms, and it is not commonly used in Chinese writing instruction in primary schools.

23.2.2 Peer Assessment

Underpinned by Social Constructivist Theory (Vygotsky 1978) and Active Learning Theory (Bonwell and Eison 1991), peer assessment is widely used in both traditional and computer-supported learning environments (Chang et al. 2011). Peer assessment, by definition, is a process whereby students grade their peers' assignments or tests based on a teacher's benchmarks (Sadler and Good 2006). The practice is employed to enhance students' comprehension of learning materials as well as improve their metacognitive skills by applying what they have learned to evaluate their peers' work. Technology considerably promotes communication across geographical and time barriers (Chang 2001) by which real-time feedback can be given from teachers and peers in order to effectively support students' learning process. Although students may be less experienced in assessment than teachers are, peer assessment is not necessarily less effective than teacher assessment. In Magin's (2001) case study, single-teacher assessment and peer assessment reached similar levels of reliability. Therefore, appropriately implementing peer assessment can attain sufficient reliability, and students can thereby receive more feedbacks to improve their performance (Chen 2010). Despite of reported reliability, effective peer assessment depends heavily on students' familiarity with the grading rubrics, and it often requires extra time that usually exceeds the time schedule of a 40-min session. Moreover, some scholar also argued that students did not necessarily achieve higher results after peer grading (Sadler and Good 2006).

23.3 Conceptual Model of Mobile-Assisted Collaborative Learning Pedagogy (MACLP)

A conceptual model is adapted from the research of Li et al. (2012) to provide theoretical guidance for the collaborative learning activities among students in this study (Fig. 23.1). More specifically, the collaborative writing process is based on Social View of Writing Process Theory (Faigley 1986; Tompkins 2008), while the peer assessment activity is supported by Active Learning Theory (Bonwell and Eison 1991), and Social Constructivist Theory (Vygotsky 1978) underpins both. This model served as the theoretical guideline for the design of the mobile learning platform and the course plan.

23.4 Methods

23.4.1 Participants

The participants of this experiment were two classes of third graders ($N = 73$; 42 girls, 31 boys) from a primary school in Hong Kong. Since this school has introduced

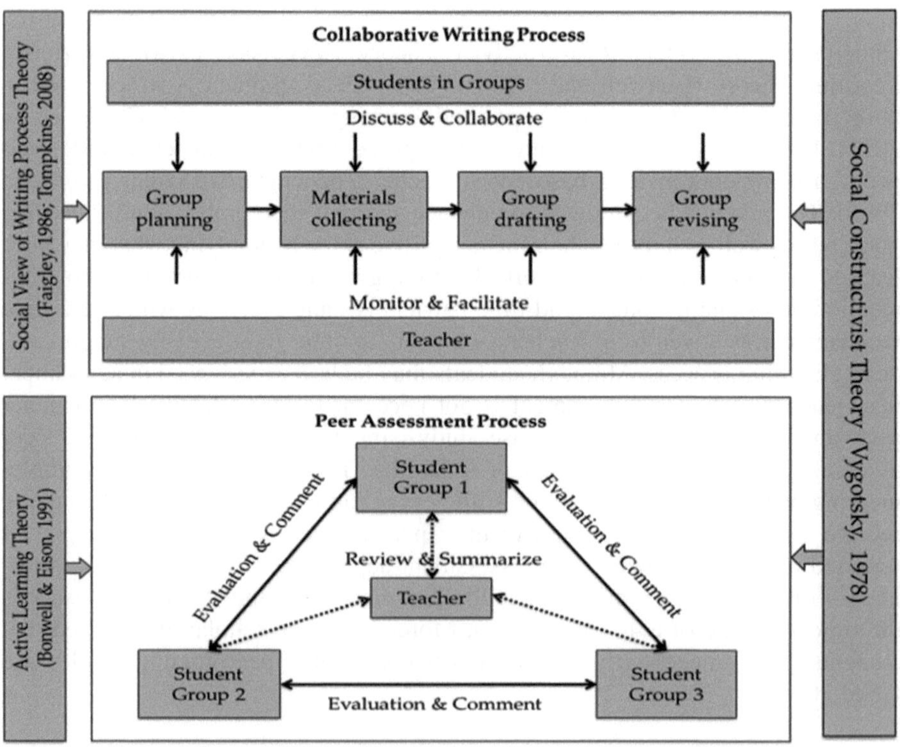

Fig. 23.1 Conceptual model of MACLP

mobile technology into Chinese writing instruction since 2012, the participants are able to operate the tablets with little technical support. In this study, the selected two classes are of equivalent academic level according to the students' average performances in the previous three Chinese language tests in school, the results of which are also used as indicator of students' prior language achievements in the data analysis procedure. During the experiment, Class A (37 students) was assigned to be instructed under MACLP, while Class B (36 students) under traditional instructional approach as a control group. Both classes were taught by the same Chinese language teacher.

23.4.2 Instructional Settings and Experiment Procedure

In this study, the authors and the Chinese language teacher codesigned a Chinese writing unit that consists of five sessions. The objective of the unit is to help students understand the definition and usage of personification with the learning task that requires students to construct a story using personification on their tablets. The mobile learning e-platform adopted in this study was developed by Modern Educational Research Society (HK) Ltd. In the experimental class (Class A), the teacher allocated students to different groups (4 ~ 5 students per group). Based on prior test scores of Chinese language, students with high language abilities were intentionally selected to mix with peers who have comparatively low language abilities. When the first session began, students in Class A were taught how to creatively use personification in story writing and assigned a learning task for them to complete in groups. As shown in Fig. 23.1, students had to discuss in groups and plan the theme, characters, and plot of their story. Subsequently, each group explored the campus within 30 min to collect writing materials (take photos or videos) using the tablets. Afterwards, each group member uploaded their files and co-drafted their story on the mobile learning platform. The drafts were posted for peer assessment according a given criteria. After each group received their feedbacks, the teacher reviewed and summarized the major problems occurred in the writing process. Students then started to revise their story before submitting the final product to the teacher. By contrast, Class B were presented the same knowledge but were required to complete the writing task individually on paper and graded solely by the teacher.

At the beginning and end of the experiment, all the participants were given a 30-min test, and selected students from Class A were invited for a semi-structured group interview to report their perceptions towards MACLP.

23.4.3 Instruments

In this study, we obtained quantitative and qualitative data by pre- and posttest, interviews and class observation. The purpose of involving multiple methods in the same research, also known as methodological triangulation (Denzin 2006), is to increase credibility and validity of the study.

The pretest and posttest were developed by the Chinese language teacher to measure students' learning gains in the planned unit. Both the tests require students to complete 15 multiple-choice items and write a short story, giving a full score of 100, respectively. To improve validity, the tests were also evaluated and modified by other three Chinese educators with average 8 years of teaching experiences. Several questions were subtracted due to ambiguity and repetition.

In order to assess the learning outcomes of students with different language abilities, we divided students in three groups—high ability, average ability, and low ability—based on their latest three Chinese language test results. After the experiment, we selected 12 students (four from each language ability group) in Class A for a semi-structured interview. The interview transcript was coded into themes by the first author and cross-checked by the second author to ensure the validity and reliability of data interpretation.

23.5 Results

23.5.1 *Quantitative Findings*

To test whether MACLP has positive influence on students' learning gains, we conducted an ANCOVA with the learning gains (gain defined as posttest minus pretest score) as dependent variable, with and without MACLP as independent variables, and students' prior language achievement (the average score of their latest three Chinese language tests) as covariate (see Table 23.1), for the purpose of controlling the effects of prior language achievement. Before conducting ANCOVA, we first examined the relationship between students' prior language achievement and their learning gains. Result shows that there is a significant correlation between participants' prior language level and their learning gains ($p < .01$), which substantiates the control of prior language achievement as a covariate. As a result of ANCOVA, there is a significant effect of MACLP on students' learning performances, $F(1,70) = 11.64$, $p = .001$, and $\eta^2 = .74$. In other words, students did improve significantly under MACLP compared with the control group.

To investigate whether students in Class A benefited equally from MACLP, a one-way analysis of variance was conducted to evaluate the learning gains of students with low (score 65~75), average (score 76~85), and high (score above 86)

Table 23.1 Students' test results with and without MACLP

		Prior achievement	Pretest score	Posttest score	Gain score
	N	Mean (SD)	Mean (SD)	Mean (SD)	Mean (SD)
Class A	37	81.11 (8.84)	78.92 (6.93)	87.95 (4.43)	9.03 (3.52)
Class B	36	83.12 (7.14)	80.11 (5.70)	86.58 (4.45)	6.47 (2.82)

Note: min. = 0, max = 100, standard deviation in brackets

Table 23.2 Post hoc tests among the means of three language ability groups

(I) Group	(J) Group	Mean difference (I–J)	Std. error	Sig. 95% confidence interval	Lower bound	Upper bound
Low	Average	.879	.967	1.000	−1.56	3.31
	High	5.903*	.934	.001	1.55	6.25
Average	Low	−.879	.967	1.000	−3.31	1.56
	High	5.024*	.912	.007	.73	5.32
High	Low	−5.903*	.934	.001	−6.25	−1.55
	Average	−5.024*	.912	.007	−5.32	−.73

*The mean difference is significant at the 0.05 level

levels of language abilities. Results show that MACLP did impose significant difference among the three language level groups, F (2,34) = 24.43, $p < .001$. High-ability group (mean = 5.64, SD = 2.37) benefited less from MACLP than average-ability group (mean = 10.67, SD = 2.81) and low-ability group (mean = 11.55, SD = 1.508) in terms of learning gains. Post hoc comparisons using Bonferroni tests were conducted to evaluate the pair wise differences among the means. Data denotes that there is a significant difference in the means between high-ability group and average-ability group, as well as between high-ability group and low-ability group, while no significant difference between average- and low-ability group (Table 23.2).

23.5.2 *Interview Findings*

To find out students' perceptions about MACLP, 12 students with different language abilities (high, average, and low) were invited for a 40-min interview. Data from the interview were transcribed and coded after negotiation between the two authors. Three overarching theme emerged from the data: cognitive, affective, and social. Eight subthemes were later identified by further analysis. Representative statements of each subtheme are given in Table 23.3.

23.6 Discussion

Underpinned by Social Constructivist Theory (Vygotsky 1978), this study investigated primary school students' performance and perceptions towards a Chinese story-writing task using collaborative writing and peer assessment as mixed scaffolds supported by a mobile learning platform, with a special focus on whether this pedagogy (MACLP) produces similar effects on students with diverse prior language abilities. The findings are summarized as follows:

Table 23.3 Students' perceptions of MACLP in writing process

Overarching themes	Subthemes	Representative statements
Cognitive	Enrich writing content	Tablets enable us to collect writing materials in different locations; we came up with creative ideas for our story when exploring the campus using tablets
	Accelerate writing process	We finished our story very fast because everyone contributed their ideas and involved in drafting the story
	Share writing skills	I looked at my group mates' writing to get more ideas when I was stuck, and I share my paragraph with them as well
	Increase knowledge retention	This writing task impressed me and it helped me to remember personification better
Affective	Promote writing motivation	I love writing when we are allowed to use tablets and take photos of what we are going to write
	Increase writing anxiety	I fear that my poor writing will slow down the process of the whole group and result in low grade
Social	Expanded audience	It is exciting to write when so many classmates are going to read our story
	Enhance collaboration	My group mates inspired me and gave me tips on certain expressions. We helped each other to modify the writing
	Instant feedbacks	I can get feedbacks from other students immediately, which is a great help to improve my writing

23.6.1 MACLP Imposes Significant Effects on Students' Learning Gains in the Writing Task

By using ANCOVA to analyze the gain scores before and after the writing task, we proved that students were better supported by MACLP with their prior language achievements controlled. In other words, MACLP benefited students in the writing practice regardless of their previous Chinese language levels. This positive result is in line with the research findings of Wong et al. (2012) of applying collaborative learning approaches to boost primary school children's Chinese writing ability. Possible factors that contribute to students' notable progress are concluded as follows: (1) heightened motivation, (2) effective collaboration, (3) instant feedbacks, and (4) increased knowledge retention.

23.6.2 Students with Average and Low Chinese Language Abilities Benefited More from MACLP

By comparing the average means of gain scores between pre- and posttests, we found that the low and average language ability groups made significant progress than the high-ability group did, although still not comparable to the high-ability group on posttest scores. The following two reasons may explain this result: (1) increased knowledge retention helped the low- and average-ability groups to tackle the true or false questions and meet the easily attainable goals of the writing task in the posttest; (2) many students from the high-ability group have previewed the unit beforehand, which resulted in high scores in the pretest, thus lower gain scores were observed than the other two groups.

23.6.3 Students Perceived MACLP as an Effective Instructional Strategy in Writing Instruction

From class observation and interview, most students in the experimental group demonstrate positive attitudes towards MACLP in three aspects: cognitive, affective, and social dimensions. In the cognitive aspect, students considered mobile collaborative learning activities to enrich their writing content, improve writing speed, and enhance writing skills and knowledge retention; while in affective aspect, all students reported heightened motivation, but average- and low-ability group expressed increasing writing anxiety; in the social aspect, multiple audience, effective collaboration, and instant feedbacks also contributed to their remarkable progress.

Conclusion

In light of the research findings, we support that using MACLP in Chinese writing instruction in primary school has positive effect on students compared with traditional scaffoldings. More importantly, students with average and low prior language abilities take particular advantage from MACLP in terms of learning gains. And most students reported positive perceptions towards this writing task under MACLP.

However, short duration of the experiment and insufficient number of participants limit reliability and hinder the generalization of the results. Future research should expand the number of participants and lengthen the experiment period. In spite of limitations, this study has important implications in both theory and in practice by filling the blank of limited research investigating the effectiveness of mobile-assisted collaborative learning strategy in Chinese writing instruction, as well as providing practical guidance for the instructional design to accommodate the needs of learners with different language abilities.

References

Bonwell, C., & Eison, J. (1991). *Active learning: Creating excitement in the classroom* (AEHE-ERIC higher education report no. 1). Washington, DC: Jossey-Bass.

Chang, C. C. (2001). A study on the evaluation and effectiveness analysis of web-based learning portfolio (WBLP). *British Journal of Educational Technology, 32*(4), 435–458.

Chang, C. C., Tseng, K. H., Chou, P. N., & Chen, Y. H. (2011). Reliability and validity of Web-based portfolio peer assessment: A case study for a senior high school's students taking computer course. *Computers & Education, 57*(1), 1306–1316.

Chen, C. H. (2010). The implementation and evaluation of a mobile self- and peer-assessment system. *Computers & Education, 55*(1), 229–236.

De Bernardi, B., & Antolini, E. (2007). Fostering students' willingness and interest in argumentative writing: An intervention study. *Studies in Writing, 19*, 183.

De Smedt, F., & Van Keer, H. (2014). A research synthesis on effective writing instruction in primary education. *Procedia – Social and Behavioral Sciences, 112*, 693–701.

Denzin, N. (2006). *Sociological methods: A sourcebook*. New Brunswick: Transaction Publishers.

Faigley, L. (1986). Competing theories of process: A critique and a proposal. *College English, 48*(6), 527–542.

Fernăndez Dobao, A., & Blum, A. (2012). Collaborative writing in pairs and small groups: Learners' attitudes and perceptions. *System, 41*(2), 365–378.

Graham, S., & Perin, D. (2007). A meta-analysis of writing instruction for adolescent students. *Journal of Educational Psychology, 99*(3), 445–476.

Huang, Z. (2008). Calling for true emotions in primary school students' Chinese writing. *Education of Science, 11*, 43.

Li, X., Chu, K., Ki, W. W., & Woo, M. M. (2012). Using a wiki-based collaborative process writing pedagogy to facilitate collaborative writing among Chinese primary school students. *Australasian Journal of Educational Technology, 28*(1), 159–181.

Lin, O. P., & Maarof, N. (2013). Collaborative writing in summary writing: Student perceptions and problems. *Procedia – Social and Behavioral Sciences, 90*, 599–606.

Magin, D. J. (2001). A novel technique for comparing the reliability of multiple peer assessments with that of single teacher assessments of group process work. *Assessment & Evaluation in Higher Education, 26*(2), 139–152.

Paquette, K. (2009). Integrating the 6+1 writing traits model with cross-age tutoring: An investigation of elementary students' writing development. *Literacy Research and Instruction, 48*(1), 28–38.

Rice, R. P., & Huguley, J. T. (1994). Describing collaborative forms: A profile of the team-writing process. *IEEE Transactions on Professional Communication, 37*(3), 163–170.

Sadler, P. M., & Good, E. (2006). The impact of self-and peer-grading on student learning. *Educational Assessment, 11*(1), 1–31.

Schultz, K. (1997). Collaborative writing in an urban elementary classroom. *Journal of Literacy Research, 29*(2), 253–287.

Shen, W. T., & Nie, D. Q. (2013). Expression of true personality: The intrinsic requirement of writing instruction. *Chinese Teaching & Studies, 13*, 77–83.

Storch, N. (2005). Collaborative writing: Product, process, and students' reflections. *Journal of Second Language Writing, 14*, 153–173.

Sun, Q. (2008). My opinion towards Chinese writing in primary school. *Journal of Educational Institute of Jilin Province, 24*(198), 152.

Tompkins, G. E. (2008). *Literacy for the 21st century: A balanced approach* (5th ed.). Boston: Allyn & Bacon.

Vygotsky, L. S. (1978). *Mind in society: The development of higher psychological processes*. Cambridge, MA: Harvard University Press.

Wong, L. H., Chen, W., Chai, C. S., Chin, C. K., & Gao, P. (2011). A blended collaborative writing approach for Chinese L2 primary school students. *Australasian Journal of Educational Technology, 27*(7), 1208–1226.

Zheng, W. P. (2008). Current challenges and strategies for writing instruction in primary schools. *The Science Education Article Collects, 11*, 109–122.

Chapter 24
The Impact of Project-Based Learning and Technology on Student Achievement in Mathematics

Leah J. Branch

Abstract The purpose of this study was to determine the effects on student achievement in mathematics when project-based learning with the support of technology is used as instructional approach rather than a traditional instructional approach with integrated technology. The research examined the differences in student achievement in mathematics between two charter schools in Chicago. It also examined teacher perceptions about project-based learning and/or technology as an instructional approach to improve learning and student achievement outcomes. The results revealed that there were statistically significant differences in student achievement between schools that used project-based learning as an instructional approach and schools that used a traditional instructional approach.

Keywords Twenty-first-century skills • Academic achievement • Project-based learning • Technology • Collaborative learning

24.1 Introduction

In schools today, there is overwhelming focus on student achievement and meeting standardized benchmarks. There is also an enormous gap between the knowledge and skills students learn in school and the knowledge needed to thrive in their communities and workplaces (P21 Century Skills 2002). The curricula, especially in the subject areas of science, mathematics, and technology, are not adequate for students living in a global, digital society (National Academy of Sciences 1997). Preparing students to live in the twenty-first century requires that educators expose them to a curriculum centered on content that would enable them to critically think, problem solve, and become efficient citizens in a vastly changing world (P21 Century Skills 2002).

L.J. Branch (✉)
Bethel University, St. Paul, MN, USA
e-mail: leajbranch@aol.com

© Springer Science+Business Media Singapore 2015
W.W.K. Ma et al. (eds.), *New Media, Knowledge Practices and Multiliteracies*,
DOI 10.1007/978-981-287-209-8_24

Schools today focus on meeting standardized testing benchmarks. However, students need to be equipped with an in-depth knowledge of core concepts in school, as well as in technology that would enable them to successfully apply their learning to real-world careers. Unfortunately, the attention on meeting testing mandates does not warrant educators to spend their time on ensuring that students acquire the necessary in-depth knowledge they need (Franklin and Molebash 2007). If educators are to meet the current needs of students, then schools need curricula that are rigorous, that cover academic standards, and that offers students opportunities to apply technological knowledge and collaborative engagement during problem-solving investigations. Therefore, the purpose of this study was to determine if there were any differences in student achievement in mathematics between schools that use project-based learning (PBL) and technology-rich instructional approach and schools that use a traditional instructional approach.

24.2 Literature Review

24.2.1 An Overview of Technological Benefits

Technological advancements are prevalent in just about every industry in our world; education should be no exception. Many of today's students are digital natives and for them, and life does not exist without a myriad of technological devices (Lavin et al. 2009). The use of technology in students' lives is highly anticipated and has been expected to be a part of the learning curriculum (Dudeney and Hockly 2012), yet a study conducted by Greaves et al. (2010) reported 80 % of the 1,000 schools it surveyed still underutilizes its acquired technology. Studies show that integrating technology can benefit learners and improve achievement (Roblyer 2003). There may be questions as to what specific factors of technological integration actually impact student achievement. Yet, it remains evident that educators need a shift in using technology to teach today's students (Blair 2012) to prepare learners for all subjects and to adequately prepare them for college and to thrive in the current workforce (America's Alliance 2006).

24.2.2 The Importance of Technological Literacy

Technology is needed for students to be exposed to various types of applicable, real-world situations in their learning environments and in order to work towards the proficiency of demonstrating these skills. It is no longer a privilege in our society; it is a necessity in order to conduct even the most simplistic business in one's daily life (Magner et al. 2011). Therefore, technology is vital to classroom instruction, and teacher utilization of technological components is critical to students' academic success (Zhao et al. 2002). Dennis Roekel (2008) noted that students are living in an era where they need to function globally in a digital society. In order for schools to meet this need, priorities must be established, and schools must constantly adapt to the ever-changing technological advancements.

24.2.3 Project-Based Learning

Research showed that a technology-rich, PBL environment could potentially expose students to learning concepts they need for their futures and increase student achievement (Lombardi 2007). In PBL environments, students are exposed to complex questions, problems, or challenges over an extended amount of time and allow teachers to create opportunities that provide authentic learning. These experiences allow students to use collaboration and communication skills, as well as foster the critical thinking and problem-solving abilities needed in navigating real-world situations (Spires et al. 2012). Attempting to understand the effects of a technology-rich PBL curriculum may help determine if the acquired higher-order thinking skills have an effect on student achievement.

24.2.4 The Role of Teachers During Project-Based Learning

According to Zhao and Frank (2003), teachers' perceptions about the use of technology affect how often and how well they integrate technological tools into instruction. Though many educators use technology in their daily lives, often their proficiency levels in managing technological tools to meet academic standards are lacking (Moeller and Reitzes 2011). However, the role of technology in an effort to improve teaching and learning cannot be realized without explicit guidance from teachers (America's Alliance 2006). Teacher facilitation is integral because they create the curricula and are ultimately the ones who construct the type of learning environments that support collaborative learning and problem-solving using higher-order thinking skills (America's Alliance 2006).

24.3 Methodology

Background Current literature has written about many theories regarding implementations schools can take advantage of to improve academic achievement (James et al. 2001). Project-based learning has been coined to improve student thinking and skills (Prince and Felder 2006); there is also sufficient literature to support the use of technology as a source of improving academic achievement (Shih et al. 2010).

Since schools have the responsibility of showing students are knowledgeable of core content by passing standardized achievement testing, and the added pressures of ensuring that students possess twenty-first-century skills, research was conducted to determine the effectiveness of project-based learning on student achievement when combined with technology in the area of mathematics.

Subjects Two charter schools in Chicago that serve middle school students were selected to participate in the study. The first sample, PBL/Tech School, included 380 students in Grades 6–8 and 12 teachers. The students in this sample are immersed PBL throughout the school year. The second sample, Tech School, included 220 students in Grades 6–8 and 12 teachers. The students in this sample receive traditional instruction and technology is regularly used to support the curriculum.

Data Collection Student achievement data was captured from two standardized tests, the Illinois Standardized Achievement Test (ISAT) and Measures of Academic Progress (MAP). The data used to compare students' academic achievement scores in mathematics and within mathematics subcategories. For ISAT, students' actual performance data was compared between schools and grade levels, and for MAP students' growth scores were compared from the beginning to the end of one academic year.

Measures The standardized scores for ISAT and MAP Tests were analyzed using analysis of variance with a mixed procedure approach. To minimize errors and to control biases due to unequal sample sizes, an F-test was conducted between variables. The covariate indicated a small *p*-value, indicating that there was a chance that the covariate actually has a meaningful relationship with the dependent variable(s).

As an indicator of statistical significance, Tukey's method was implemented with a cutoff of .05.

24.3.1 Research Questions

The review of literature made several connections that identified both project-based learning and technology as resources to improve student achievement. To guide the research in this study, the following research questions were addressed:

Q1: Is there a difference in student achievement in mathematics between schools that use project-based learning (PBL) and technology-rich instructional approach compared to schools that use technology with a traditional instructional approach?

Q2: Does the use of PBL and a technology-rich instructional approach have any effects on student achievement in specific mathematic subcategories?

24.3.2 Hypotheses

In line with this discussion and research questions, the following hypotheses were conjectured to examine the effects of project-based learning and technology on student achievement in mathematics.

H1: There is a difference in student achievement outcomes when project-based learning and technology are used for instruction versus a traditional instructional approach with technology in mathematics.

H2: There is a difference in student achievement outcomes within specific mathematic subcategories when project-based learning with technology is used for instruction versus a traditional instructional approach.

24.4 Discussion of Findings

24.4.1 Overview of the Purpose

Researchers (Shih et al. 2010) have claimed that project-based learning and technology can improve students' thinking, communication skills, and content knowledge and, as a result, have a positive impact on student achievement. In Chicago, there are many underperforming schools (Bogira 2013). Reports have indicated that only 8 % of Chicago's low-income students graduate from college and several claims that urban schools fail students and leave them unprepared for college and life (Bogira 2013). Therefore, the charter schools responded with rigorous curricula, research-based practices, and the proper resources within its schools to improve the achievement performances of students to help ensure they are equipped for college and beyond. Understanding the effects of PBL and technology versus traditional instruction was important as it guides schools to develop and implement instructional practices that provide students the necessary foundations for learning and the technological skills for living.

24.4.2 Summary of Participants

PBL/Tech School is a Chicago Charter School that serves students in Grades 6–8 and focuses on providing rigorous and engaging instruction that increases student knowledge, interests, and individual strengths. The approach to instruction at PBL/Tech School is to engage students in project-based learning activities that align with

Table 24.1 Demographics of PBL/Tech School

Race/ethnicity	Percentage of students (%)
Black	97.9
Hispanic	0.5
White	0.2
Low income	83.5
Special education	16.0

Table 24.2 Demographics of Tech School

Race/ethnicity	Percentage of students (%)
Black	95
Hispanic	0.3
White	0.3
Low income	82.9
Special education	10.7

the curriculum as well as utilize technology. The sixth grade population within this school used iPads and laptops at a 1:1 student to technology ratio and students in Grades 7 and 8 used laptops. The sample population at PBL/Tech School included 379 students in Grades 6–8.

Tech School is a Chicago Charter School that serves students in Grades 6–12 and emphasizes curricula that focus on research, design, and creativity. Beginning at Grade 6, students are acclimated to research practices and are exposed to instruction that draws upon students' cultural backgrounds and their development of knowledge and skills. Tech School uses a traditional instructional approach and incorporates technology to support the curriculum. The sample population at Tech School included 219 students in Grades 6–8. The demographics of each school were similar and are presented in Tables 24.1 and 24.2.

24.4.3 Results

NWEA MAP Test When comparing actual achievement outcomes between schools for the MAP test in mathematics, PBL/Tech School and Tech School showed typical growth at each grade level. In eighth grade, PBL/Tech School's growth score was higher than Tech School's growth score. The p-value revealed statistically significant differences in growth scores between students in eighth grade (Tables 24.3 and 24.4).

Table 24.3 NWEA MAP math test growth scores between schools

School	Math fall	Math spring	Fall to spring growth	National norms	Growth compared to norms
PBL/Tech -6	215.2	221.6	6.4	6.0	0.4
PBL/Tech -7	218.1	223.1	5.0	3.4	1.6
PBL/Tech -8	221.2	226.8	5.5	3.1	2.4

Table 24.4 Analysis of NWEA MAP math test scores between schools

Grade	School 1	School 2	Mean difference	*t*-value	Pvalue
8	PBL/Tech	Tech School	3.86	2.89	.004

Table 24.5 ISAT math mean scores between schools

School	Mean score	(%) of students meeting/exceeding
PBL/Tech School	255.29	46
Tech School	251.14	37

Table 24.6 Analysis of ISAT math test scores between schools

School 1	Mean score	School 2	Mean score	Mean difference	Pvalue
PBL/Tech	255.29	Tech	251.14	−4.14	0.003

ISAT Test When the overall achievement performances were observed for math, PBL/Tech School had a higher overall mean score (252.29) than Tech School (251.14) in Grades 6–8. The data for PBL/Tech School also showed that its mean scores were higher at each grade level than the mean scores at Tech School (see Table 24.5). The analysis showed that the results were statistically significant (Table 24.6).

ISAT Subcategories In order to further investigate the differences in student achievement among PBL schools and traditional, mathematic subcategories were examined on ISAT testing. The researcher sought to determine if the differences in instruction between PBL schools and traditional schools had specific effects in categories such as measurement, number sense, algebra, data and statistical probability, and geometry.

In the subcategories for mathematics, the percentage of students who met and/or exceeded the particular subcategory goal at PBL/Tech School was consistently higher than the percentage of students at Tech School in the measurement, number sense, algebra, and data and statistical probability strands (see Table 24.7). Of these subcategories, the statistically significant differences were seen in the measurement

Table 24.7 ISAT subcategory math scores between schools

Mathematic subcategory	PBL/Tech percent of students meeting/exceeding standards	Tech percent of students meeting/exceeding standards
Measurement	52	47
Number sense	58	55
Algebra	51	47
Data/statistical probability	59	57
Geometry	50	51

strand in sixth grade ($p = .0002$) and in the algebra strand at seventh grade ($p = .05$). In the geometry strand PBL/Tech School's percentages were higher than Tech School's percentages for sixth grade. For seventh and eighth grades, Tech School performed higher than PBL/Tech School, but none of the differences in percentages were statistically significant in this strand.

As a result of the analysis, the hypotheses was supported and accepted in each case. H1 stated there were differences in student achievement outcomes in schools that used project-based learning with technology versus schools that used traditional instruction. H2 stated there were differences in student achievement outcomes within specific mathematic subcategories when project-based learning with technology is used for instruction versus a traditional instructional approach.

24.5 Discussion

24.5.1 Summary and Analysis of Findings

This study provided insights to the theories presented by several researchers (Shih et al. 2010) about the use of technology and project-based learning to increase student achievement. In examining the differences in student achievement between PBL/Tech School and Tech School, the analysis showed that there were statistical differences within the academic performance between schools and at specific grade levels. The results from this study show statistically significant achievement differences in mathematics for overall MAP and ISAT tests as well as nearly all subcategories in mathematics. NWEA (MAP) is an adaptive test that conforms to students' actual knowledge and indicates what students are ready to learn regardless of grade levels. The real value of this measure is in monitoring the growth of students, as opposed to traditional standardized testing, such as ISAT, which only indicates proficiency within grade-level content. Likewise, if students are generating higher growth scores, it is because they have been successful at responding to questions with a greater level of difficulty (NWEA 2011). Though both schools experienced growth at typical norms according to NWEA's normative data (2012), the higher growth at PBL/Tech School was statistically significant and indicates that the PBL approach may be just as effective as the traditional instructional approach.

Although these findings do provide evidence of the effectiveness of PBL in increasing student achievement, it is important to note that these outcomes could also be influenced by several factors ranging from increased student motivation (Shih et al. 2010), the teacher's role in project-based learning experiences (Johnson and Johnson 1998), or teacher attitudes about using technology in the classroom (Zhao and Frank 2003). While further research needs to be conducted, the research revealed that student achievement according to standardized benchmarks was visible while simultaneously exposing students to the necessary technology skills needed for living and working in the twenty-first century.

24.5.2 Recommendations for Further Research

Project-based learning and technology have great potential to improve classroom practices and student learning as stated in the literature and as seen within the data analysis of this study. In this study, to protect the identity of human subjects, teachers were only linked to their specific schools. However, a recommendation for future research would be to replicate the study in a way that links teachers with the students in their classrooms to truly evaluate the diligent use of project-based learning with technology compared to classrooms with traditional instruction. Since this study also included a significant difference in the number of special education students being served in each school, a study could also be conducted with data coded to identify special education students to determine if project-based learning efforts are improving student achievement for all students or to determine if the academic achievement scores would be higher as a result of excluding the scores of special education students.

The researcher recommends that replicated studies utilize an assessment that accurately assesses the outcomes of project-based learning on student achievement as standardized assessments are not entirely designed to evaluate the necessary twenty-first-century proficiencies gained from the use of instruction that focuses on preparing students for college, careers, and thriving in a digital society.

Conclusion

In today's society, students need more exposure to tasks that allow them to be engaged in inquiry, collaboration, and communication and technological skills that will enable them to perform successfully in areas of their lives beyond the classroom. However, many schools are still tied to meeting academic standards and focusing on students being able to demonstrate learning during standardized testing. It was beneficial to determine that the PBL approach with technology, when used as an instructional approach, was effective for meeting student achievement outcomes while still exposing students to the authentic learning experiences needed in their lives.

References

America's Promise Alliance. (2006). *Every child, every promise: turning failure into action*. Alexandria: Author.

Blair, N. (2012). Technology integration for the new 21st century learner. *Principal, 91*(3), 8–11.

Bogira, S. (2013, November 13). *A better goal for CPS*. Retrieved from http://www.chicagoreader.com

Dudeney, G., & Hockly, N. (2012). ICT in ELT: How did we get here and where are we going? *English Language Teachers Journal, 66*(4), 533–542.

Franklin, C., & Molebash, P. (2007). Technology in the elementary social studies classroom: Teacher preparation does matter. *Theory and Research in Social Education, 35*(2), 153–173.

Greaves, T., Hayes, J., Wilson, L., Geilniak, M., & Peterson, R. (2010). *The technology factor: Nine keys to student achievement and cost effectiveness*. Shelton: MDR.

James, D. W., Jurich, S., & Estes, S. (2001). *Raising minority academic achievement: A compendium of education programs and practices*. Washington, DC: American Youth Policy Forum.

Johnson, D. W., & Johnson, R. T. (1998). Making cooperative learning work. *Theory into practice, 38* (2), 67–73.

Lavin, A., Korte, L., & Davies, T. (2009). The impact of classroom technology on student behavior. *Journal of Technology Research, 2*, 1–13.

Lombardi, M. (2007). *Authentic learning for the 21st century: An overview*. ELI Publication, 1. Retrieved from https://neteducause.edu/ir/library/pdf/ELI3009.pdf

Magner, T., Soule, H., & Wesolowski, K. (2011). *The partnership for 21st century skills-framework for 21st century learning*. Retrieved files.eric.ed.gov.ezproxy.bethel.edu/fulltext/ED543030.pdf

Moeller, B., & Reitzes, T. (2011). *Integrating technology with student centered learning*. Education Development Center. Retrieved from http://www.nmefoundation

National Academy of Sciences. (1997). *Preparing for the 21st century: The education imperative*. Retrieved from http://www.nas.edu/21st/education

Northwest Evaluation Association. (2011). *RIT scale norms study*. Retrieved from http://legacysupport.nwea.org/sites/www.nwea.org/files/resources/NWEA%202011%20Norms%20Report_01.17.2012_2.pdf

Partnership for 21st Century Skills. (2002). *Learning for the 21st century: A report and MILE guide for 21st century skills*. Washington, DC: Partnership for 21st Century Skills. Retrieved from http://www.p21.org/storage/documents/P21_Report.pdf

Prince, M., & Felder, R. M. (2006). Inductive teaching and learning methods: Definitions, comparisons, and research bases. *Journal of Engineering Education, 95*(2), 123–138.

Roblyer, M. D. (2003). *Integrating educational technology into teaching*. Upper Saddle River: Merrill Prentice Hall.

Roekel, D. (2008). *Technology in schools: The ongoing challenge of access, adequacy and equity*. National Education Association Policy Brief. Retrieved from http://www.nea.org/assets/docs/PB19_Technology08.pdf

Shih, J. L., Chuang, C. W., & Hwang, G. J. (2010). An inquiry-based mobile learning approach to enhancing social science learning effectiveness. *Educational Technology and Society, 13*(4), 50–62.

Spires, H. A., Hervey, L. G., Morris, G., & Stelpflug, C. (2012). Energizing project-based inquiry: Middle-grade students read, write, and create videos. *Journal of Adolescent and Adult Literacy, 55*(6), 483–493.

Zhao, Y., & Frank, K. A. (2003). An ecological analysis of factors affecting technology use in schools. *American Educational Research Journal, 40*, 807–840.

Zhao, Y., Pugh, K., Sheldon, S., & Byers, J. L. (2002). Conditions for classroom technology innovations. *Teachers College Record, 104*(3), 482–515.

Author Index

© Springer Science+Business Media Singapore 2015

W.W.K. Ma et al. (eds.), *New Media, Knowledge Practices and Multiliteracies*,
DOI 10.1007/978-981-287-209-8

MIX
Papier aus verantwortungsvollen Quellen
Paper from responsible sources
FSC® C105338

If you have any concerns about our products,
you can contact us on
ProductSafety@springernature.com

In case Publisher is established outside the EU,
the EU authorized representative is:
Springer Nature Customer Service Center GmbH
Europaplatz 3, 69115 Heidelberg, Germany

Printed by Libri Plureos GmbH
in Hamburg, Germany